Praise for *THE DITCHDIGGER'S DAUGHTERS*

"Inspirational."—*The New York Times Book Review*

"Inspiring . . . how the strength of values has enabled black families to survive and thrive."—*Washington Post Book World*

"Entertaining yet inspiring. . . . A welcome antidote to the many recent books that have shown the underside of growing up black."—*Cleveland Plain Dealer*

"Dr. Thornton's story shows that a family that stays together, that holds fast to traditional values, can make a quantum leap up the social mobility scale in a single generation."—*Wall Street Journal*

"*The Ditchdigger's Daughters* is more than a labor of love. For anyone who has ever had a dream, it is a guide to success. Sure to give the reader hope for the future."—*Newark Star-Ledger*

"Inspiring. . . . A moving family biography."—*Detroit Free Press*

"It will rekindle your belief in the American spirit."—*New York Daily News*

"Inspirational . . . how determination and strength encouraged a family to excel beyond its conditions and fulfill the dreams of the parents."—*Booklist*

"Heartwarming. . . . The family is plagued by hardship, but they are willing to laugh at themselves while showing that being poor isn't an excuse for failure."—*American Visions*

"As much a memoir of a father's love, determination and common sense as it is a testament to six women whose parents' 'single-minded' devotiion enabled them to overcome the odds of racism and sexism."—*Milwaukee Journal*

The Ditchdigger's Daughters

A BLACK FAMILY'S ASTONISHING SUCCESS STORY

Yvonne S. Thornton, M.D.
as told to Jo Coudert

Dafina
Books

KENSINGTON PUBLISHING CORP.
http://www.kensingtonbooks.com

For Mommy and Daddy

We wouldn't have been anything
or done anything without you.

DAFINA BOOKS are published by

Kensington Publishing Corp.
850 Third Avenue
New York, NY 10022

All Kensington titles, imprints and distributed lines are available at special quantity discounts for bulk purchases for sales promotion, premiums, fund-raising, educational or institutional use.

Special book excerpts or customized printings can also be created to fit specific needs. For details, write or phone the office of the Kensington Special Sales Manager: Kensington Publishing Corp., 850 Third Avenue, New York, NY 10022. Attn. Special Sales Department. Phone: 1-800-221-2647.

Dafina Books and the Dafina logo Reg. U.S. Pat. & TM Off.

ISBN-13: 978-0-7582-2588-7
ISBN-10: 0-7582-2588-1

First Hardcover Printing: January 2002
First Trade Paperback Printing: March 2008
10 9 8 7 6 5 4

Printed in the United States of America

◆ Contents ◆

◆ Introduction ◆

Many have asked about the impetus for writing *The Ditchdigger's Daughters*. The seed was innocently planted when I was an OB/GYN resident, during a conversation with my mother. She told me that all she wanted was to have our story told in a book that would be in the library. She wanted to let the world know that with education, focus and determination, how her little "nappy-headed" daughters from the housing projects became successful independent women of whom she was so proud. When my mother told me her request, I was somewhat taken aback because I wasn't a writer. I delivered babies for a living. I told her that I had little time to sleep much less to write a book. However, my mother's wish became my quest, my obsession, my new goal in life.

I had asked a reporter, Georgia Dullea, from *The New York Times,* to help me write this book. She had done a story on women in OB/GYN a few years earlier, but she informed me that she was a journalist and didn't write books. After listening to my parents' story, she told me it would make a wonderful human-interest article and perhaps someone who did write books would read the story and become my collaborator.

The first article about my family appeared in *The New York Times* on Father's Day in June 1977. After the article appeared, television and movie offers quickly followed. But, there was no one who wanted to write a book. Finally, in an arrangement with Columbia Pictures, we insisted on having a book written as part of the movie contract. A prominent screenwriter, book publisher and writer for the book were selected for the project. I was finally going to see my mother's dream become a reality. However, the producer responsible for our film project, was asked to leave Columbia Pictures for reasons unknown and our story was abandoned.

The years went by and I went on with my life and the demands imposed upon me by my own career and family. Serendipitously, I received a box one day from the book publisher who had since declared bankruptcy. The box was filled with audiocassette tapes of the interviews my father gave in preparation of the original book that was never written. I had already established a scholarship in their name at my alma mater, but a book about them seemed to be more and more elusive. For years, I had searched for just the right person who had substance, writing talent and a unique understanding of my parents' struggle. Writer after writer came and went. Either they wanted an enormous amount of money to help me write a book or their writing skills and temperament were not suited to convey my parents' insights and wisdom responsible for our success.

One day, I saw a reference in *The New York Times* to the American Society of Journalists and Authors and its Dial-a-Writer service. Dorothy Beach, who ran the service, put me in touch with one writer who had too many assignments to take on another, a second writer who wanted a year's salary in advance, and a third writer who said she wasn't interested in writing a book but thought the *Reader's Digest* might want to run an article about the family. That writer was Jo Coudert. Ironically, Jo Coudert had authored my husband's favorite book, *Advice from a Failure*. While an undergraduate student at Princeton, he had referred to her book so often that he had to keep the highlighted pages together with Scotch tape and rubber bands. When we were both medical students, he would quote chapter and verse from Jo Coudert's book daily as if it were a bible on the self-analysis of human emotions and behavior. I finally had to ask: "Who is this Jo Coudert?" My husband had never met Jo Coudert but I was about to meet her.

I met Jo for a long interview in my office. As I reminisced about my family, Jo, without the aid of a tape recorder, just listened and would occasionally write a sentence or two in her notebook. The story was written, and the *Reader's Digest* published it in February 1987 as "Donald Thornton's Magnificent Dream." That was that, at least for Jo Coudert. But, I still didn't have a book written. I had finally found the writer I knew could do justice to my parents' story, but she wasn't interested. I was relentless. Once or twice a year for the next five years, I would call Jo to ask if she might possibly change her mind about writing the Thornton story as a book. Jo was as resolute as I was persistent. The answer was always the same: "I have no intention of writing a book, but if I do, it will be my book, not someone else's."

One evening when I was at a medical symposium, I was watching *The Court Martial of Jackie Robinson* on television. The movie reminded me of my father, Donald Thornton. From my hotel room in Denver, I picked up the phone and called Jo Coudert in New Jersey. The answer had not changed, but for the first time I mentioned the old tapes of the interviews with my father. "I'll send them to you," I said. "Just listen to them. That's all I'm asking you to do."

As well as being a writer, Jo is an amateur watercolorist, and she let the tapes run while she was painting. But after a while she left her brushes standing in the water jug and simply listened. Her attention was caught by Donald Thornton's folk wisdom and worldly insight. Jo finally consented to collaborate in writing the story about my parents. Jo and I began meeting all day every Saturday, Jo making notes and taping, while I retold the story of the ditchdigger's daughters: how we were born and grew and were molded into becoming successes by a father who labored at two jobs and a mother who cleaned houses.

With the book outline and representative chapters in hand, our literary agent approached many publishers. To our chagrin, no one wanted to publish the book. The publishers said it wasn't marketable because the book had no conflict. But persistence does prevail and a small publishing house in New York did take a chance and published the book in March 1995.

Judging by the letters from readers and the comments from young people who come up to me after hearing me speak, the book has made an impact on lives of many people. One reader wrote that she was returning to school and planning to go on to college because "I now realize I can do anything I want to as long as I am determined—the gospel according to your dad, Mr. Donald Thornton." A thirty-one-year-old just admitted to

Michigan State University of Dentistry wrote: "As I start school this fall, I am keeping your book on my desk. When I am feeling overwhelmed, I will read it again and again. I can't thank you enough for sharing your experiences. I truly admire you and your family. If I were to be asked who my hero is, the answer is simple—I have two: my husband and Donald Thornton." A mother wrote: "My name is Lakshmi. I am a citizen of India. I live in the southern state of Tamil Nadu. I have two daughters. Whenever they feel dejected about studying, I tell them to remember you and most importantly your dear dad. Your book told such a touching story and it changed our way of thinking." A fifth-grader from Sarasota, Florida, wrote: "I just wanted to write you this letter to let you know that you made a difference in my life and to thank you for writing this book so all of us will be able to have something to refer to."

The Ditchdigger's Daughters is an American story. Its popularity has been due to "word of mouth" rather than multimedia marketing. I had objected to the subtitle, *A Black Family's Astonishing Success Story,* because it implied that the Thornton family was unique. There are millions of black families, as well as families of all races, colors and creeds with working class parents who just want a better life for their children and are willing to make the sacrifices needed for their children to succeed. We thank Kensington Publishing and Dafina Books for reintroducing our book in hardcover, and we thank all of our readers who have laughed and cried with the Thorntons and drawn courage and inspiration from the story of my family who struggled and won. On a personal note, when the book was named as one of the "Best Books for Young Adults" by the American Library Association in 1996, I had a feeling of personal satisfaction and said to myself: "Mommy, you finally have your book in the library."

Yvonne S. Thornton, M.D.
January 2002

The Ditchdigger's Daughters

◆ 1 ◆

The Beginning

"YOU KIDS ARE BLACK," Daddy sometimes said to us. "You're dark-skinned and ugly."

"Daddy, don't you love us?" we wailed.

"I love you. I love you better than I love life," he assured us. "But I'm not always gonna be around to look after you, and no man's gonna come along and offer to take care of you because you ain't light-skinned. That's why you gotta be able to look after yourselves. And for that you gotta be smart."

Daddy had a bet on with the world, and this was one of the arguments he used to make us study—and study hard. He worked as a laborer and Mommy as a cleaning woman, and since this was the early 1950s, before the days of equal opportunity and affirmative action, the odds against his winning his bet were fairly astronomical. Nevertheless, Daddy had set his heart on the improbable notion that his five black daughters would grow up to become doctors.

The idea had not come out of pride and ambition; it started as a joke. Daddy dug ditches at Fort Monmouth, New Jersey, and when Mommy gave birth to a fourth and then a fifth girl, his fellow ditchdiggers kidded him about having nothing but female offspring. What kind of a man is it, they teased, who can't produce even one son for himself?

Another man, stung by the taunts, might have said to his wife, "Five daughters and no son, five girls and no boy, I'm outa here." But Daddy dearly loved Mommy, and although he longed for a son, he had no intention of walking away from his family. He took the kidding from the other laborers; he took the sly snubs from his brothers, who disparagingly referred to our family as "Donald and his six splits," and one day he hit upon a way of making five daughters sound not so bad.

"You won't be laughin'," he predicted, "when my little girls grow up to be doctors."

"Who're ya kiddin'?" the men jeered. "Your girls'll be having babies by the time they're fifteen like the rest of 'em in the projects."

"Not my kids," Donald said. "My kids'll be wearing white coats and have them scripperscraps hangin' 'round their necks, and people'll be bowin' and sayin', 'Yes, Dr. Thornton' and 'No, Dr. Thornton.'"

"Get outa here."

"You is crazy, man."

Now the ditchdiggers had something else to needle Daddy about. His preposterous claim was tossed up, shot down, bandied about, buried, and dug up again. Since he was not going to be allowed to forget it, Daddy took to defending it, and the more he defended it, the more firmly the idea got wedged in his mind. He found he liked it. He liked it a lot. Doctors. *Doctors.* What a grand sound. Black doctors didn't dig ditches or clean houses. God must have given me all daughters for a reason, he figured to himself. Why don't I just see what I can do with them?

Daddy didn't have much idea how doctors were made, but Mommy said, and he agreed, that first his girls would have to do well in school. Mommy cared passionately about education, but before this, Daddy had scarcely given it a thought. Growing up in the Depression years in Long Branch, New Jersey, his strongest feeling about school had had to do with clothes. When he was a small boy and a charity provided him with a pair of shoes, little Donald only felt proud of his new shoes, but as he got older, he grew self-conscious about his patched clothes. The wheat starch his sister put in his shirt collars to glue down the frayed threads made his neck itch. He suspected that people guessed his underwear was ripped. He knew he was occasionally laughed at, and he sometimes imagined he was pitied.

"It kind of drove me to saying I was going to run away," he remembered, describing those days. "Me and my friend headed toward California. We got fifteen, twenty miles down the road before our feet lost their nerve and turned us back. Then we got the idea we'd go to New York. We worked around at odd jobs and a lady gave me a dollar and a half for cutting her grass, which was a lot in those days, so we caught the bus to the city.

"We took the subway up to Harlem, and when we came out on 125th Street, I'd never seen so many black folk in my life. It scared me so that I started to go back down the steps. 'Look at all them colored people,' I whispered to my friend. 'Where are the white people?' That's how your mind runs as a child. But then I began to like it and I said, 'Oh, gee, I'm not going back home.'"

After a day or two he did, though, and his mother was pleased enough to see him that she made sure he got chicken for dinner. That meal stuck in Daddy's mind because it was one of the rare times he didn't have to eat oatmeal. His father's pay as a laborer was eighteen dollars a week, which had to feed nine children, and even when meat and potatoes were on the table, the servings stopped at Daddy's older brother. Daddy got oatmeal.

"I always wondered why the good things couldn't have stopped after me," he would tell us. "It kind of drove me to do a little stealing. I'd go to the Acme or the A & P and sneak cheese and salami and crackers into my pockets. That's why when I bring something home now for you kids, I always make sure there's enough for everybody. I don't want nobody to get the feelin' of bein' left out like I had."

Daddy was fourteen and in the tenth grade when he dropped out of school in 1939. "I figured I'd be all right because I had common sense and I knew basic things, like you got to love other people and thou shalt not steal—which I did and I knew was wrong." He got a job working beside his father, helping to build jetties of huge rocks to protect the beach at Sandy Hook, but every payday he headed for Harlem, reveling in the blackness and the color, the music and the swirling street patterns, the conked hair and zoot suits, the pointy-toed shoes and swinging watch chains, and people, people, people everywhere, people with skin like his.

As winter came on and the icy salt spray that so often made his father arrive home with icicles in his hair began to split the skin on his own fingers and freeze the flesh of his nose, Daddy made up his mind to look for work in the city. On Chambers Street in New York, he handed over five dollars to a straw boss and in return was awarded a job in a commercial laundry, wringing the water out of sheets.

"Pretty soon the guy told me, 'Look, you're a hard worker, Donald, but you're too light for the work.' I felt bad that he fired me. I was livin' at the Y, and just about that time my mother sent a detective to get me. I told the detective I was almost fifteen years old, and he said, 'Still an' all, you're too young to be off in the city by yourself,' and he rode me back home."

But as soon as the fare and a little something extra jingled in Daddy's pocket, he was back on the New York bus. This time he bought a job as a porter at the Theresa, the biggest and finest hotel in Harlem, and from this base he swaggered forth nightly in pursuit of his twin passions: jazz and jitterbugging. On a night when Coleman Hawkins was playing at the Savoy Ballroom, he eyed the girls without partners lined up against the walls and singled out one with high cheekbones.

Mommy always picked up on the story at this point. "This skinny little kid comes over and asks me to dance. I thought to myself I was crazy to give him the time of day, but okay. And, wow! Did he turn out to be a dancer! We jitterbugged like you wouldn't believe—up, down, in, out, over the shoulder, through the legs. Oh, what a great time that was!"

Between sets, Daddy discovered that Mommy was also at the Theresa Hotel, working as a chambermaid. Her name was Itasker Frances Edmonds, and she too had dropped out of school that past fall. Itasker, however, had left school with passionate regret and much further along than the tenth grade. She had completed three years at Bluefield State Teachers College in West Virginia, where she had grown up, one of thirteen children of a coal miner who stretched his pay by growing potatoes and raising chickens, rabbits, and pigs. A self-ordained Baptist minister, her father lined up all the children every evening when he returned from the mine and whipped them, contending that each had more than likely done something wrong during the day when he hadn't been there to see it.

The younger children tended to the farm chores, while the older boys followed their father into the mines. As for the older girls, since there wasn't enough land to make it worthwhile to keep them home to farm, they were expected to marry and leave or find work and leave. When Itasker did neither but brewed the curious plan of going to college to become a teacher, her father, who could neither read nor write himself, merely nodded. He did not have to say the obvious: She would get no help from him.

Itasker, always called Tass, owed both her high cheekbones and her name to a Native-American great-grandmother, a full-blooded Cherokee married to a Negro slave. By the time Tass was born, no one remembered what the great-grandmother's name had been, but with a vague thought of acknowledging that admixture of different blood, her parents decided she should have an Indian name. The only one they knew was the name of a source of the Mississippi River, Lake Itasca, but they had heard it pronounced Itasker and that is the way they spelled it.

Less clear than the origin of Tass's name was the genesis of her liking for poetry. If it could be traced to a particular teacher or book, Mommy never told us kids about it, only about her determination to go to Bluefield State Teachers College, a black college in West Virginia, and major in English. To earn her tuition, Tass worked in the school's kitchen, scrubbing floors and scouring pots so large that she climbed inside them to scrape the sides down. This she did willingly for three years—and took it for granted she would do it for her senior year's tuition as well. That last September, however, suddenly and unexpectedly she was informed that seniors were not permitted to work, that the jobs had to go to incoming students. Tass was directed to come up with the tuition or leave school.

Stunned and weeping, Tass called an older sister. "That's okay, Tass," Beatrice said reassuringly, "I'll send the money so you can finish." The college allowed Tass to stay on in an attic while she waited for the check to arrive—not attending classes, not studying, just waiting day after day. The check never came.

"I was brokenhearted," Mommy said. "I'd worked so hard, I had an A average, I wanted so much to be a teacher, and here it was, all slipping away from me. I didn't blame Beatrice. She didn't want me to cry, so she told me she'd send the money, and she would have if she'd had it, but she just didn't. But, oh, it was hard."

Often enough, there were tears in Mommy's eyes when she repeated this story, which she did to impress upon us how important it was to earn a diploma, because without it her three years of college had counted for nothing and she had had to earn her living as a cleaning woman. I understood that well enough, but what I secretly took away from the story was the conviction that I must never make a promise I cannot keep and I must keep every promise I make lest someone else suffer through the drying up of hope, as Mommy had done while she waited in that stifling, empty attic.

With no choice but to leave Bluefield, Mommy headed north. Another sister, Ellie, went with her. Their plan was to buy sailor suits, polish the song-and-dance routines they had invented for themselves as children, and earn money in show business. While they charmed club audiences at night, Tass imagined, she would attend a New York college during the day and earn her degree. Reality blew holes through their sails before the wind had a chance to fill them even once. New York City colleges laughed at Tass's credits from Bluefield State Teachers College; she would have to start over again as a freshman. As for show business, that dream died when they saw their first show at the Apollo Theatre.

Even in East Beckley, West Virginia, Tass and Ellie had heard about Amateur Night at the Apollo. They pictured themselves winning the required four Wednesday nights in a row and being awarded a week's paid engagement, thus launching their show-business career. As it happened, on the Wednesday night they went, a female singer was trying for her fourth win. At the end of the evening, the MC held a white envelope with the prize money over the heads of each of the acts in turn, and when he came to the young singer, the audience screamed, shouted, whistled, and stomped. Flashbulbs went off. Reporters rushed up the aisles. A star named Ella Fitzgerald was being born, and the audience knew it. Tass and Ellie knew it—and knew, too, that they were out of their league. They found work scrubbing bathrooms at the Theresa Hotel.

So it was that Donald Thornton and Tass Edmonds met, first at the Savoy Ballroom and then in the back halls of the hotel, as Tass emptied wastebaskets and Donald emptied garbage pails, as Tass pushed a vacuum cleaner and Donald pushed a broom, as Tass polished tiles and Donald polished brass. They talked, they laughed, they shared sandwiches on the back stairs.

Donald commuted to Long Branch on weekends to reassure his mother he was all right, and one Sunday evening he returned to the city to find that Tass had been taken to Bellevue Hospital. A heavy period had turned into hemorrhaging, and she had had to have a transfusion. The sight of Tass lying still and drawn against the white sheets of a hospital bed rooted her unshakably in Donald's heart as his to take care of.

Donald was sixteen years old. Tass was twenty-six. Years and years later, when I myself was grown, I discovered that Mommy had been born in 1915, Daddy in 1925; but whether Daddy was aware that the woman he had elected himself to guard, protect, and cherish was ten years older than he, I never knew. Perhaps not, for her age on their first child's birth certificate was given as only two years more than his. In any event, it would have made no difference, for Donald loved Tass.

"It made me feel good, like a big man, to look after her," he said, speaking of those times. "I liked having her need me. She was always like one of my children."

For eighteen dollars a month, he rented a cold-water flat in a tenement and took Tass there when she left the hospital. For two years they lived and worked in Harlem. "When we had a nickel, we shared a hot dog," Daddy said. "Sometimes we were so hungry we sucked each other's thumbs." When there was a knock on the door and Donald heard his mother's voice, he would shout that he couldn't find his pants and not open the door until Tass had had time to go out a window and up the fire escape to the roof. The two women never met, and if Donald's mother suspected her son was not living alone, she could not prove it.

So determined was Donald to stick by Tass that when he turned eighteen on March 14, 1943, he ignored the draft notice that came. He and Tass were aware that World War II was on, but it did not seem to have much to do with them and they went about their lives as calmly as bottom-fish do with waves churning and crashing remotely above them. In September a second draft notice arrived, and this one was too specific to be ignored. It ordered Donald Thornton to report on September 30 to have a physical and be inducted. On September 29, he and Tass went to a Woolworth's on Lenox Avenue and bought a ring for $1.50. Then they stopped in at a little church and asked the minister to marry them.

"Tass, getting married is in case I die," Donald told her. "Half the benefits will go to you and half to my mother. In the meantime, if you get in trouble or need any help, you go to my mother's in Long Branch. She'll take care of you." Did he know then that Tass was pregnant? He never admitted it to us, his children, whom he daily, direly warned against "foolin' 'round" all through our childhood.

Tass's sister Ellie had also married by this time, and after Donald left, Tass slept on a couch in Ellie's flat for two months. Then she decided to go to Long Branch, to Donald's family.

When she got off the bus, she observed with satisfaction that the Thornton house on Lippincott Avenue was solid and substantial: two stories plus an attic and cellar and a fenced-in yard. She knew from Donald that there were only four or five black families in Long Branch, which in the days before automobiles had been an oceanfront resort for the rich. Lillian Russell and Diamond Jim Brady, who rode in their carriage up and down Ocean Avenue, were the best known of the summer visitors. Woodrow Wilson's summer White House, Shadow Lawn, now a college, was in a quiet part of town filled with large old houses, ancient trees, and landscaped grounds. The servants who staffed the houses and maintained the grounds lived, for the most part, in the black section of nearby Asbury Park, but somehow the Thornton family, which had been in New Jersey since long before the Civil War (Robert Carter of Nomony Hall, Westmoreland County, Virginia, in a deed of manumission dated August 1, 1791, freed his slaves, among them one Tom Thornton), had acquired this house in a middle-class neighborhood.

Tass rang the bell and was taken aback when the door was opened by a light-skinned, cold-eyed woman who was almost six feet tall. Donald, like Tass, had skin the color of dark chocolate, and he was short and stocky and friendly, the opposite of this unsmiling giant. Tass timidly introduced herself as Donald's wife.

"No, you're not," the woman said flatly. "My son's not married."

Tass showed her the ring on her finger and the marriage license she was carrying in her pocketbook. While Donald's mother stared at the license, searching for evidence that it was fraudulent, Tass explained that Donald, inducted into the navy and now in training at Great Lakes Naval Training Station in Illinois, had told her to go to his mother if she needed looking after and that she was five months pregnant, none too well, and unable to work.

The formidable woman finally allowed grudgingly, "All right, you can come in." She clearly believed Tass had trapped her son into marriage through her pregnancy, and Tass, not wanting to betray Donald, kept silent about the two years she and Donald had been living together. She suspected that Nanna, as we were later to call our grandmother, had detected with one shrewd glance that Tass was older than Donald, which automatically gave her grounds for believing that Tass had led a young and credulous boy astray. Tass realized, too, because she was familiar with black mores, that Donald's mother disapproved of her violently as a wife for her son because of Tass's shade of darkness. In black circles, it is acceptable for women to marry darker than themselves, but men, to marry well, have to marry lighter than themselves. If Donald was really married to this woman, he had married beneath him.

Only Donald's father, as dark as Donald, a squarely built, strong, sweet man thoroughly dominated by his queenly wife, welcomed Tass into the family. The others, Donald's brothers and sisters, took their cue from their mother, as they were to do in most things all their lives, and set about despising Tass—to the extent that snapshots from that time have Tass's face scratched out. In her misery in this hostile household, Tass slept with her marriage license under her pillow to remind her of Donald and reassure her.

One day the license was missing. Tass went to Nanna to ask if she'd seen it. Nanna pulled the ripped pieces from her skirt pocket. "Now you're no longer married to my son," she announced. "Get out of my house."

Tass, now seven months pregnant and with complications that led to heavy bleeding, returned to her sister Ellie's place in New York and stayed there until the baby was born. Donald was in the South Pacific when word reached him that he had a daughter. "We'd been moving up, moving up," he remembered. "New Caledonia, Guadalcanal, New Hebrides. All of us blacks jammed in together. White officers. Fight, fight, victory, victory, that's all we heard. I said to myself, Fight, fight, my eye. My wife's had a little baby. I don't want to die. I want to see that baby."

He described how: "On one of them islands they got me in the hospital, and my papers had done caught up with me. You see, back in Great Lakes, I was supposed to go to the hospital and have my jawbone cut. They said I had malocclusion; my upper and lower teeth didn't meet up with each other. But we was getting ready to ship out and I wanted to stay with the guys, so I acted like

I wasn't supposed to go to the hospital and I shipped out with my buddies. I didn't get caught until New Hebrides. They looked at my papers and says, 'You ain't supposed to be over here anyhow.'

"A major says to me, 'What we're gonna do is send you back to Mobile 5, which is another hospital, and we're gonna take an inch and a half of bone out of your face and you'll be eating through a straw.'

"'Not me,' says I.

"'You sadsack,' he called me.

"I said, 'Yes, sir, I may be that, but I still didn't say you could cut my face.'

"That made him mad, and he began filling out papers to send me back to the States. All the better, I says to myself. I'll get to see my baby."

In San Diego, in 1944, because he again refused surgery on his jaw, Donald was discharged from the navy. The government provided one hundred and forty-eight dollars for a first-class, sleeper ticket to New York. Instead, Donald bought a coach ticket, planning to sit up for the four nights and have a hundred dollars in his pocket when he arrived back East. He had barely settled in a seat, however, when a porter came through and asked if he'd be interested in working his way to Chicago washing dishes for seven dollars a day, his meals, and a place to sleep. Working hard but eating and sleeping well, Donald arrived in Chicago, cashed in the unused part of his ticket, caught the Trailblazer to New York, and in New York, hailed a taxi.

He knocked on the door of Ellie's apartment and Tass opened it. "Yes?" she said. "Hello," Donald said, smiling as wide as it is possible to smile. When he had gone away a year earlier, Donald had weighed 140 pounds. He stood there now at 210 pounds. Tass said, "Yeah, what do you want?"

Donald reached for her hand. Her eyes, darkening with fear, shot to his face. Then, like footlights coming up in a theater, radiant recognition crept in. "Donald? Donald…oh, Donald!"

He held her, hugged her, swung her, kissed her. "Now, where's my other baby?" he said. "Where's my Donna?"

He exulted to Tass that he had so much money in his pocket that she could go out and buy mud flaps for the baby's carriage if she wanted. What she wanted, she answered with all the pent-up longing in her for a place of her own, was a home for the two of them and the baby.

The next morning Donald rented an apartment at 75 East 119th Street for twenty-three dollars a month, and by nightfall had moved them in. The day after that, he had two jobs: one an eight-hour-a-day, five-day-a-week job in a commercial laundry, the other an eight-hour-a-night, five-night-a-week job in a meat-packing plant. On weekends, when the laundry was closed, he went into the building and cleaned the machines. Two jobs, sixteen hours a day, odd jobs on the weekend—it was a routine Daddy was to follow for the next twenty-five years.

Donna had been born in 1944. In 1945, Jeanette was born. In 1947, when Mommy was pregnant again, Daddy said, "If this one isn't a boy, I'm going to drown it, Tass, I swear." It was not a boy. It was me, Yvonne, the third daughter, and Daddy arrived at Mommy's bedside in Columbia-Presbyterian Medical Center carrying a bucket with water sloshing in the bottom. Mommy heard the splashing and burst into tears.

Daddy grabbed her and held her close. "Oh, Tass, I was only funnin'," he whispered. "She's a sweet little girl. She's got this little dark spot on her cheek shaped like a cookie." From then on, in the family, I was Cookie. Because something Daddy could not explain happened when he went to fetch Mommy and me home from the hospital, he sometimes said, "Whatever pertains to you, Cookie, it's like there's been a magic. Maybe it was luck sloshing around in that bucket and it splashed on you."

Daddy had twenty dollars in his pocket when he went to collect Mommy and me. "When you're poor, Cookie," he explained when he told this story, "you always know exactly how much money you have, and I knew I had twenty dollars in my pocket. On my way to the hospital, it came to me that I better get something to keep the baby warm, so I stopped in a store and bought a blanket. It cost five dollars. Okay, so now I have fifteen dollars. I get to the hospital and tell them I've come for my wife and baby and they say I've got to pay them twenty dollars. I tell them I don't have twenty dollars; I've only got fifteen. 'Well,' they say, 'you can't have your wife and baby until you get the other five dollars.' I reached into my pocket to show them that fifteen is all I've got, and out comes twenty dollars. Now, where did that extra five dollars come from? From that day to this, I can't tell you, Cookie. I only know it wasn't there and then it was, and from that day to this, I've got to think there's somehow magic mixed up with you."

I loved the story. It's been like an umbrella keeping the rain off my parade all my life. It is so wonderful for a child to grow up with a belief in her specialness, her luck, it provides such courage to risk, to overleap, that I have sometimes wished that all parents could tell comparable stories to their children, even if they have to invent them—stories to serve as a talisman all their lives.

When Donna was five, Jeanette was four, and I was almost two, Daddy came home one day and found Mommy looking grim. "What are you so down in the mouth about, Tass?" he asked.

"Didn't you hear?" she said softly. "A little girl no bigger than Donna here was raped outside the building last night."

Daddy sat down heavily at the kitchen table. He put his head in his hands. When he looked up again, it was to tell Mommy to start packing, they were leaving the city.

"Going where, Donald?"

"You want to go back to where you come from in West Virginia?"

"I sure don't."

"Then we got to go to Long Branch where I come from."

"Your family doesn't like me."

"Tass, honey, I don't know no other place for us to go, and we can't have the girls growin' up here. Like it or not, we got to go to Long Branch."

And that very day we did.

◆ 2 ◆

The House That Donald Built

THE FIRST THING DADDY DID IN LONG BRANCH was to apply for a job at Fort Monmouth, an army base on the outskirts of town. The hiring office didn't say yes and didn't say no. "They just kept sauntering around, sauntering around," as Daddy described it, and he grew so fretful and so concerned about no money coming in that he called New York and arranged to return to his jobs there, resigning himself to the time and expense of having to commute an hour each way. Tass suggested, "Give it one more day, Donald. Go back to Fort Monmouth on Monday."

He did—and waited around, waited around. A major said, "Come back tomorrow." Daddy fumed to Mommy that if he did that, he would miss a second day of work and how were they going to buy food and pay rent? "Just one more day," Tass urged. Daddy went back and hung around and grew even more frantic. If there was anything he hated, it was to waste time because, "When you lose time, it's something you can't never get back." He was pacing the floor like a German shepherd on a chain when a secretary emerged from an inner office and commented, "I can see you're unhappy, Mr. Thornton, but it's okay. You went on the payroll as of yesterday."

On the payroll as a ditchdigger. "But I didn't care what it was," Daddy said, "so long as I was close to home and didn't have to pay the money to go back and forth to New York." Because the wages were ditchdigger's wages, he began asking officers if he could wax their cars on the weekends, their wives if he could wash their windows or polish their floors. Any odd job, any repair, the minute he heard about it, he'd say, "Yes, indeed, I'll get that done for you as soon as I get off work," and when people discovered

16

how willing Daddy was and how pleasant, they called on him often and felt friendly toward him. "Don, can you use this piece of furniture?" they offered. "Don, would you like to have these clothes to take home to your children?"

"But when it came time for me to advance, to be something more than a laborer," Daddy recalled, "they didn't know me. I caught on then to what part I played. I played subserviency. I played Uncle Tom. They tossed me what they wanted me to have, and I thanked them."

He was not being sarcastic about his thanks; he had no time or use for resentment. The broken tables and chairs were braced and painted and used to furnish our two-bedroom apartment in Garfield Court, a low-income housing project in Long Branch that Daddy qualified for as a veteran; and Mommy, who was clever at sewing, ripped the seams of the clothes, cut the cloth down, and made outfits for us kids.

Even with such shifts to make do, by Wednesday or Thursday of each week, the money Daddy brought home had been spent. "Don't keep asking me where it went," Mommy protested to Daddy. "If you think you can do better, you try buying the food."

"Well, why don't I just see if I can make the money stretch some," said Daddy, and from then on, he did the shopping and managed the family finances. In Asbury Park he bought day-old bread for a nickel a loaf; at Freddy's meat market on Broadway, he got a markdown on the ends of rolls of salami and bologna and on cuts of meat and chickens that had lingered in the case too long. Scraps and soup bones were thrown in for free.

Sometimes Daddy took us kids along with him to the butcher shop. "These are my girls I brought for you to see," he would say as though to show the butcher that the bargains he gave Daddy were going into the making of sturdy, well-behaved children. If the butcher needed his sidewalk patched or his showcase polished, Daddy did these things as a favor in return. He was never a trimmer, only a man at the bottom of the heap scrambling to make ends meet.

Daddy diced and sliced the scraps and cut the mold off the

meat. Occasionally he hesitated with his knife in the air. "I don't know, maybe I shouldn't cut the green out; it's like filled with that penicillin that keeps you girls healthy," but I think he said that to tease us. He made stews and spaghetti sauce out of the scraps and fried up the chickens, serving the backs and necks to himself and giving Mommy and us the breasts, thighs, wings, and legs. He wanted us to have the best of what he could get, and he made sure of two things: there was always enough for seconds and Donald's kids never ate oatmeal.

One night we were having pork chops for supper when a woman selling encyclopedias came to the door. Mommy had no money to buy, but always hospitable, and perhaps in need of some adult conversation after a day spent with small children, she invited the woman in. Jeanette, at four, had other ideas. She planted her small self in the doorway and told the saleswoman firmly, "Go home and eat your own pork chops."

That feisty little girl looking out for her own interests was a blueprint for the teenager and adult to come. Donna, the first-born, was pliant; I, the middle child, eager for love and approval, was well behaved; and Rita and Linda, the fourth and fifth girls, were malleable. Jeanette was the spirited one, the rebel, the freethinker. Only Jeanette defied Mommy and Daddy's ban against playing with the other kids in the project, and when she was promptly struck in the head with a brick, that was quite enough to confirm for the rest of us that we must do what our parents said. But Jeanette, then and later, went her own way, even if it meant taking a hit.

Except for Donna, we were all named after celebrities: Jeanette MacDonald, Rita Hayworth, and Linda Darnell were movie stars of the day. My name, Yvonne, came from one of the famed Dionne quintuplets. The odds against quintuplets—one in 65 million births—were about the same as the odds against any of us amounting to anything in this world despite our elegant names. There was irony in plump little black girls bearing the names of sleek white stars of the silver screen, but to us at the time, it all seemed perfectly natural and rather flattering, as though some of the glamour of the famous would descend to us even if Daddy did say we were black and ugly. Jeanette, when it became fashionable in the 1960s, toyed with the idea of taking an African name, but the rest of us just laughed. We liked our names, and besides, even if our forebears had come to this country involuntarily, that was at least two hundred and fifty years ago. We had been here far longer than most Americans, so how could we be anything but American?

About the time Donna was ready to start school, we moved to a larger apartment in Seaview Manor, another housing project in Long Branch. Liberty Street School was a convenient two blocks away, but Daddy checked it out and discovered that it had a black principal, black teachers, and a virtually all-black student population.

"The thing of it is," he reasoned with Mommy, "the white people see to it that they get the best, so if we want our kids to do well, they've got to go where the white kids are." This meant, not to Liberty Street School, but to Garfield School, which was a mile and a half away. Somehow Daddy wangled it so that Donna, and later Jeanette and I, started out there. Daddy's theory was that we should go to school with children who had goals, or whose parents had goals for them. "Our kids'll watch the white kids," he predicted, "and they'll hitch a ride on their wagon."

As each of us started school, he solemnly instructed us to "pick out a rabbit." He explained how, in greyhound racing, the dogs ran their hearts out because they were chasing a rabbit that whizzed around the track ahead of them, and that's what he wanted us to do: study our hearts out to come in first. He said, "You'll go to class and pretty soon you'll notice one of the kids does real good, is out in front of the rest. That's your rabbit. If that kid gets an A, that lets you know you can get an A too. You just have to try harder." He was right. A girl named Patricia was my rabbit, and however good her grades were, I worked until I caught up with her, and sometimes my momentum carried me right on past her.

Other than having a crush on a boy named Carl, who was the

only other chocolate chip in a sea of vanilla faces at Garfield School, I remember nothing about my year there except the wretched morning I had an "accident." Mommy had drilled it into all of us that, "When the Lord's Prayer is being said, or the Pledge of Allegiance, you're to be as still as soldiers." Being a conformist, I did not dream of going against this dictum even on a morning my bladder was full to bursting. I held out until the end of the ceremony, but release from soldierdom came too late. The part of my clothing that escaped soaking, I then proceeded to drench with tears. Mommy was sent for, and when she came to get me, I assured her through mortified sobs that I would never set foot in school again.

"If you let yourself be stopped when something bad happens," she said quietly, "you won't be around when something good happens." Mommy bathed me and dressed me in my best little pleated skirt and a starched white blouse, and I felt so pretty that somehow it seemed all right when she delivered me back to the classroom.

In its way, this episode was as emblematic of me, the conformist, as the pork chop incident was of Jeanette, the rebel. Both foreshadowed the parts we were later to play in the central drama of our family life.

Under the GI Bill, Daddy was also attending school, studying at night to be an automotive technician. He completed the course, only to find that advancement was closed to him as a black man at Fort Monmouth. He maneuvered a switch to janitorial work on the night shift and landed a second, civilian job during the daytime making home-heating-oil deliveries. On weekends, for fifty cents an hour, he worked as a hod carrier for a mason, and as soon as he learned how to run a straight course of bricks and knew how much sand and water went into the mixing of mortar, he began making plans to build a house for us.

A lot on Ludlow Street, at right angles to Lippincott Avenue where Daddy's parents lived and close to Gregory School where he wanted us to go, came up for tax sale. Daddy had saved the transportation money that came with the GI Bill, and he asked his father to bid on the lot for him, since he himself would be at work. His father did—and won the bidding at two hundred dollars.

Deed in hand, Daddy went to the Shadow Lawn Bank in Long Branch and applied for a mortgage. He was refused. Politely, he asked a bank vice president the reason. "Don, you seem like an okay fellow," the bank officer told him, "but we don't give loans to blacks, and I'll tell you why. There are not too many colored people in town. Suppose you can't keep up the payments on your loan and we have to take your house. Who are we going to sell it to?"

Daddy had to accept the man's reasoning, but he refused to accept that he could not build a house just because the bank did not want to give a black man a mortgage. With the last of the little bit of money he had saved, Daddy hired a man who owned heavy equipment to dig a hole for the cellar. With stakes and strings he marked a rectangle fifty feet back from the street where the house would stand.

"Why you leavin' so much space in front?" the bulldozer operator objected.

"On account of my kids," Daddy said. "Suppose they come runnin' out the front door or 'round the side of the house. If the house is close to the street, they're out in the road and maybe gettin' hit by a car 'fore they know it. This way, puttin' the house fifty feet back, their little legs'll get tired and they'll fall down before they run out into the street."

It was part of Daddy's philosophy that, "You should always be thinking ahead. Otherwise you'll hear yourself saying 'Oh,' and let me tell you, *Oh* can be an awful big, awful mournful word."

With the hole for the cellar dug, every time Daddy earned a few extra dollars, he bought ten or twenty concrete blocks, and with Mommy acting as his hod carrier, bringing him wheelbarrows of mortar while he laid up the blocks, he started work on the foundation. I still have a snapshot from that time, and Mommy, pushing a wheelbarrow, is visibly pregnant.

All of her pregnancies had been difficult, with a great deal of bleeding, caused, she always claimed, "by you kids lying on my right kidney." From how prominent her cheekbones became, Daddy could recognize when she needed a blood transfusion and he would bundle her off to the clinic at the hospital. Whether it was because of the heavy work on the foundation or the cumulative effects of five pregnancies, it took eighteen pints of blood to bring Mommy through this pregnancy—blood donated by men at Fort Monmouth, both black and white, which touched Daddy to the point of tears. The doctor informed Daddy that, at peril to Mommy's life, there must be no more pregnancies. He and Mommy agreed to a tubal ligation, although Mommy wept, not for herself, but because now Donald would never have a son. Donald turned the sharp thought over in his mind long enough to wear off its bitter edge. One day he sat by Mommy's bedside and cupped her hand like an injured bird in his thick, work-hardened fingers. "Tass," he told her, "for me to work hard for myself is no purpose. But for me to work hard for my wife and my children who need me, that has come to be my purpose and that's all I need. It don't matter that we don't have a boy. There's nothin' I could do with a boy that we can't do with our girls."

It was this talk with Tass. It was the ribbing Daddy took about having yet another girl. It was being immeasurably grateful to the doctor for pulling Tass through. It was the thought Daddy had that: "I can't imagine nothin' greater than knowin' how to make someone well. People are bound to respect you if you can do that, it don't matter what color you are." It was these things coming together in the unconscious well of his mind that made the claim that his five daughters were going to grow up to become doctors rise up and jump out of Daddy's mouth, surprising him almost as much as it did his hearers.

It don't matter what color you are if you can make people well. As Daddy replayed his brave joke and realized that his daughters might indeed transcend their color if they became doctors, his tossed-off statement hardened into the determination that fueled his life from then on.

With so little money to buy building materials, progress on the house was almost imperceptible after two years, and the city sent a notice that the cellar hole must be filled in; trapped rainwater was turning it into a breeding ground for mosquitoes. Daddy went to city hall. "I didn't challenge the man," he told Tass. "I didn't argue. I just said, 'Look, I've got a family. I've got five little girls and I'm tryin' the best I can to build a house for them.' The guy looks at me a long time. 'Forget the notice,' he finally says. 'Go back to work.' That's what I've done all my life—I've never challenged the other guy; I've just tried to make him understand where I'm comin' from and where I'm goin'."

Chatting with the Italian owner of the building-supply yard one day, Daddy mentioned the order from the city and the reprieve he had been granted. Mr. Calabretta asked a few questions, and Daddy explained what he was trying to do, that he was building the house on Ludlow Street so his daughters could go to school in the white part of town to get a start on a good education and become doctors.

"Don," said Mr. Calabretta, "I don't hear young fellows talk like you. I'll tell you what—you get anything you need from my yard and you pay me when your house is done."

Daddy read in Mr. Calabretta's face that he meant it. "Oh, that made me feel good," he remembered. "I said to myself, this is some guy to talk to me like this. Now I can really go to town." He ordered five hundred blocks and bags of sand and cement, and they were delivered without a bill. He ordered five hundred more. The house began to rise around him.

Now that Daddy knew he was really going to get the house built and that we actually would be living there someday, he wanted us transferred to Gregory School. The principal checked and said there was no such address as 174 Ludlow Street. Daddy told her that he was building the house and that, in the meantime, we were living with our grandparents around the corner on Lippincott Avenue. The principal could not prove that we weren't, although almost every afternoon she drove down Ludlow Street to check that black people really were building a house in that section of town.

In September 1954, Donna began fourth grade, Jeanette

third, I second, and Linda kindergarten at Gregory School. The school was a block away from our grandparents' house, and because Mommy was working as a maid for a Mrs. Egan in Red Bank, every afternoon at three we had to go to Nanna's and stay there until Daddy picked us up at six.

Those three hours a day were the worst time of our lives. Nanna, whom we secretly referred to as the wicked witch of the east, would not allow us to play outdoors. Instead, we had to sit all in a row on a couch across the room from her big chair by the front window. While she watched the comings and goings on the street, we were permitted to do our homework but not to talk or move. If we crossed our legs, she snapped, "Stop that trickin'," implying that we were masturbating, and—whack!—she reached out and hit us with a switch on the side of the head. If we worked up enough courage to clear our throats and whisper that we were hungry, she would grudgingly order us to get a piece of bread from the kitchen. The bread was invariably stale and the kitchen filthy because Nanna was too regal to do housework.

When Daddy honked the horn for us at six o'clock, a wedge of little girls catapulted out of that house like missiles from a slingshot. The worst day of my life was the day I was in the bathroom at six o'clock and Daddy didn't notice I was missing from the pack. I ran screaming down the street after his truck, but it turned the corner and disappeared from sight. One of my aunts dragged me, crying frantically, back to the house.

"What's the matter?" Uncle Kenny said. "You can stay with us tonight, Cookie."

"Call Mommy! Call Daddy!" I pleaded. I was close enough to hysterics that finally Uncle Kenny did telephone. Daddy consigned me to hell by casually agreeing that the easiest thing was for me to stay where I was.

I spent the night scrunched into the smallest, tightest ball I could manage in the corner of a bed that reeked of mouse droppings, feeling—or imagining, I didn't know which—the light, quick feet of roaches rummaging in my hair and skimming across my face. It was a toss-up which was more horrible: the nightmare of lying awake in that bed or the nightmares that played out in the Grand Guignol theater of my mind when I dozed.

After that experience, I felt doubly sorry for Rita, who was too little to go to school and had to spend all day at Nanna's. As soon as she could walk and talk, Rita clung to the picket fence in the corner of Nanna's yard every morning, yearning after us as we set out for school and plaintively begging, "Don't leave me here! Don't leave me here!" We sympathized desperately but off we went to school, never absent and never late, so eager were we to be away from that house and that despotic woman, who, I suspect, never forgave us for being our mother's dark daughters. Nanna was even harsher to Betty than she was to us. Betty was a foster child whom Nanna was being paid by the state to raise but whom, in reality, she used as a servant, although Betty was not much older than Donna. "Massage my feet, Betty," Nanna would say. "Betty, give me my slippers." "Get the witch hazel, Betty, and rub my back." "Betty, get a bucket of water and clean up Bobbie."

Bobbie was another ward of the state boarded at Nanna's, one for whom she received even more payment because Bobbie was severely handicapped. She had cerebral palsy, and Nanna kept her in a sort of cage, or pen, because Bobbie had no control of her arms and legs or her bodily functions. Whenever Bobbie soiled herself, Betty would be ordered into the cage to clean up after her.

Even after Bobbie died, there was no letup in Betty's chores, for Pretty Aunt Yvonne and Aunt Dollbaby Joy (neither of whom would answer unless addressed in exactly those terms) also used Betty to fetch and carry. Of the grown-ups, only Daddy treated Betty like a person with feelings. One day he spotted a long, broad, rawly oozing scrape on her leg and insisted on knowing how it had happened. When he discovered it had been caused by a boy pushing her over a desk, he boosted Betty into the front seat of his truck and drove up and down the neighborhood streets, all the while patiently arguing against her timid disinclination to identify the boy until, in a burst of courage, she pointed him out lounging on a street corner. Daddy stopped the truck, clamped his hand on the boy's collar, bent him over his knee, and handed Betty a rolled umbrella.

"Now," he said, "you beat this rascal with that umbrella until you're pretty sure he ain't never gonna give you or any other girl such a shove again."

Betty, who had never once answered back in her life, never once fought back in her life, was slow to warm up, but then she made a satisfying job of it. After that, she worshipped Daddy, and since she was our age and we were with her so much and were so fond of her, we considered her our sister and Mommy and Daddy came to speak of having six daughters, as was eventually the case.

We, of course, were desperately anxious to have the house finished so we would not have to stay at Nanna's in the afternoon, but no snail could have been slower at constructing a shell than Daddy, who was able to lay blocks only on weekends, and not then if someone offered him an odd job that would bring in money. Daddy building the house was like a woman sewing her first dress: she's been wearing dresses all her life so she has a pretty good idea of what one should look like, where the collar and the pockets and buttonholes properly go, but getting them all assembled without a hitch here, a pucker there, and an off-center seam down the back—well, that is a matter of experience that she doesn't yet have. Daddy similarly lacked experience at building houses, so the house, although it was solid and still stands, had a homemade, somewhat improvised look.

For one thing, the kitchen was located in the cellar. Even Daddy's doggedness didn't permit him to contemplate building a second story on the house, and with a living room, three bedrooms, and a bathroom having to go on the ground floor, he figured that the kitchen might best go in the necessary, but otherwise mostly wasted, space of the cellar. He built the kitchen entirely of brick, not just the floor and the walls but the bases for the sink and stove. He said he did this because brick never needed maintenance, but I suspect that seeing the mosquito-breeding water seeping through the foundation after every rain had given him the hint that a kitchen below ground might not always be perfectly dry, which proved to be the case. I remember us kids in bathing suits and Daddy in rubber boots sloshing around in the kitchen after spring storms.

Because the stovetop was electric, I asked Daddy once if we weren't in danger of being electrocuted. "No, Cookie," he said. "I thought of that and had the guy run the wires overhead. There ain't nothin' electric closer to the floor than four feet."

The men Daddy worked with at Fort Monmouth listened to talk about the house while Daddy was building it, and when the time came, a co-worker who was an electrician and another who was a plumber volunteered to do the wiring and the plumbing. "You see how it is, kids," Daddy said to us. "People aren't gonna throw their time or money away on somebody who gets a bottle of Thunderbird wine and lies down on the sidewalk, but if you show people you're tryin', they're gonna want to help."

We children were too small to lend a hand, but sometimes a couple of us would carry one end of a plank while Daddy carried the other. In those days houses were dismantled by wrecking crews rather than being smashed to bits by machines, and Daddy, when he saw a house coming down, made a deal for usuable lumber, which was then dumped on the front of our lot and had to be carried around to the rear. True to his philosophy of always thinking ahead, the same was true of logs when Daddy spotted a fallen tree being cut up.

He told us, "This house has a fireplace because maybe there'll be a time when we can't right away come up with the money for heating oil, so then we got the fireplace to keep us warm." Although I can't remember it, years later he said that we did heat the house with wood the first few years we lived there, but I do remember the struggle to lug all the logs from the front to the backyard.

There came a day, after four and a half years, when the house was completely roughed in, a roof on it, Sheetrock on the walls, subflooring laid. Was it sheer exuberance—I don't know—but for the first and only time in our lives, Mommy and Daddy played with us. The heavy rope Daddy had been using to haul buckets of mortar to the top of the walls became a jump rope, with Mommy and Daddy swinging it while we kids ran in and out doing Double Dutch and Hot Pepper. When we faltered and that thick rope caught us on the legs, it raised such welts that by the end of the afternoon we looked like severely abused children, but we were so delighted to have our parents play that there wasn't a murmur out of one of us.

With the house recognizably a house and with the credibility of having had the persistence to build it, Daddy decided to try again for a mortgage. He went back to the same bank. It was four years later and Daddy was four years more experienced at dealing with people. Fort Monmouth had taught him what was expected from a black man, and time had shown him that he was willing to do it for the sake of his goal. He put on a suit and tie. He walked into the bank. He asked for the president. No, he didn't want to be helped by an assistant manager. He would wait until the president was available to see him. So saying, he settled himself in a chair and folded his arms and looked serenely determined.

When he was finally ushered into the president's office, he waited respectfully until the president looked up from his papers. "Yes, Mr. Thornton, what can I do for you?"

Daddy looked him straight in the eye so the president would see he was honest and then he lowered his eyes so the president would appreciate that he knew his place. "I wonder, sir, do you have children?" Daddy asked him.

The president looked vaguely surprised. "I do."

"Then, sir, you'll understand why I want to do good by my children. I have five little girls and I've built this house myself in this nice part of town so they can go to a good school. I'm a veteran and I've got two jobs and I'm workin' hard..." He was groveling and he knew it and he meant to, something we never realized until years later when we were grown and sat around talking about how it had all come about. He'd say then, "I have put up with so much stuff for you kids," and he'd describe scenes like this and explain his thinking at the time—how you go to the top person because he doesn't have anyone over him to cause him worry about making the wrong decision, how you establish your common humanity by talking about something you have in common like children, and how, when you get around to making your request, you switch to being humble so he can feel like a big man helping you.

The bank president leaned grandly back in his chair and said, "What do you need, Mr. Thornton? What do you think you need?"

"Well, sir, if you'd give me a mortgage on this house I've built, I could finish it up inside and pay off on the materials Mr. Calabretta done let me have on credit."

The bank president wasn't so seduced that he didn't check with his own eyes that the house on Ludlow Street was roofed and windowed and wired and plumbed, that it was substantial, and that final money really was needed for paint and trim and wall-to-wall carpeting over the plywood subflooring. Having verified all that, he issued an order for a mortgage to be granted to Donald Thornton, the first mortgage the Shadow Lawn Bank of Long Branch had ever granted to a black.

There's a postscript to the story. The man who originally refused Daddy the construction mortgage wrote him a letter of apology twenty years later when it became apparent what Daddy had accomplished. Daddy said the man did it to relieve his own mind. "He couldn't wash it out. He couldn't drink it out. He had to confess that what he had done was wrong. He had to say, 'Hey, I'm sorry, you didn't deserve what I did to you twenty years ago,' so he could get back to feelin' right with himself." Perhaps contrition also played a part in the bank's hiring one of Daddy's nephews as its first black teller.

With September coming around, Daddy decided we should move into the house before the inside was finished; indeed, it was several years before the Sheetrock walls received a coat of paint. Daddy went to the office of the manager at Seaview Manor and gave notice that the Thornton family was giving up its apartment in the project.

"Where you going to?" the manager asked, somewhat surprised, because people, once they were granted an apartment in the projects, were more than likely to stay put.

"I built a house over to Ludlow Street," said Daddy.

"Get out! *You* built a house? Where'd you get the money to build a house?"

The manager went to Ludlow Street later that day and peeked through a window of the house. "There wasn't nothin' but a picture of Jesus tacked up on the wall," Daddy laughed. "But your Mom and I were there cleaning up, getting it ready to move into, and we waved and he could see it really was ours."

My memory of the move is of a red saxophone, a tiny toy that Donna had gotten as the prize in a box of Cracker Jack. Mommy packed it, saying, "I want to save this," as though she foresaw its importance as a family icon. All that was to come in our lives had its origins in that toy saxophone.

When Donna won it as a prize in a box of Cracker Jack, she ran to Daddy to ask what it was called and how it was played. Daddy told her, and, a lover of jazz, he described how a fellow named Charlie Parker played a real one and made fantastic sounds come out of it. After that, Donna blew and blew on her toy, trying to make it produce wonderful sounds, and as young as she was and as careless as any child, she nevertheless didn't let the little red saxophone out of her hands. "Daddy," she begged, "get me a real one. I want to play a real one."

Donna was so insistent that Daddy began asking around and found that one of his buddies at Fort Monmouth had an old saxophone that Daddy could have for twenty-five dollars, payable at the rate of five dollars a week. When he laid his hands on the first five dollars, Daddy went around to Kenny Wright's house, and Kenny brought the saxophone down from the attic. On the way home Daddy thought to himself: *Gee, Kenny's parents probably went through a lot to buy him a horn and pay for lessons, and now here he is, selling it out of the attic where it's been laying who knows how long. I don't want that to happen to me.*

"Anything that came to my attention," Daddy always said, "I

tried to think about it and see if it had something to tell me about my life."

He decided to take the saxophone back to Kenny Wright if Donna lost interest in it after a couple of days, but day after day Donna persisted in blowing on it, trying to force sounds out of it. The sounds she did get were so ghastly that Mommy and Daddy, who both had an ear for music and strong memories of Dizzy Gillespie at the Savoy Ballroom, felt they would go crazy if she didn't get some instruction. They made a deal with Mr. Winthrop, the music teacher at Garfield School, to teach her for two dollars a half hour.

And that is the way it all began.

◆ 3 ◆

Sweet and Sour Notes

JEANETTE WENT ALONG when Mommy took Donna to her music lessons and very soon was announcing her determination to play an instrument too. Mr. Winthrop suggested the trumpet, but when Jeanette's efforts to blow one produced little in the way of sound and much in the way of spittle flying in Mr. Winthrop's face, he shifted his recommendation: "The guitar, I think, because the child has long and graceful fingers." He introduced Jeanette to a guitar of his own, and when it became apparent that she did indeed have an affinity for the instrument, Daddy made a trip to the pawnshop in search of the money to buy her one.

The only items he possessed that he thought might have some value—and it was more wishful thinking than conviction—were memorabilia brought home from the war. He spread the medals and buttons and buckles and a bayonet on the pawnshop counter. "Mr. Moss," he said, "I've got five little girls and I'm tryin' to do good by them. The oldest one, she's learnin' to play the saxophone, and my next, she's beggin' me to get her a guitar. Now, what do you think, can I get a bit of money for these here souvenirs?"

Even Daddy didn't expect he would be allowed more than ten dollars for his trophies, but Mr. Moss looked them over carefully and pronounced them worth sixty dollars. Daddy then visited Mr. Scott at the music store down the street and described his need for a guitar for his little girl. Mr. Scott found a fine one that he could discount to sixty dollars, explaining that he could afford to give Daddy a bargain because Daddy already bought reeds for Donna's saxophone at his store and would be buying guitar strings there as well.

Years later I listened to Daddy tell a young black man about those early times. "I think back when I hear guys like you saying 'those white motherfuckers, those honkies, we should blow 'em all away.' These people, who happened to be white, they knew I was searchin' for somethin' and they was ready to help. So, when black people say whites are no good, don't you listen. Yeah, there's some out there that'll put you on fire, but that's not the people you look for. There's a lotta good white people out there with good hearts. They know the struggle."

Daddy cobbled together two more odd jobs he could do on weekends to pay for the music lessons. Once I asked him why he worked on Sundays instead of going to church with us. "Cookie," he said, "you eat on Sundays just like any other day, so I work on Sundays just like any other day." He was matter-of-fact, not sighing or sounding sorry or tired, I think because Daddy was a man lucky enough to know instinctively that work is not a burden but a boon, that it is work that builds a solid sense of self.

For Mommy, because of her religious indoctrination by her hell-fire preacher of a father, Sundays were for churchgoing. She made sure we went to Sunday school, which was conducted in the basement of the Second Baptist Church on Liberty Street. Whenever *Liberty* or *Lincoln* is in a name, the street, school, or building is bound to be in a black neighborhood, and, for all I know, that may be true of Second Baptist, too, because when I asked Daddy what happened to the First Baptist church, he said "White folks got that. Coloreds get the Second Baptist churches." Daddy didn't care for churches—"Religion is in your heart"—and he argued with Mommy that he did not want people talking to his kids on Sunday who would get in the way of his doing good by his children on Monday. But Mommy, who didn't often argue with him, quietly said, "Donald, I want them to go," and that settled that.

Because Mommy made no distinction between everyday schoolwork and Sunday schoolwork, insisting that we study as hard for one as for the other, we could be counted on to have memorized the lesson and we were called on often to recite and to read the Bible stories aloud. Except for one Sunday when a newcomer appeared in the doorway of my class, a pretty girl just up from the South. "Little Miss Sunshine," purred our black teacher. "Come in, come in. Sit here by me."

"How come?" I asked Mommy when I got home, describing how I knew the lesson but wasn't called on once, how it was all: "We'll let Little Miss Sunshine do this. We'll let Little Miss Sunshine read that." Mommy asked what the newcomer looked like, and when I said she was light-skinned, much lighter than the rest of us, Mommy nodded. "High yella," she said. "That's why the teacher favored her."

When Daddy heard about this favoritism, he began our acquaintance with black-on-black prejudice, telling us about things like the paper-bag test—how being black doesn't necessarily guarantee you entrance to a black affair; at the door you lay your hand on a brown paper bag and if your skin is darker than the bag, you're turned away. "White, you're all right; black, step back; brown, stick around," was how it went, he said.

I remember protesting, "But, Daddy, we can't do anything about the color of our skin."

"That's why I'm tellin' you, you got to get smart," he said. "When you're grown, this society is gonna look at you as an ugly black female—not just white people but black people, too, are gonna see you that way—and the only thing that's gonna get you above that is if you're educated. Light-skinned people generally have everything given to them. They don't have to bother 'bout learnin'. But you are not light, so studyin' is the only way I can see you gettin' ahead of this."

When Daddy was through work on Sundays, he would take us to Asbury Park to have ice cream and walk on the boardwalk, but first he would drive up and down the streets and he and Mommy would point out people. "See that black woman wheeling that expensive baby carriage?" Mommy would say. "There's a white baby in that carriage, and that's what happens when you don't have a diploma. You take care of white ladies' children. You clean white ladies' houses."

Daddy would say, "Look at that black lady sloppin' along there in her turned-over shoes. She looks uneducated, don't she? But now, vision her as a doctor. Vision her as shufflin' along 'cause she's tired from being up all night savin' a little baby's life. She looks different, don't she? She looks different 'cause now you're lookin' at her with *respect*."

Again, Daddy would say, "See that white man crossin' the street in his shiny shoes? He looks elegant, don't he? He's rich and he looks right through people like us. But s'pose a car comes barrelin' 'round that corner and hits him and he's lyin' there all hurt and bleedin'. Then s'pose a slimy green monkey runs over to him and says, 'You're hurt, you're dying, I'm a doctor, I can save you.' That rich, wealthy man would beg, 'Please help me, Doctor,' without even noticin' he's reachin' out to a slimy green monkey. Same thing if that tired black lady in her turned-over shoes leans down to him and says, 'I'm a doctor, I can help you.' He'd grab her hand, no matter than if it was darker than ten paper bags, and he'd look up at her like a baby looks at his nursin' mother 'cause she's somebody can keep him from dyin'."

Daddy made the scene so vivid that we stopped caring we weren't cute and light-skinned and felt proud that we were going to be doctors and even rich white men would see us as angels. We listened to Daddy when he said: "When all you got goin' for you is cuteness and then you get bags under your eyes, they forget about you and get someone younger. When all you can do is play basketball and you break your knee, they forget about you and give your place to someone else. But when what you got goin' for you is inside your head, that's something nobody can take away from you. Nobody. Ever. 'Cept by killin' you, and then it don't matter no more 'cause you're dead."

Second-born Jeanette, the brightest and best of us, was quick to latch on to Daddy's theme. "I'm gonna be a doctor," she chanted. "I'm gonna be a doctor with a scripperscrap hangin' 'round my neck and everybody'll grab my hand and love me."

"And call you Doc," Daddy applauded.

She savored the idea. "Doc. They'll call me Doc."

"In fact, I'm gonna start callin' you Doc right now," Daddy proclaimed. We were all going to become doctors, but Jeanette was the one who was going to be a doctor beyond the shadow of a doubt. It's unlikely that any of us wondered at this point if we could actually make it to becoming doctors, for we knew even less than Daddy about what it took to ascend to this exalted state, but if we did have misgivings about ourselves, we had no doubts about Jeanette. "Doc" she was, and doctor she would become.

Curiously enough, though, it was Jeanette who came home one day with a C on a test. Prior to that, B was the lowest grade any of us had gotten, and even a B caused Mommy to shake her head and ask, "Did anyone in the class get an A? Then you can get an A, too. You just have to study harder." But this time she looked at the C on Jeanette's paper and said nothing. Wasn't she going to lay into Jeanette? Was Doc so special that she could get away with anything? The rest of us were stunned. I, for one, resolved that if that's the way it was going to be, I was darned if I was going to work so hard at studying from then on.

Then Saturday came. Mommy roused Jeanette at 6:00 A.M., told her to dress in old clothes, and ordered her to the kitchen, where she handed Jeanette a bucket and scrub cloths. "You and I are going to clean the kitchen from top to bottom," Mommy announced. "I'm going to teach you how to do it and do every bit of it right because that's what you're going to be doing for a living when you grow up."

Jeanette was outraged. "I'm going to be a doctor!"

"Anybody who gets a C on a test is either too dumb or too lazy to be a doctor. You're going to end up working in somebody's kitchen, so you'd better know how to do it. Now, start by scouring the oven. And I want it spotless."

Neither tears nor argument moved Mommy; she remained stony, and for all of that day, Jeanette scrubbed the stove, the sink, the cupboards, the walls, the floor. Mommy was relentless. What was not done perfectly had to be done a second time, a third time. Jeanette's hands grew raw and cracked. "Yes," said Mommy inflexibly, "that's what happens when you do cleaning." Jeanette looked like pulled weeds and the rest of us were as meek as baby bunnies when Mommy lined us up on the living room couch at the end of the day.

She surveyed us with all the usual softening lines absent from her face. "Your father works. I work," she said slowly and emphatically. "The job you children have is to study. As long as you work at your job as hard as your father and I do at ours, we'll take care of the house. We'll do the cooking and the washing up and the cleaning. But if you don't do your job, if you fool around or get lazy, then you'll do the housework because that's what you'll be doing the rest of your life."

I looked at Jeanette's cracked and bleeding hands, at her slumped, defeated posture. Right, I thought to myself. I get it. I'll study.

Mommy had only one threat worse than that of becoming a cleaning woman, which was that we would be "shaking sheets at the Star Laundry" where she herself had once worked. She never failed to invoke the possibility of this hellish, if somewhat mysterious, fate when we drove past the establishment, just as she never failed to breathe heavily and conjure up the smiting hand of God when we drove past Monmouth Park Race Track. Gambling away good money was a sin, she declared, a sin with dire consequences, as she had searingly learned from her one experience with it.

When she and Daddy were living in New York, Mommy had gone into a numbers parlor to play a combination she had dreamed about, and while she was there the police raided the place. She tried to chew up her ticket but her mouth was too dry to swallow it, and she was threatened with arrest. She trembled all over when she confessed her sin to Daddy, and something of that same trembling emotion crept into her voice each time we passed the entrance to the track and she sounded her warning against going in. When I did finally go to the races one day twenty years later, goaded into it by a teasing remark that I was surely no longer under my mother's sway, I found that I was miserably uneasy every moment, quite certain that a horse would stampede, the grandstand collapse, or a madman shoot up the place, aiming the first bullet at me.

Teachers say: Give me a child at an impressionable age, and she's mine for the rest of her life. I gladly suspect that I am Mommy's and Daddy's for all of my life, for I am forty-seven now and not only can I not comfortably go to a race track but the other night in a restaurant, asked to wait in the bar until our table was ready, I was the only one in the party who didn't perch on a bar stool. Couldn't. Mommy had proclaimed, "Ladies do not sit on bar stools."

Such injunctions were burned into us, for Mommy felt strongly about proper behavior; about sitting with a straight back, knees together, legs crossed at the ankle; about walking with shoulders back, head high. "A person meeting you for the first time judges you by how you walk, how you speak, and how you're dressed," she told us. On our Sunday excursions to Asbury Park, she would watch for an example of what she called "a black walk." "See that?" she'd say. "I don't know that man from Adam, but I can tell from his walk he's stupid, dumb, a no account." Then she'd point to another man. "I don't know him either, but that's an educated person. His back's straight, he's walking straight, not slumping and slouching and oozing along."

She had us walk up and down the hall at home with books on our heads, all the while giving us instructions: "Always enter a room with your head up. Right away that tells people you're your own person. If your head is down, that lets people feel they can do anything they want with you. When you talk to somebody, white or colored, always look him straight in the eye. First of all, it's honesty. Second, he knows he can beat up on you if you don't make eye contact."

According to Mommy, not looking somebody in the eye, not having a strong handshake, and not holding your head up were character flaws. "But you have to be a lady," she always summed up. A lady never enters a room without saying "Good morning," and never leaves without a "Goodbye" to all present. A lady always speaks to inferiors just as readily and cordially as to superiors. A lady is never loud or obstreperous. These were articles of faith to Mommy, and she passed them on to us as if they were written on tablets of stone.

Because she was our mother and children assume a parent knows the ways of the world, it didn't occur to us to question where she had learned the commandments she was passing on to us, but I think back now and realize that it was extremely unlikely that she had gleaned them as a coal miner's daughter in West Virginia, only slightly less unlikely that she'd acquired them scouring cauldrons at Bluefield State Teachers College. I think she must have absorbed most of her ideas about etiquette, behavior, and the correct way of doing things from her white employer, Mrs. Egan.

Mrs. Egan, who had a large and lovely house in New Shrewsbury, New Jersey, an opulent town north of Long Branch, taught Mommy that forks go on the left, knives on the right; that you serve from the left and take away from the right; that when a fork is turned over on the dinner plate, the person has finished eating; that when a cup is turned over, the guest doesn't wish coffee and is to be asked if he or she would prefer tea. Mommy passed this information on to us. We even had some elegant things to practice setting a table with, for when a piece of china or crystal became chipped, Mrs. Egan gave it to Mommy. Our cutlery was the cheapest that could be bought in the dime store, but we acquired a sense that finer things existed from the sight and feel of Mrs. Egan's chipped etched goblets and bone-china dishes.

Along with the finer things, Mommy also brought Mrs. Egan's stale marshmallows home for us to eat. It struck us as odd when people remarked that a pillow was as soft as marshmallows or puffy clouds looked like marshmallows. Marshmallows, in our experience, were rock-hard and crunchy; delicious but you wouldn't want to rest your head on them. Not until we were grown did we become acquainted with their true nature.

Nor with the true nature of orange juice. Daddy diluted one small container of frozen orange juice with a gallon of water to stretch it into enough for all of us. When I finally tasted orange juice as it should be, I thought it was quite awful, rather like drinking almond extract.

Mommy cooked for birthdays and holidays, but Daddy did the everyday cooking. He liked to, I think, but also he probably felt that he coped better with the bargain chickens and meat than Mommy did. "So long as they make food," he used to say, "they'll make expensive cuts and what's left'll be cheap, and I can make the cheap cuts taste just as good as the expensive." None of us, so far as I remember, ever got sick from eating the overage food. In fact, we seldom fell ill from any cause. If we did develop a fever or come down with a cold, we weren't taken to a doctor. Daddy had his heart set on our becoming physicians, but he didn't want to have anything to do with the medical profession in the meantime because it swallowed up dollar bills.

"Get the doctor book," Daddy would tell Mommy when she greeted his homecoming with the news that a child was in bed. He would feel a fevered forehead. "High temperature—what do it say?"

"Musterole and aspirin," she would read from the home medical encyclopedia.

"Musterole and aspirin is what the book says? Okay, then that's what we gotta do."

On the night Daddy came home and found the sick child looking a little less peaked, he would gently suggest, "You want Daddy to fix you some nice fruit salad and maybe a nice piece of cake?" If the tempted child agreed that she could manage to choke down these treats, Daddy would sit by the bed until the last piece of fruit had been swallowed, the last cake crumb picked up on a moistened finger, then he'd roar, "Okay, you're well! Get outa that bed!"

Home doctoring didn't extend to home dentistry, except for baby teeth, which Daddy extracted in the time-honored way by looping strong thread around the loose tooth, tying the other end to a doorknob, and then slamming the door shut. Linda, when she was four or five, having seen Daddy perform this operation on us older ones, undertook it for herself, bravely and successfully, which so impressed the rest of us that we immediately predicted she was destined to be a dentist when she grew up. After establishing that dentists also have *Dr.* prefacing their names, she complacently agreed.

We were conscious of dentists because of Mommy's and Daddy's troubles with teeth. Both of them had more false than real ones in their mouths. Mommy lost her teeth through neglect, the common treatment for an aching tooth in East Beckley, West Virginia, being not to fill the tooth but to "treat it with cold steel," i.e., to pull it, and Daddy lost his because of his malocclusion. Of the five of us, Jeanette and I inherited Daddy's jaw structure, and since he was determined for us not to be dentally crippled as he was, he managed to materialize money enough for us to have teeth pulled and teeth added to align our bites so that the rest of our teeth would not drift, loosen, and fall out. About the time we needed this work, the brother of the owner of a garment sweatshop where Mommy worked as a presser graduated from dental school, so Daddy was able to arrange for a bargain rate.

Mommy's and Daddy's teeth, no matter how long and how often they soaked them in Polident, never gleamed whitely, for they were dedicated, devoted, enthusiastic smokers. Daddy came home in the morning from his all-night job, and before he went off to his day job, he and Mommy sat drinking coffee and smoking cigarettes while we kids ate breakfast and got ready for school. This was, in effect, our family roundtable talk time. Problems with schoolwork, that was Mommy's department, but problems with people, that's where Daddy held forth.

"Daddy," I said one morning, "a boy at school called me a thick-lipped bitch."

"I'll tell you what, Cookie," he advised. "When somebody says somethin' mean to you like that, you tell him thank you very much."

"I'm supposed to thank him? He isn't doing me any favor!"

"But you don't want him to know that. You want to confuse him. He's said somethin' that's s'posed to make you feel bad, and you say thank you very much, now he don't know what to do. He might try it once more jus' to make sure he understood you right, but when it still don't work to rile you, he's gonna give up and leave you alone."

He added, to drive his point home, "You never want to let nobody know they've pushed your buttons 'cause once they know they can do it, they'll keep doin' it. But if you don't ever let them know you even got buttons, that's it, that's all. There ain't nothin' they can do."

Daddy made everything into an object lesson—even the death of our much-loved dog, Butch, a German spitz who had been with us at Garfield Court and Seaview Manor and now at 174 Ludlow Street. Usually Butch was companionably in the midst of wherever we were, but one day we heard the screech of brakes and the heart-sinking howls of a badly injured dog. The truck driver had tried to stop and Butch had tried to scoot from under the wheels, but he hadn't quite made it; his pelvis was smashed.

"See," Daddy said a couple of days later at the breakfast table when our grief had become a little more manageable, "it's like I tell you, hormones is trouble. Butch went runnin' after that female dog across the street and got hisself killed. Same thing with men and women. When they get to runnin' after that taste of honey, they get themselves in trouble. Lotsa trouble."

Listening, I imagined myself crushed and bleeding like Butch if hormones got me to running after a boy.

Mommy, as determined as Daddy to vaccinate us against becoming dropouts at fifteen, added her own dark view. "Boys get girls pregnant, and what's the difference to them? It's no difference to them, but the girl's life is over. All the lovely things you were going to do, all the wonderful things you were going to learn, all the exciting places you were going to go, there's none of that now. Your life as you know it is ended. The only time it makes any sense to get pregnant is when you can tell yourself that if you died the next day, you've already done most everything you wanted to do."

Hearing this made us feel a little bit as though we had ruined

Mommy's life. "Mommy," we said, "don't you love us? Don't you like having us?"

"It's not that I don't love you," she said. "I just want you to understand that your life changes when you have kids, so you've got to decide when it's okay for it to change, not let some boy talk you into a taste of honey when it's not to your advantage."

"Boys don't care you're gonna be doctors," Daddy followed up. "They're lookin' out for what they want, so you gotta be lookin' out for what you want."

Sometimes Jeanette would buck whatever it was Daddy was trying to teach us by quoting a friend or teacher, "Well, so-and-so said we should do this or so-and-so said we shouldn't be doing that," which didn't go down well with Daddy.

"Doc," he would say, "you look in the mailbox on your way to school and see if there's a certified check in there to pay for your food and the nap you're wearin' off the carpets in this house. If there is, you bring it to me and I'll listen to the person who's got his name on that check about how to raise my kids."

What Daddy hated most was the possibility that we might hear from other people that because we were black, we daren't dream, mustn't plan to go places, shouldn't bother to study, because how much do you have to know to clean houses and dig ditches? "I don't want no one dilutin' the message," he told Mommy, who had more of a sense of us as children and would have let us go to the playground to rollerskate and play ball. Daddy would have none of it. "There's five of them," he argued. "They can play with each other. What do they need to go outside the family for?" He wanted us to look only to each other for help and companionship. "If we stick together," he said over and over, "there's nothin' this family can't do."

If we stick together...and, he might well have added, if you do what I say, for that was the implication: that we should listen to and be guided by him. If we didn't, trouble was quick to follow, almost as if he had planned it. Like the time we went to the beach. Neither Mommy nor Daddy could swim and we were under strict orders not to go in the water, but Jeanette, being Jeanette, defied the ban. Venturing into the surf up to her knees, she came screeching out, stung by a jellyfish and with a crab clamped on her big toe. Incidents like this made Daddy seem prescient and kept the rest of us enthusiastically in line.

One morning Jeanette, bucking Daddy on some point, hit on the argument probably every child in the world has used against his or her parents: "I didn't ask to be born."

Daddy had an answer for it. "I know you didn't ask to be born, honey, and as your father responsible for gettin' you into the world, I owe you somethin'. I owe you three hots and a cot, which is to say, I owe you three meals a day and a place to sleep. That's what I'm obliged for, and that's what I'm lookin' to see you get." He nodded several times, overcome by the seriousness of his obligation, then leaned back in his chair with a curl to his mouth like a villain's mustache. "'Course, nobody says the meals has got to be chicken. S'pose I just give you bread and water? An' s'pose I let you sleep on the floor?"

"No, Daddy!"

"That's all I'm obliged for, honey. Everything else is gratis. Everything else I do for you is 'cause I want to, not 'cause I have to."

For days afterward, because Daddy had a tenacious mind of the sort that doesn't easily turn loose one idea and go on to another, he would set a plate in front of Jeanette with, "See, I ain't obliged to give you this. I could give you bread and water and soup with just a little bit of fat floatin' in it, just to keep you alive. That's all I'm asked to give you. But you get more, right? You get this nice plateful, and I imagine when it comes to dessert, you'll have some of that, will you? All right, dessert, and all the other good stuff. But just remember, the good stuff I do for you is because I want to, because I'm your daddy and I love you and I want to, not because I have to."

The subtext to this was that it was not enough for us, the children, to behave in minimal ways either, that filial respect and dutifulness might be all that was basically required of us, but the good stuff, like doing well in school and sticking together as a family and paying attention to what Mommy and Daddy were trying to teach us, we would do because we loved them and wanted them to love us.

Perhaps because Donna and Jeanette were paired, and Linda and Rita were paired, and I was just sort of in the middle by myself, I was particularly anxious for love and approval from Mommy and Daddy. It occurred to me, as it had to Jeanette, that playing a musical instrument was a way to ensure their attention. Donna, progressing in her lessons, had set her heart on a larger and deeper-toned tenor sax, and when Daddy finally managed to buy her one, I begged for the old alto sax.

"You, Cookie? You ain't but five. You can barely breathe, honey, let alone blow in that horn."

"Yes, I can, Daddy. I can blow it." The sax was too heavy for me to hold, but I got it braced on a chair, then I blew. And blew. And blew. I blew so hard that I passed out. When I came to, Daddy allowed as how he had been planning to sell the horn, but okay, I could have it and he would figure out a way for me to go to Mr. Winthrop for lessons, too.

So, that was three of us studying music. Daddy and I reminisced about it years later: "I didn't want to see those horns go up in the attic after I spent for them and the lessons, so the challenge went like this: if Donna got me a nice song and I praised it, then you, Cookie, the next day, you can bet you had a nice song for me, too, because you wanted the same praise.

"Now we got two horns and a guitar goin' in the house, and to be honest with you, Cookie, sometimes the noise would drive me nuts. I'd go into the living room where you was practicin' and I'd say, 'Oh, that was so nice. Daddy loved it,' then I'd go down to the kitchen and say, 'Oh, God, it's driving me insane.' I'm talkin' 'bout the time you thought you had learned how to blow the horn but the only thing that was gettin' out was noise. You knew how to set your lips to get a big sound, and you got it, never mind whether it was in the right key or not. But I knew you were young and it would come."

From the beginning, Daddy was against our learning to play

by ear. He wanted us to learn to read music, be taught theory, and acquire such a soild foundation that we would be able to play jazz, which he loved. As we got better, he began looking for teachers beyond Mr. Winthrop. The 389th Army band, staffed with skilled musicians and good enough to be called on to play at the White House, was stationed at Fort Monmouth. Daddy took to hanging around the servicemen's club when members of the band played for dances.

He stood off to the side of the bandstand and watched and listened. "I picked out who I thought played the best. I'd go up to the fellow and say, 'I got three little girls learnin' music. Could you come over to my house and teach them 'cause I don't want them to learn by ear?' Like, I picked out this guy—he played the guitar and it sounded so sweet and full of life—and I asked him and he said, 'Sure, where do you live?' I told him Long Branch and offered to pay him three dollars an hour, which he said was all right. He was the kind of person that didn't watch the time, which I liked, and whenever Jeanette asked him something, he never said, 'We'll get to that later, not now, you're too young,' so that gave her a good edge and she played very, very good.

"I always made sure Tass was there or I was there for the lessons so that what the guy said one of you girls was weak on, we would know. Kids want to please you, so if we'd sent you to the music studio, you'd have come home and told us the man said you played great. This way, we heard it when the man said, 'Donna, you gotta be stronger on your . . .' whatever. When he comes back again, we're sittin' there again, and he says, 'No, I told you last week you gotta . . .' Now Donna knows I've heard this twice and it's costin' me three dollars, and she's gonna make sure I don't hear it one more time."

As soon as I got far enough along on the alto sax, Donna, Jeanette, and I began playing together. "They're good," one of the army musicians eventually told Daddy. "You wouldn't know it was little girls playing. But they need a rhythm section."

Daddy thought this over. "Linda's five now and she likes to

beat up on things," he mused. "Maybe I can get her goin' on drums."

Daddy got hold of drumsticks and a rubber pad and hired a soldier-drummer to teach her. Linda learned the right way, not the lazy way of holding both sticks between thumb and fingers like a hammer, but, rather, by laying the left stick easy between the index and middle fingers and letting it rest against the thumb. Linda quickly mastered the paradiddle, a type of drum roll. The instructor was impressed. Daddy asked if she was promising enough for him to go into hock for a trap set, and when the instructor said she was, back he went to Mr. Moss with the war memorabilia, which had been redeemed, pawned again for Donna's tenor sax, and redeemed again. Now the money went down the street to Mr. Scott for a drum set.

With Linda playing drums to provide the rhythm, with the guys from the Army band treating us not like kids but like real musicians, somewhere in that time there came into being the concept of our being a band. There is something special about people closely related by blood playing or singing together, like the Lennon Sisters or the Mills Brothers, and that wordless communication made the music sound better than anything we could have produced alone, while the sense of being in sync made us enjoy practicing. We didn't mind that Daddy didn't want us to run with other kids. Our world became exclusively study and practice, and we loved it.

Did Daddy plan it that way so that our attention would be turned inward to the family and our satisfactions would come from each other? Like most things in life, it was probably some planning and some happenstance: the happenstance of a little red saxophone in a Cracker Jack box; then his seeing a way of capitalizing on Donna's interest to pull the rest of us into a shared, absorbing, and rewarding pursuit, and his keeping it going by making sure we had praise and rewards, encouraging words and ice cream.

Did he anticipate that music making might someday pay the

tolls on the road to our becoming doctors? I think not. Daddy was on such unknown terrain that, like Robinson Crusoe on his island, he simply used whatever came to hand to help him in his blind but determined quest to equip us to build better lives for ourselves.

◆ 4 ◆

The Thornettes

A LIFE PIVOTS ON INCIDENTS. Aunt Gloria, one of Daddy's older sisters, trained as a nurse at Monmouth Memorial Hospital in Long Branch, and when I was eight, she took me on a visit there. We were in an elevator and a woman with a huge belly got on. She seemed to me to be fat in an unusual way, and I was staring at her when suddenly she screamed, squatted on the floor, and a bloody creature dropped from under her skirt. The creature looked like an animal but not like an animal. It started to cry, and I whispered to Aunt Gloria, "I think it's a baby."

The elevator doors opened, and hospital personnel rushed in and whisked mother and child away. Wow, I thought to myself, she got on the elevator one person and got off two people. At that moment I knew that was what I wanted to do when I became a doctor: I wanted to deliver babies. I didn't know the word *obstetrician*. I had never heard of a "maternity ward." How babies were delivered was unknown to me. I simply knew that I wanted to be present when one person became two.

Why did Aunt Gloria take me to the hospital that day? I cannot imagine, for we seldom saw her. Donald's relatives took little interest in Donald's children. He was the only one of all his brothers and sisters to marry young; the others were in their late twenties before they managed to wobble out of Nanna's orbit long enough to take a spouse, and we were teenagers before a single cousin was born.

Sometimes an aunt dressed in her Sunday finest would stop by, and later Daddy would say, "She's just showin' off. Don't worry about it. You might have a little hole in your dress here, a little patch on your sleeve there, but you're clean." And he would go on to turn the visit into one of his lessons for us.

"She's comin' over here all dressed up and she don't even bring you so much as a piece of chalk for a present. Now, what does that tell you? She ain't comin' over here to see you; she's comin' over here for you to see her." Then he would tell us: "Don't listen to what people say. Look at what they do. When these same people come to you later on when you're grown up and ask for your advice, don't deny them. Just remember that when they had the chance to be nice and give you things, they didn't do it. I don't want you to hold any sort of hostility. Malice wears you down. It makes you evil. It wastes your time that you could be doin' something positive with. But it don't hurt to remember back."

Sometimes when we were out driving, we would see the shades up at an aunt or uncle's house, but when Daddy tooted the horn, the shades slowly descended. We knew they were saying, "Oh-oh, here come Donald and his six splits."

"They're home but they don't want us to see them," Daddy said. "That's okay. We'll go for a ride and I'll buy ice cream for everybody. Don't worry about these small-minded people. You'll show them when you grow up."

If it happened to be around New Year's, we knew for sure that no one would welcome us because in the black subculture there was, and still is, a superstition that if a female crosses your threshold first, you'll have bad luck the rest of the year. Even though Daddy could have gone through the door before us, the relatives were not likely to take a chance. Nor did we see them at Christmastime. "You'd think they could at least bring the kids a little toy or a set of jacks from the ten-cent store," Mommy and Daddy said to each other every year. But the relatives never did.

Because our family had so little money for Christmas presents, we would each draw a name and buy one sister a present, and all of us kids would go together on a gift for Mommy and Daddy. With Mommy it was okay; we could get her Evening in Paris perfume or Sweet Pea cologne from Woolworth's. But Daddy was difficult. We couldn't buy him aftershave lotion because he didn't have a beard. He said it was because he had Indian blood, just like Mommy, and Indians don't have facial hair, or so little that it isn't worth shaving.

For Christmas decorations we would string popcorn and wrap empty shoe boxes in colored paper with ribbons and bows. After dinner on Christmas Eve, when most Christmas tree sellers were about to close up, Daddy would go downtown and get a tree for next to nothing. He would bring home this scraggly, picked-over tree that nobody had wanted. We would set it up, and miraculously, after Mommy decorated it with bubble lights, ornaments, and a star on top, it was transformed into something beautiful. We would arrange the empty boxes under it so it looked like there were lots and lots of presents.

Once somebody came to the house after Christmas and was curious about why we hadn't opened all our gifts. We improvised desperately. "Oh, they're for relatives coming up from the South," we said. *"Way* down South. They won't be here for days yet."

We couldn't use our allowances to buy gifts because we didn't have any. "Allowances?" said Mommy blankly when we suggested them. "What's allowances?" We made do, instead, by collecting bottle money. In those days there was a two-cent deposit on Coke and Pepsi bottles and a five-cent deposit on large ginger ale bottles. We pounced on the empties whenever we spotted them in gutters and weedy vacant lots and trundled them in a little wagon to the candy store on the corner. The returns provided our pocket money and money for the collection plate at the Second Baptist church.

After the "Little Miss Sunshine" incident, Mommy decided we would bypass Sunday School and attend the regular service with her. Because the minister had a captive audience, his sermons—frequently interrupted by shouts of "Yes, Lord!" and "Oh, Jesus, I've got the spirit!"—tended to go on and on. We were often restless and bored, but we behaved in a thoroughly disciplined fashion, neither playing with the fans with the names of funeral parlors printed on them nor whispering to each other nor kicking the pew in front of us, because we had done all of these things the first time Mommy took us to church and when we got home, she had given us the whipping of our lives.

"House of God!" she roared, lashing at us with a broken, hard-rubber belt from her sewing machine. "House of God and you're kicking and whispering and fooling around! Next time you'll be quiet!" Whomp. "Next time when the minister's talking, you'll be still!" Whomp. And whomp again. And again—the hard rubber raising welts wherever it landed.

She was right: next time, and every time thereafter, she had only to look at us with one eyebrow slightly raised, and no matter how hot it got and how furiously the funeral parlor fans waved, we never moved through all the amens and announcements of the arrival of the spirit.

So confident was Mommy of our behavior after that one whipping that she sometimes sent us to church alone. It was on one such occasion that the Reverend Williams descended upon us after the service and ordered us to stand over to the side until the rest of the congregation had filed out. "Are you putting pennies in the collection plate?" he demanded.

We looked to Jeanette to answer him. "It's our bottle money," she said, and started to explain how we collected it.

"We don't take pennies!" the reverend thundered.

Chagrined and shamed, we ran home with this news. Daddy exploded. "Tass, I told ya! These kids work hard to put together their pennies, an' he don't want 'em. He don't want 'em!"

That was the last time we went to the Second Baptist church, but not the last dealings we had with the Reverend C. P. Williams. Several years later, in 1961, Nanna died. She had been ill with diabetes for a long time and had made Betty, the foster child she was supposed to be caring for, leave school to take care of her, to sit by her bed for hours massaging her feet, and to cook and clean and be a slavey for the aunts and uncles. It distressed Daddy, but there wasn't anything he could do about it. He had always had a soft spot for Betty and felt protective toward her ever since a time when he had taken his mother and Betty to Asbury Park to see Betty's mother. He told me about it years later.

"I was driving and I blew the horn and Betty's mother came out. My mother said, 'We brought your little girl around so you could see her.' The woman glanced in the car at Betty, turned and stalked back into the house, and slammed the door. Now, I was young—it was before I was married—but I said to myself, 'How can anybody do this to a little child? How can anybody do this to a baby?'"

When Nanna died the child welfare system offered anyone in the family the option of keeping Betty. All the aunts and uncles announced they wanted her, but Daddy knew they would use Betty as a servant just as Nanna had, so he said he would take her. "You've got all those girls already, Donald," they objected.

"Let Betty decide," Daddy said. "Let her say where she wants to go."

"With Donald," Betty whispered. "I want to go with Donald." Cowed by years of browbeating, of being told she was stupid and worthless, Betty had just enough spark to stick to her decision when the child welfare representative questioned whether she wouldn't be wiser to go where there were fewer children and a larger house. The representative then had to investigate whether the house and people were fit to have her.

"Mr. Thornton," said the investigator, "you already have five daughters."

"I do," he said, "and you look at my daughters and you won't see none of 'em in turned-over shoes or actin' unmannerly or lookin' nothin' but healthy."

"Your sister wants Betty and she can do more for her than you can afford to."

Daddy started to say, My sister don't mean Betty no good, but he told himself he couldn't rat on his sister, so he said instead, "I can handle another girl. I can give Betty a carin' home. I want to put her back in school."

Daddy told us, "I think it was my sayin' I wanted to put Betty back in school that made up the lady's mind. Plus I told her that Betty only had a certain length of time before she would be ready to be a wife and she hadn't oughta be goin' into marriage thinkin',

'Nobody loves me. They can do this to me, they can do that to me, and I got no right to stick up for myself.' Those thoughts hadn't oughta be there, and if it was God's will, I wasn't gonna let 'em be there."

Daddy went on: "People aren't dumb, specially the state. They figured, Hey, this guy here, maybe he wants to do right for Betty, and they said, 'Okay, but you got to have three or four references and a blood test and a chest X ray.' I thought, what the heck is this? I got five kids at home already and I didn't need to get a blood test. But I went to the hospital and went through this, and I put down the banks I owed money to and the pawnshop where I pawn my stuff when I need money and the Second Baptist church 'cause you have to go to church if you're gonna take a child.

"So after a while the lady from the state, she called me up and she says, 'Mr. Thornton, everyone gave you a wonderful character reference, but I'm gonna tell you something—maybe I shouldn't but I'm gonna tell you anyhow. The only one you got to watch out for is Reverend Williams. He talked about you like you were a dog. He said you didn't send your kids to church and he didn't think it would be a nice home for Betty to go to because you're not a religious family. But you know what we decided? We've decided to send Betty to your house anyway.' I said, 'Thank you very much. Now I got six daughters.' "

The role of self-effacing caregiver had been laid out for Betty by Nanna. It was what she knew how to do and she did it automatically. But when Daddy found her slipping into the same subservient role in our house, he called an immediate halt to it. We were older by then and took turns drying the dishes after dinner, but there came a Thursday followed by a Friday on which Betty was drying the dishes both nights. "Betty," Daddy hollered, "didn't I see you dryin' last night?"

"Yes, sir."

"Then it can't be your turn tonight. Whose turn is it?" No one answered, so then he really bellowed. "WHOSE NIGHT IS IT?"

"Jeanette's," Donna told him.

"Jeanette, if you don't get yourself down here, I'll pick up this shoe and I'll… Betty, you get upstairs."

One night Daddy came home and Betty wasn't there. Mommy explained that his brothers had called and wanted her at their house. "They did, eh?" Daddy said, and wheeled and marched over to what we still referred to as Nanna's house. He was yelling at Betty when he walked in the door. "What're you doin' here? If you don't get up and get out of here and get back home…!" Betty was already up and running out the door as Donald turned on his brothers. "You take care of your house and yourselves," he told them. "I'm takin' care of Betty."

Daddy was driving an oil truck then, and soon after Betty came to us, he hoisted her up on the front seat beside him and drove her to school. The two went to the principal's office. "Betty's one of my girls now and I want her in school," he announced. He was prepared to argue, but the principal volunteered that they were only too glad to have Betty back. "Not in the stupid class," Daddy said. "My mother's been callin' her dumb all her life, but Betty's not dumb. My wife and my girls'll help her till she catches up."

Betty went on to graduate from high school. But long before that, Daddy, who believed in setting goals, discussed her plans with her. Coaxed to express her wishes, Betty guessed that she liked taking care of people. Instead of saying, "Well, you can become a day worker," Daddy suggested, "Why don't you become a nurse?"

"I think I'd like that," Betty admitted, and that is what happened. She became a licensed practical nurse and went to work at Monmouth Medical Center. When, at twenty-two, Betty married, Daddy gave her a wedding reception at the Garfield-Grant Hotel in the center of town. The social worker who had placed her with Daddy stood up at the dinner and made a little speech about Betty's godfather, Mr. Thornton, who put her back in school and encouraged her to enter a profession and now was giving her this lovely reception to celebrate her wedding. The social worker had given Daddy a wink when she started to speak, and when she said these things, she was looking right at the Reverend C. P. Williams, who was sitting there stuffing himself with veal at a feast paid for by the man he had said was a heathen and not fit to provide a good Christian home for Betty.

But long before all this came to pass, we loved having Betty with us because she had always seemed like a sister to us and she was another person in our circle. Daddy didn't like us to have friends. If one of us started a sentence with: "My girlfriend..." Daddy interrupted.

"What girlfriend? You mean your sister?"

"No..."

"Your *sister*?"

"Oh, yeah, my sister," we would give in, knowing that Daddy wanted us to stick together, not to go outside the family.

"That's what you got the music for, so you can be playin' with each other."

"But, Daddy, what if we want to play with dolls?"

"No dolls! I don't want you playin' with dolls, you hear?" He wouldn't allow a doll in the house. "Girls get dolls," he said, "and as soon as they get big enough to have babies, the doll baby picture comes back and they have a baby. There's a time for babies. Now's the time for learnin', for gettin' your music. We're a poor family so we got to know which way we're goin'."

That they could have babies at fifteen was a big disadvantage of girls, in Daddy's opinion. On the other hand, he had discovered a real advantage to them. As he later said: "Girls are very determined to win and keep the love of their daddy. For me to smile was like Santa Claus coming to a child on Christmas. When I was frownin', they begged me, 'Daddy, what's the matter?' I wouldn't tell them. 'Daddy, *please* tell us what's the matter.' I'd say, 'You've been bad girls.' 'Daddy, we'll be good. Just talk to us. Just smile.' And when I'd smile, they'd say with satisfaction, 'Daddy's happy.' A beating only matters to a child when you're beating them. But when one of my girls said, 'Daddy?' and I said sternly, 'Yes?' instead of, 'What you want, sugar?' they didn't like that. So then I told them, 'You want me to be a good daddy, you got to be a good daughter.'

"I told them, never ask of a person what you can't give of yourself. In other words, if you expect me to be nice and give you the things you want, you got to be nice and give me what I want. I want you to study. I want you to do good by your music lessons."

One day I came home from school and bragged, "Daddy, I got an A."

"That's good, Cookie."

"That's all you're gonna say, Daddy?"

"Well, there's A+, isn't there?"

So then I came home with an A+ and he said, "Very good, honey. Now get A+ +." He wasn't being harsh. He knew that, as black children, we had a long, long way to go, and he believed that, "When you reach the point where you think you got it, you lose it. You've always got to keep in your mind that there's more to be grasped."

He never made the mistake of thinking that his daughters were geniuses. He always said we were just average, run-of-the-mill children, nothing smart, nothing brilliant about us. "But," he said, "they are children given the chances that every child should be given. When people say they aren't smart like my kids and so they can't do what my kids are doing, I tell them they're wrong. If you want to do it, if you put your mind and your thoughts and your heart and your soul to it, you'll do it. It's when you don't want to be bothered to work hard that you'll find all kinds of excuses."

Daddy was like the coach of an all-girls' team, motivating, punishing, rewarding, pushing sternly, and prodding gently; never letting us forget that our ultimate aim in life was to become doctors and giving us nearer goals, like A+ + +, to shoot for along the way. To give us goals in music, every several months he would scrape together a hundred dollars to pay for us to make a record at the Bell Sound Studios on West 54th Street in New York City. The record was never intended for sale or for any other purpose than to let us hear our own progress, to provide us with evidence that we were getting better, that all the practicing was paying off.

We practiced in the late afternoons after we had straightened up the house and finished our homework. Mommy would come home from Mrs. Egan's. Dead-tired, she'd slump down on the couch and say, "Play 'Some Enchanted Evening' for me, kids," and we would and she'd fall asleep. We figured we weren't hitting any sour notes if she could sleep like that, but maybe it was just that she was so exhausted.

A few years later, she began working as a presser in a garment factory in Long Branch. For a while she had done piecework sewing. She would bring home a big bag of material for cuffs and pockets, and we would help her with the sewing, but when she found that pressers made much more money, she went to work on the steam machines in the factory.

Daddy kept asking, "Tass, why are you gettin' so thin?"

"Because of sweating so much at that pressing machine," she'd tell him.

Daddy got angry one day. "Enough of that stuff! How many times I got to tell you to quit?"

But Mommy liked to have her own money. If she asked Daddy for a dollar to buy a pair of stockings, he would say okay, but then he'd fish around and fish around in his pockets until he'd put together ninety-nine cents, and he'd say, "Here. You can find another penny somewhere."

He would do the same thing to us kids. We'd say, "Daddy, the school pictures cost two dollars," and he'd go in his pocket and come up with a dollar. "Daddy, they cost *two* dollars." He would root around some more and find a quarter, then he'd pick the lint off a nickel, and scratch around and there'd be a dime, and finally he'd get up to $1.97 and hand it over, saying, "You can find three cents someplace, kids."

If you came back and said, "Daddy, I can't. I can't find a single cent," he'd say, "Okay, I just found a couple of pennies," and he would hand them over and now you had enough, but the whole process was agonizing.

We were poor, of course, but I don't think it was that so much as he loved having all of us dependent on him. "Donald and his six splits" could just as well have been "Donald and his six spokes," with Daddy as the hub of the wheel around which we all revolved.

Whether it was conscious or not, I think another way of keeping us dependent on him was by making us fat. He had a lunch break at three o'clock in the morning from his all-night shift at Fort Monmouth, and he would scoot home and wake us up. "Hey, kids, Daddy's home. Daddy's got blueberry pie for you." He would cut big wedges from a leftover pie he had been given by a friend who worked in the mess hall, pile ice cream on the slices, and wave the plates under our noses.

"Is it fattening, Daddy?"

"Naw, it's good for you."

If he thought he detected a slackening off in appetite, he insisted we take something called Father John's Tonic. The predictable consequence was that, except for Jeanette, we were all heavy. Linda in particular was a very fat little girl. But that was fine with Daddy because he figured that the more overweight we became, the less attractive we would be to boys.

Mommy came home from a PTA meeting one evening and mentioned that someone's child had played a piano piece. "You tell them that at the next meeting the Thornettes'll play," Daddy said.

"What's the Thornettes, Daddy?"

"That's you, kids. You can play 'Some Enchanted Evening' for them like you do for Mommy."

An almost solidly white PTA audience responded delightedly to four plump little black schoolgirls solemnly playing "Some Enchanted Evening" with grace and feeling and not a single wrong note, and we were immediately invited to play for a PTA fund-raising dance. Our instructors from the Army band provided us with what musicians call "the fake book," a collection of all the standard songs, with parts for the saxophone, piano, guitar, etc. Daddy made us music stands out of cardboard boxes, and with the fake books propped in front of us, our musical training was so good that we could sight-read any song that was requested. With Linda on the drums providing a gentle, swishing, rustling, whispering background beat, the Thornettes were a combo easy to listen and dance to.

It was 1955. Linda was six, I was eight, Jeanette ten, and Donna eleven. Were we paid for the many PTA meetings and dances we played at? I don't know. Money was Daddy's province. It went into his pocket; it came out of his pocket. He ran the family.

Perhaps he thought the Thornettes needed a piano player or perhaps he just wanted to be part of the music. In any event, he decided that he would learn the piano. He bought one on time for thirteen dollars a month and hired a German woman married to an American soldier to come to the house to teach him.

As he remembered it, "This lady is tellin' me what I got to do, and I'm tellin' her, 'You mean, all my fingers got to move that way?' So I knew I couldn't do that. So I'm lookin' over at Rita, my youngest, who's sittin' there, and I says, 'Maybe you ought to try to teach my daughter.' The teacher says, 'How old is she? Four? Wait another six months until she starts school, then I'll take her.' After six months I contacted her again to have her start givin' Rita music. She said Rita's fingers were too small to hit the keys, but she'd try. And Rita took to it. I mean, her four sisters were the Thornettes and Daddy was takin' them to play Friday nights at the canteen at Fort Monmouth and Saturday nights to the Elks Club in Asbury Park and the soldiers was comin' to give them lessons and write arrangements for the band, and you can bet she wanted to be a part of that."

Somehow we kids heard that the Paramount Theatre in Long Branch had an amateur show every week and that the prize for coming in first was a radio, exactly what Mommy would love to have for the mantel over the fireplace in our living room. We made plans to enter the contest and win it as a surprise for her. We enlisted the help of our grandfather, who owned a pickup truck and promised to deliver the drums and our instruments and us to the theater, and we practiced "Rock Around the Clock," the song by Bill Haley and the Comets that ushered in the rock and roll era.

We were confident we would win because we had been playing in public for a couple of years, everybody loved us, and we could hear from the records Daddy took us to New York to make that, once we started to get good, we had gotten really good fast. But we lost. A little girl twirling a baton came in first. "How come?" we asked our grandfather as we left by the stage door. "She wasn't as good as we were."

Grandfather jerked his head in the direction of the little girl's mother, who was whispering head-to-head with the theater manager. This was our introduction to the notion that the world is not necessarily a fair place. We were terribly disappointed not to capture the radio for Mommy, but we felt good about what we had done. Before this, it was Mommy and Daddy taking us to the PTA meeting, taking us to the Elks Club. This time it was like: *Here we are. We're doing it! We're good. It didn't work out, but, hey, we're on our way.*

When we practiced now, particularly something like "Shout" by the Isley Brothers or "I Feel Good" by James Brown, all up and down the street people opened their windows and danced in their living rooms or out on the sidewalk, as though they couldn't help it, as though the music got in their feet and they just had to move. When Daddy saw that, he began hiring a hall and charging admission for Saturday night dances. Because he was always food oriented, he would make up big batches of sausage and meatballs in tomato sauce to sell in the back of the hall, and in between sets we'd be back there helping him serve up the plates. We never said no when he told us to do something. We never even questioned it. Daddy said this was a way of making money, and we just went ahead and did it.

He made one more attempt at becoming part of the band himself. He decided he would play the bass. This was the late 1950s when electric bass guitars had come on the market, but Daddy wanted a jazz bass, the upright acoustic bass with four strings and no frets, like a cello—the most difficult kind to play. As usual, he found a first-rate instructor to come to the house. All through those years, from the time I was nine until I was in high school, he had serious musicians coming every Saturday to teach us. Reuben Phillips who conducted the Apollo Theatre orchestra made arrangements and wrote original compositions for us. Another fellow, who had gotten out of the army and was teaching at Juilliard, worked with us on counterpoint and composition. Again, I don't know how or whether Daddy paid them. All I know is that he was a master at persuading people to do what he wanted them to do.

Daddy had two lessons on the bass. As she had done through the years while we were being taught, Mommy sat in the room crocheting and listening. After the second lesson, the teacher said, "Donald, you're going to have to practice more." Daddy was working two jobs, hiring halls, cooking sausages. When was he going to find time to practice? Mommy didn't say anything. The next week the teacher came. Mommy had the book; she had practiced. She played for the teacher, and Daddy was out, Mommy was in.

Mommy came in on bass. Rita came in on the piano. When we practiced in our tiny living room, Linda on drums was in front of the picture window, Jeanette on guitar and Donna and I on tenor and alto sax were in front of the fireplace, Rita on piano was against the wall, and Mommy on bass was at the top of the stairs going down to the kitchen so she could smell if dinner was burning. We would practice and practice and practice. We loved it. All of us. We were family and it was fun.

◆ 5 ◆

Show Biz

WHATEVER MONEY THE THORNETTES were bringing in, that much and more was going out on lessons, music arrangements for the band, maintaining the instruments, and material for the dresses Mommy made for us to wear when we played, which meant that Daddy kept right on working his two jobs: as a janitor at Fort Monmouth on the night shift from midnight until eight in the morning and during the day making deliveries of home heating oil. He lived in dread of missing a mortgage payment, for fear the bank would immediately foreclose on the house he had labored so hard to build, and his worst nightmare threatened to come true the day his supervisor at Fort Monmouth, a civilian, called him in, saying he had heard a rumor that Daddy was moonlighting on a second job.

"This is your main job," the supervisor said.

"I know that, sir," Daddy told him respectfully. "I'm just tryin' to make a little extra money. My kids are fixin' to go to college someday...."

The supervisor cut him off. "I'm putting you on days."

Daddy pleaded with him. "But the more I begged," Daddy reported later, "the more he just kept sayin', 'This is the job. Be here Monday morning.' He got me so upset, I went to see the army officer in charge and explained it to him why I had to stay on nights, and the major went back to the supervisor and told him, 'You leave Thornton alone. He don't take no sick leave. He don't take no annual leave. You let him stay where he's at.'"

So, all was well...until a Friday night six months later when the major sought Daddy out to shake his hand and tell him he was retiring. "Oh, my God, the super's got me this time," Daddy

63

moaned to himself, and, sure enough, he was called in on Monday and told to report at eight Wednesday morning.

"I begged him again," Daddy said. "It's the only time I ever got down on my knees to a guy. I told him, 'I've been drivin' the oil truck all winter through the cold and the ice and the snow. Just let me work two more months. If the oil company has to get a new man now, he don't know the stops, the tanks is covered with snow and he can't find where they's at, and I'll miss out on my end-of-season bonus which I really need for my kids.'

"He just looks at me and says, 'Report on Wednesday morning.' The guy wanted to screw me, really wanted basically to make life hard for me. He could've said, Yes, Donald, I understand you're strugglin'. That's what I say: There's some white people that are very good, and there's some white people that when you're tryin' to do something, they'll knock you down.

"So now I had to tell the oil man I had to quit. He says, 'Don, this is a bad time to be leavin' me,' and I says, 'I know it is, but I got no choice.' I really felt bad. I began to go down in my mind because everything I had planned seemed to be goin' out from under me. I knew I had to have more money. The bank isn't gonna understand that guy givin' me a hard time, and they're gonna take my house if I can't meet my mortgage."

There was a diner across the street from Fort Monmouth, and Daddy walked in there and asked if he could wash dishes at night. "I asked in such a way that the man said, 'All right, you come on in.' So when I was through during the day at Fort Monmouth, I started washin' dishes at this diner at night."

Daddy also began to cast around for a way for the band to make more than just break-even money. We had been watching *Ted Mack and the Original Amateur Hour* on TV for years, and when one of the contestants who had won became famous overnight, he said, "Hm-m-m. That's it. That's us." He told Jeanette to write the program a letter about the Thornettes, except to refer to us as the Thornton Sisters because it sounded more professional, like the King Sisters and the Andrews Sisters.

The "Amateur Hour" answered, telling us to come to New York for a tryout. We piled into our old car—Mommy, Daddy, five kids ranging in age from seven to fourteen, all the instruments; we looked like gypsies—and drove to Radio City in New York. It was 1959, the era of teeny boppers, and the place was jammed with mothers and kids, the kids jumping around with nerves and excitement. We were just as excited but did as we were told and sat with Mommy and Daddy until it was our turn.

"Don't call us, we'll call you. Next!" shouted the man doing the auditioning.

"That's all right," said Daddy, driving home. "We'll go back and we'll make it the next time."

We had already been practicing one and two hours a day as a band, in addition to each of us practicing individually for our lessons. Now we upped the practice sessions to two and three hours a day, and back and back we went to audition.

One day the magic words came. We were in! We were accepted! The Ted Mack Amateur Hour! TV! The whole school prepared to tune in. All of Long Branch. Daddy went to his Fort Monmouth supervisor and said, his tongue in his cheek and wanting to get even with him, "I got to thank you for putting me on days 'cause that's given me the chance to get my kids on television."

Daddy studied the Ted Mack show as though he were the coach of a team on its way to the Superbowl, searching for an edge, an advantage we could exploit to win. "Whatever it takes, kids, that's what we got to do." After a time he announced, "I got it. That Ted Mack is Irish, and what wins on his show is people doin' the Irish jig. You're gonna have to learn to do an Irish jig."

"We're gonna dance and play at the same time?"

He pointed out that Linda had a drum solo in "Jumpin' with Symphony Sid," the song that was our specialty, and while she was doing her turn, Donna and I could put down our saxophones and dance a jig. It didn't occur to us to say that doing an Irish jig to a jazz tune was incongruous, only slightly less incongruous than little black girls doing an Irish jig at all. We were so used to taking Daddy's word that it never crossed our minds to say, "Hey, that's stupid."

We did object to our costumes, however, complaining that we would die of the heat under the lights, but Daddy insisted that every inch of us had to be covered, everything but our faces and hands. "Nobody's starin' at my girls," he growled, stipulating that the skirts of our jumpers must cover our knees and that we must wear tights under the jumpers, along with high-collared blouses, blazers, and loafers.

The big day arrived. Waiting backstage to go on, we were keyed up but not nervous because we weren't one person going out there but a unit, all of us sisters and Mommy supporting and strengthening each other. Daddy had often illustrated the strength there is in numbers by grabbing a stick from the pile of kindling by the fireplace and snapping it in two. "See how easy it is to break one of something?" he told us. Then he would pick up five sticks and try to snap them and they wouldn't break. "See, kids, if you stick together, you can't get broken. So long as you help each other, cover for each other, support each other, you'll be okay."

So, going out onstage, we felt good about ourselves, and because of Daddy's insistence on solid training, we had great confidence in our music. We stepped into the spotlight expecting to win.

"And now, from Long Branch, New Jersey, an instrumental group—the Thornton Sisters!"

Ted Mack singled out Mommy. "Are you all really sisters?"

"They certainly are, Mr. Mack. I'm their mother and I should know."

"Does Mr. Thornton play a musical instrument?"

"No, he just buys them for us."

"Ah, he buys them. Well, he ought to be entitled to listen then. All right, let's hear you."

The scripted lines were not great, but the audience chuckled appreciatively. And then we were playing. And jigging.

We came in second. The real Irish jig dancers came in first.

Even so, driving back to Long Branch, we were ecstatic. This was show biz! We were in it!

"No, you're not," cautioned Daddy. "Come Monday morning, you're back in school. You still got to do your studyin'."

With that native astuteness of his, Daddy sensed that the way to get to an ultimate goal is to set intermediate goals along the way. The next goal he targeted for us was Amateur Night at the Apollo Theatre in Harlem. If an act won four Amateur Nights in a row, the prize was a week's engagement at the Apollo on the bill with stars.

Practice and study. Study and practice. That's all we did. Friends, dates, social life, none of these existed for us. If a girl invited one of us over, we said no, we had to practice. If a boy invited one of us to a movie, we said no, we had to practice. Rather than feeling deprived, though, we were actually a bit smug. I used to wear the neckstrap of my saxophone to school so the kids would whisper, "She plays saxophone. She's one of the Thornton Sisters."

We let it drop that we were going to New York to record, carefully not mentioning, of course, that we were recording for ourselves in order to detect where we needed to practice more. We begged Daddy to buy us an electric metronome, one that had a light, because with Linda on the drums, we couldn't hear the ticking of the old metronome. When he priced the new kind of metronome and found it cost a whole week's pay, he moaned and groaned, but he and Mommy decided that if that was what the band needed, he had to get it for us.

One day we found the metronome in pieces on the floor. "Who broke the metronome?" Mommy demanded. "Who broke the metronome?" No one answered. Four of us didn't know, and the guilty one wasn't saying. "Every one of you is getting a beating if you don't tell me who broke that metronome," Mommy warned. Nobody confessed. "All right, I'm going down to the kitchen to do the ironing, and I'm coming back up in an hour. You'd better tell me then who broke it. If it was an accident, I can understand that, but I cannot accept not being told the truth."

Mommy stalked down the stairs. We looked at each other. We sort of assumed that Rita had done it because she was the youngest and most likely to have been horsing around, but she denied it. We decided to stage a mock trial.

"Okay, Donna, where were you?"

"Down in the basement."

"Jeanette, where were you?"

"I was studying."

At the end of the hour we heard Mommy's heavy tread on the stairs. She looked from one to another of us. No one spoke. "Get in the back room," she ordered. She locked the door, pulled down the shades, and waded into us with Brown Betty, the broken sewing machine belt, roaring as she lay about her.

"Your father works so hard...." Crack! "You kids don't appreciate...." Crack! "I'll teach you to be truthful...." Crack! "Nobody's talkin'—who can I trust?" Crack! And crack! And crack! We were crying and screaming. Mommy was hissing through clenched teeth. Then suddenly the whipping was over. Mommy unlocked the door and went back to her ironing without another word, and when next we saw her, she simply called us to dinner as if nothing had happened. When Daddy got home and heard about the metronome, he didn't ask if we had been punished; the welts and the silence were eloquent enough. He took the metronome to be fixed, and from then on we surrounded it with pillows and no one could go near it without the rest of us chorusing, "Watch out for the light!"

The only other time I remember such a whipping was when Mommy had apparently called me for lunch and I was too busy preening in front of the mirror in the room I shared with Linda and Rita to hear her. The next thing I knew she was at me with Brown Betty, hitting me anywhere she could strike while I screamed, "What did I do? Mommy, what did I do?"

"I called you twice. You didn't answer. You didn't say, 'Mommy, I'm coming.' When I call you, you'd better say you're coming or you're in the bathroom or whatever because I'm not screaming my lungs out. You got to have feelings for other people.

It's rude and inconsiderate not to answer when someone's calling."

I'm a swift learner. From then on, when she yelled, "Cookie!" I answered instantly, "Yes, Mom, what do you want? I'll be right there."

A strict family rule prohibited us from taking a shortcut across the railroad tracks to get to school because over the years several children had been struck by trains. But one day Donna and Jeanette were late and reasoned that Mommy was at work and wouldn't see them crossing the tracks. Nowadays you have to worry about neighbors molesting your kids, but not so long ago they looked out for them, and what the neighbors saw quickly reached Mommy's ears. Donna and Jeanette knew better than to deny their wrongdoing, which saved them from a whipping but earned all of us one of Mommy and Daddy's lectures.

Always when we did something wrong, they sat us around the front-room table elaborating on what could happen to us if we didn't listen to them. "We've told you time and again not to cross those railroad tracks, but you're late and somebody says to cut across, and a train could have come and killed you." And, with a sudden shift of subject, "That's why teenagers get pregnant— because somebody says, 'Oh, this one time's not gonna hurt.' Or somebody says, 'Oh, one drink isn't gonna hurt you.' If you listen to that, you're weak minded, and weak-minded people end up in trouble. You have a mind. You got to use it. If somebody comes along and says, 'I'm gonna lead you to the Promised Land,' you got to say to yourself, 'Now wait a minute. Where is this guy comin' from?' You have to think things over because you could get hurt."

Their lectures were far more effective than whippings. When a whipping was over, it was over and the pain eventually subsided, but their words stuck in our minds. It could be years later when something would happen and you'd say to yourself, "Hey, I'm not going to do this because Mommy and Daddy said..." Their precepts never left us because there was nothing abstract about them; they were vivid and memorable.

In the summer of 1959, a few months after "Ted Mack and the

Original Amateur Hour" show, Daddy decided we were ready to try for the Apollo Theatre. The Apollo was like Mecca to black people. Everyone knew about Lena Horne, Cab Calloway, Ella Fitzgerald, Pearl Bailey, Billy Eckstine, Charlie Parker, Sarah Vaughan, Sammy Davis, Jr., and all the other greats who had gone on to stardom from the Apollo. Everyone knew that theatrical agents and record companies were on the lookout for new talent at the Amateur Nights. Everyone knew that the audience was discriminating and that if you could win four Wednesday nights in a row and earn a week's paid engagement with the stars, you had solid talent and were on your way to fame and fortune.

We knew it, too, and every Wednesday morning for two months that summer, we piled ourselves and our instruments and our hopes into the old car, trundled over the Pulaski Skyway, past the American Can Company, through the Holland Tunnel, up to 125th Street in Harlem, and waited in the basement of the Apollo Theatre to be allowed to audition. Daddy asked the guy in charge, "What does it take?"

The guy shrugged. "Keep coming back," he said.

We did. Every Wednesday morning we were there, people— all blacks—breathing on us from every side, everybody tense, restless, praying to be called to audition and become one of the five or six acts that would go on that night. There were singers, tap dancers, comedians, couples, quartets, but no other bands, particularly no other groups as young as we were. We looked like the schoolgirls we were; perhaps it was hard to take us seriously. Until we finally got a chance to audition. We were taken seriously then, and we went on that night, playing "Funny Face," an upbeat jazz tune in which each of us had a solo, but this time no Irish jig. Tradition at the Apollo had it that amateurs going out onstage touched a wooden stump for luck, the remains of a chestnut tree under which unemployed entertainers had once gathered on a street corner hoping to pick up jobs from booking agents. That first night we went on, we touched the stump, and when the master of ceremonies called all the acts out onstage at the end of the show and held the envelope containing the winning prize of twenty-five dollars over the heads of each of the acts in turn, the Thornton Sisters got the most applause. We had won! We could come back the following week.

When we left the Apollo that night, a man came up to Daddy and said he had just heard us perform. He then leaned down and kissed nine-year-old Linda on the cheek and said that, despite her age, she was one of the best drummers he had ever heard. That man was Illinois Jacquet, the great jazz saxophonist.

We told Daddy that touching the stump had worked, it had brought us luck. He snorted. "You make your own luck. That piece of wood's got nothin' to do with it." After that, we just pretended to touch it when we went on stage. Instead, we had a ritual of our own: We would stand in a circle backstage, like a team in a huddle, and each of us in turn put out one hand, stacking them one above another but not touching—touching would break the spell. We would concentrate. Break away. And make our entrance.

We went back the next Wednesday and won again. And the next. The third time we won, we were saying, "Okay, this is it. One more time and we'll have a week with the stars."

"And," Mommy predicted, "they'll be running down the aisles with the cameras from *Life* magazine and *Time*, like the night Ella Fitzgerald won."

On the Tuesday before the Wednesday of the fourth week, Daddy got a call from the manager of the Apollo Theatre. "It's not gonna be four weeks," he said. "It's gotta be six weeks."

"Hey, wait a minute," Daddy protested. "It's been four weeks ever since I was a kid."

"The rules have been changed," the man told him and hung up.

Daddy raged, but Mommy said, "We'll show him, Donald. We'll go out there and win six times. Then they'll *really* be runnin' down the aisles with the flashbulbs poppin'."

We won the fourth week.

We won the fifth week.

The sixth week they brought in another band to play against us. That band went on first and they were good, so good that we whispered to each other in dismay that they were surely professionals. The applause for them was thunderous. Backstage we stacked our hands, not touching, concentrated, broke away, and ran out onstage. We played—oh, my, how we played that night. And we won! Six Wednesday nights in a row at the Apollo! In front of the toughest audience in show business!

But where were the flashbulbs? Where were the reporters racing down the aisles? Those days were over, it seemed.

More important, where was our contract for a week with the stars? Frank Schiffman and his son Bobby owned the theater. "You don't have a week," they said. "That was only verbal. There's nothing in writing."

Daddy was in shock. An honest person himself, he assumed other people were honest and couldn't believe the Schiffmans were telling him that because there was nothing in writing, they weren't going to book the Thornton Sisters for a week's engagement. "It's not right," he kept saying. "We worked too hard. First it was four weeks and we won. Then it was six weeks and we won. We've earned our paid week with the stars."

My dad, a black man, a ditchdigger, a laborer, a janitor, went out and hired a lawyer. That was the first time I saw my father fight, fight in the way that people with money fight. We'd been wronged and he was not going to say, Yassuh, massa, that's all right, we'll go someplace else. He said, "It's wrong to do this. Especially to my kids." Ira J. Katchen, our white attorney, agreed, and based his brief on the argument that even though there was no written agreement, the prize of a week's engagement on the regular bill was a long tradition, well known far and wide.

At the end of a year and a half, the Schiffmans settled out of court and scheduled the band for a week in October 1961. "Naw," Daddy told them, "the week's gotta be in summer. I'm not takin' my kids outa school."

Daddy drew the moral for us. "Don't back off from people because they're white and we're black. What's right is right."

We never knew why the Schiffmans didn't want us. Because we were kids? Because at Daddy's insistence we wore such cover-up, schoolgirl outfits? Most likely it was because there were five of us and the rules of Local 802 of the musicians' union stipulated they had to pay five salaries instead of the one they would pay for a single's act.

By the time we played our week at the Apollo, Donna was seventeen, Jeanette sixteen, I thirteen, Linda eleven, and Rita nine. Rita, who had been too young to play the Amateur Nights with us, now came in on piano, so the Schiffmans were actually getting one more Thornton sister than they were paying for. And Jeanette put a stop to the little-girl outfits.

We were on the bill at the Apollo with Fats Domino singing "I'm Walkin'," Dee Clark singing his hit record, "Raindrops," Carla Thomas singing "Gee Whiz," Phil Upchurch playing "The Happy Organ," Ernie K. Doe singing "Mother-in-Law," and Shep and the Limelights singing their hit, "Daddy's Home." It was the year of A-line dresses and spaghetti straps, and Jeanette persuaded Mommy that that's what we should wear for a gig at the Apollo.

"Spaghetti straps!" Daddy screamed. "Not my daughters!" Mommy finally brought him around, and forever after "spaghetti straps" was our code phrase for whatever Daddy disapproved of in the way of outfits.

We played thirty-one shows that week at the Apollo, and we loved it. Once the limelight hits, it is as though it changes your whole molecular structure. You're never the same again. The applause, the adulation make it almost impossible to go back to being the nobody you were before.

Daddy wouldn't let us leave the theater between shows—no running around 125th Street—but we could go out in the lobby and look at the pictures of the Thornton Sisters taken by J. J. Kriegsmann, "Photographer of the Stars." Black or white, every star had photos by J. J. Kriegsmann. The marquee didn't blaze out THE THORNTON SISTERS, but if our name wasn't up in lights, our faces were in the lobby and we felt like we were *it*.

For Daddy, being at the Apollo was like recapturing part of his youth, and for Mommy it was the fulfillment of the dream she and her sister Ellie had had when they came north. Her eyes sparkled and danced while she was onstage playing the bass. As for us, we were having the time of our lives, and there was great, great esprit de corps, a sense of solidarity and love among the sisters. Of course, we said things like, "Who stole my slip?" but accusations didn't lead to raised voices. Mommy had never allowed any quarreling, no hitting, no saying, "I hate you!"

"Strangers do that. You don't do that in the family," was something she had always made perfectly clear to us. "Each of you is part Daddy, part Mommy, so that really makes you closer to each other than I am to your father because you are bound by blood." If one of us struck another, she came in and hit both of us. It convinced me that in families where a child says, "I hate my brother" or "I can't stand my sister," it is because the parents did not put a stop to bickering and battering in the very beginning before it escalated to hating.

That year we played the Apollo was the year Donna graduated from high school. She yearned desperately to go to the senior prom, but Daddy had never allowed her to go out on a date. She had no boyfriend, and there was no one to take her. When he became aware of just how unhappy Donna felt about missing the dance, Daddy told Mommy to design Donna an evening gown and he would ask a soldier from Fort Monmouth to escort her.

The prospect of Donna going out with a fellow prompted Daddy to embark on one of his soliloquies over morning coffee at the round table. "This neighborhood is just waitin' for the Thornton girls to get into trouble, to come home pregnant. Oh, that would be really juicy. Oh, wouldn't they like that. Niggers are like crabs in a basket. Let me tell you somethin', you have all these crabs in a basket and they're okay, jus' millin' around aimless, until one crab decides he wants to go up the side and try to get out of the basket. Then, all of a sudden, the other crabs who was doin' nothin' rush to that side of the basket and start pullin' him down."

Years later I was in a Maryland market and spotted a basket of softshell crabs. I stood and watched and, sure enough, one of the crabs started climbing up the side and the others scrambled over and pulled it down. So, Daddy's words were literally true. He said that's how black people are. "They see somebody tryin' to rise up and they tell bad things about you, they talk behind your back. If you're a nice-looking girl, they try to get their sons to date you and lead you out of the path you're followin'. There are always people who want to pull you down. It's human nature. You have to make sure you know that's what's gonna be happenin' and plan so it don't happen to you."

Daddy hammered into us the belief that women can do anything, that they are brighter than men, and then he turned around and called us stupid. "You stupid women," he excoriated us. "Women are stupid emotionally. You can't help yourselves because God made you that way. Women are to have kids. Men are to run around. That's the natural order of things. You're not gonna change that, so you have to select the time you're gonna be stupid. In every hour there's about three seconds that you're weak. For fifty-nine minutes and fifty-seven seconds you can be strong. The boy's kissin' your ear and he's doin' this and that and you can be strong, but for three seconds you're weak. The next hour that three seconds becomes six seconds. If you're on a date for three hours, that's nine seconds that you're weak, and the fella zooms in and gets you. You can't help yourselves. God made you that way. But you can select the right time to be stupid, and that's what you gotta do. You gotta pick the time."

He described kissing to us as "swapping spit," which made it sound disgusting, but at the same time we had an idealized, romantic vision of being kissed by a boy and we couldn't wait for Donna to get home from the senior prom and give us a moment by moment description of what it was like. We hadn't reckoned on Daddy, however. As Donna was being escorted up the front walk by her date, the porch light snapped on and there stood Daddy in his boxer shorts. There was to be no kiss for Donna.

For days Donna talked about how handsome the soldier was, what a fine dancer, what a polite and well-mannered man. She was starry-eyed with the pleasurable wonderment of having been in a man's company and arms. "He liked me. He really liked me," she mooned. "I'm sure he's going to ask me out again." So often did she say the soldier this, the soldier that, that Daddy grew impatient.

"That soldier didn't do nothin' without his gettin' paid," he snapped.

"No!" Donna protested. "He'd never accept money for taking me out."

"How do you know what he'd never do? You're so smart, look at this." Daddy pulled out the box where he kept his papers and thrust a canceled check under Donna's nose. "That's his name, ain't it? That's what I paid him. I hired him and I paid him, and I ain't hirin' him to take you out again so you can just stop talkin' about him."

Donna was crushed. Only the excitement of starting her first job eased her past this blow. Rather than go directly on to college, she and Daddy decided she would work for a year until Jeanette graduated and then the two of them would go to college together. In the meantime, we had signed a recording contract with Roulette Records. Rhythm and blues had come on the scene—Ike and Tina Turner, the Shirelles, the Crystals, the Ronettes—and the band plunged into that kind of music.

There was the Top Ten, and then there was the black Top Ten. If a manager thought one of the black songs had potential, he would give it to a white artist. That's what happened with many of what are now thought of as Elvis Presley songs. Elvis was the "cover" for a number of black songs. Because he was white, the song would get wider play and go over bigger, and everybody except the black artist made more money.

"Tutti Frutti" was one such song. First recorded by Little Richard, it became a big hit when it was covered by Pat Boone. Even when a hit recording happened to be by a black artist, unless the artist was as famous as Ella Fitzgerald or Duke Ellington, the black face was not on the record jacket. Instead, the jacket illustration would be of moonlight or the ocean or mountains, or if it was a black group, there would be little white cartoon figures.

The first recording we made for Roulette was "Doin' the Waddle," which was supposed to be a new dance. It was also the last record we made for them. They tried to send us on tour to promote the record and Daddy would have none of it. "My daughters stay in school," he informed Roulette.

"You've got a contract," he was told.

"Nothin' in that contract says I gotta take my daughters outa school, so you can just rip it up."

And they did.

Atlantic Records then signed us as a novelty group, but Daddy again vetoed traveling to promote a record, so that contract was dissolved as well.

I had no regrets about any of this because an incident in my freshman year in high school validated my belief that I was going to become a doctor. My biology teacher, Rollo Galbraith, was a tough taskmaster, but he softened enough one day to comment that he had never seen any student take such voluminous notes as I did.

"It's because I love your class, Mr. Galbraith," I told him. "I really like biology. I want to be a doctor."

He looked surprised, maybe because the only black girl in his class was the student who was aiming highest. "A doctor?"

"Yes. I want to deliver babies. I want to be an obstetrician."

A few nights later, after dinner, a car we didn't recognize pulled into our driveway and a man got out and rang the doorbell. I switched on the porch light. "Mr. Galbraith!" I exclaimed, startled.

He asked me to come out to his car, where he opened the trunk and gestured to boxes of books. "These are obstetrical textbooks and journals I inherited from my uncle," he said. "I thought you might like to have them, Yvonne."

He helped me carry the boxes into the house and expressed the hope that the books would be useful to me in studying to become an obstetrician. I was overwhelmed. It was a gesture that carried a world of meaning for me. It said: Here is a white man, a teacher, who takes you seriously, who believes you can reach your goal.

I thanked him for his gift. And my heart thanked him for his far greater gift: his faith in my ability. From that moment on, I never doubted that I was going to become a doctor, that someday I would be an obstetrician.

◆ 6 ◆

Weekend Dates

"DADDY, PLEASE!"

"What do you wanna go out there for?"

"So we can get mobbed like the other performers. So we can sign autographs and give interviews."

We were in our dressing room at the Brooklyn Fox Theatre, and on the street below kids swarmed behind barricades in a line snaking around the block. We longed to appear among them and be treated like celebrities. Daddy threw us a disdainful look, draped a towel over his head, and saying, "Watch this," strolled over to the window. He stood there with his arms outstretched like a winning prizefighter and in a loud baritone began to sing: "I keep forgettin' you don't love me no more." Down below, a teenager screamed, a sea of faces turned upward, and the mob surged toward the building, wailing, "Chuckie! Chuckie!" They thought Daddy was Chuck Jackson, the idol of black teenagers that summer of 1962.

Daddy moved away from the window. "See that, those heifers down there will scream at anybody. The screamin's worth *nothin'!*"

A disc jockey known as Murray the K had booked us for a week's summer spectacular at the Brooklyn Fox, an annual event known as Murray the K and His Swinging Soiree. It was a class show. On the bill were the Four Seasons, the Crystals, Tommy Roe, Fabian, and Chuck Jackson. And the Thornton Sisters, this time on the marquee. We weren't famous yet but we were getting known because Murray the K had been plugging our recording of "Wild Childhood" several times a day on his radio show.

With everyone else on the bill performing their number-one

79

hits, we felt that we shouldn't just be playing an instrumental, and Daddy gave in, agreeing that the Contours' Top Ten record called "Do You Love Me?" was a better choice.

When it was our turn to go on, Linda, on the drums, was already seated onstage, then the rest of us twirled out and Donna said, "You broke my heart 'cause I couldn't dance. You didn't even want me around. And now I'm back, to let you know I can really shake 'em down....da, da, da, da," and as we turned to go to our instruments, Linda, who had a big voice, came in with, "Do you love me?"

One night Linda lost her voice and Daddy yelled from backstage, "Cover! Cover!" Donna covered for her, and after that we knew to come in for each other, Jeanette for Donna, me for Jeanette, and so on.

We played four shows a day and were paid five hundred dollars for the week, money which, according to Daddy, had already been spent on clothes for the act, so we couldn't go out to a restaurant to eat like the stars of the show. Instead, we brought bologna and salami and liverwurst from home and made sandwiches in the dressing room. But I think Mommy and Daddy had another reason for confining us to the dressing room. We were curious, quick-eyed kids, and when we came offstage after doing our set, we spotted drugs changing hands, numbers betting, pickups, but only in glimpses because Daddy would be waiting in the wings and he and Mommy shooed us upstairs to the dressing room like ducks to a pond.

"Okay, kids, come on, come on," they urged with little claps and clucks. And when we protested that we wanted to talk to the fans hanging around the stage door, Daddy said, "Those little wenches, they'll scream for anybody. I already showed you."

"Daddy, they love us. You should hear the applause and the shouts and whistles when we do our numbers."

"Today they love you. Tomorrow they'll love somebody else."

We tried to turn his argument against him. If they loved us today, we said, why didn't it make sense to cash in today? The way it looked to us, we had broken into show business and found out we were really good, audiences liked us and would pay to see us, so why not drop out of school and hit the circuit? We were a poor black family. Daddy especially, but Mommy too, had worked like dogs to pay for our instruments and musical training and get us this far. And now, here was our family's chance at a big payoff.

The remarkable thing, it seems to me when I look back on it now, is that Daddy didn't see it that way too. But if ever he wrestled with the temptation to go for the money and let the doctor dream die—or at least be postponed—he gave no hint of it. "You look nice and you're talented," he agreed. "You're young, you're shakin', and everybody likes you. But you're not always gonna be cute kids. You're gonna turn into forty-year-old women. And a forty-year-old woman blowin' a horn ain't a pretty sight."

He gave us time to imagine this before going on. "Now you take a forty-year-old woman with a scripperscrap 'round her neck. People'll pay to see a doctor who can make 'em well, but they're not gonna hand over a dime to see a gray-haired, wrinkled old lady blowin' a horn."

We had to admit that was probably true. "Men can get old," Daddy told us. "Even when they're sixty, women'll look at them and say, 'Oh, you're so mature. I like older men.' But you women, you only got a certain amount of time to make it and you got to move fast. After twenty-five, it's all downhill."

One afternoon, between shows, a casually dressed white boy came backstage to speak to Daddy. The fellow said he thought the band was great and wondered if there was any chance of our playing for his eating club at Princeton. As the social chairman of the Cap and Gown Club, he had bands booked through January and would like us to play on a Saturday night in February. He was hesitant when he asked about our fee because he assumed we were making star-type money, while, in truth, we were playing around Long Branch and Asbury Park for thirty-five and forty dollars a night.

"I'm afraid the best we can do is one hundred and twenty-five dollars an hour," the student said apologetically. "For four hours."

Daddy did a quick calculation. Four hours at one hundred and twenty-five dollars an hour. Five hundred dollars for one night's work! Not wanting to look too anxious, he frowned and slowly shook his head. "I'll have to talk it over with the band."

Afterward, Daddy told us that he leaped over three chairs in his rush to get to our dressing room. "Kids! Kids! There's a college boy out there who wants to pay us five hundred dollars to play at Princeton for four hours!" He was exultant. "Princeton ain't even that far. It can't be more'n an hour from home. And it'd be a Saturday night. It don't take you outa school."

When he'd calmed down a little, he strolled back and told the waiting social chairman that the fee was not what we had been accustomed to being paid but, nevertheless, we would be agreeable to performing at Princeton. The young man beamed. He shook Daddy's hand and said he would call us to make the final arrangements.

"Tell me this," Daddy said, "do other colleges have dances on the weekends?" When the fellow said that indeed they did, then and there Daddy caught a glimpse of a possible future. Perhaps playing colleges on weekends was the stone he had been looking for to kill two birds: a way for the band to make money to pay for our education while at the same time we stayed in school and got that education.

When September came, we were back in school. I entered the tenth grade in senior high and found myself assigned to a history class with kids who were wearing baseball caps indoors and blowing bubblegum and sailing paper airplanes. That night I wailed to Mommy that I must be in the wrong class and would she please go to school and talk to the principal for me. Her answer was that I should try to straighten it out on my own, that I was old enough to fight my own battles and that she and Daddy would intervene only if no one would listen to me.

The principal referred me to Miss Apostalocus, the guidance counselor, who had known our family for years. She asked why I thought I was in the wrong class. "Because the work is too easy," I told her. "Last year I was in a class where everybody was very bright and did their homework and paid attention. This is probably a very low class and I want to be with the smart kids."

"You think you can handle the work in a more advanced class?"

When I assured her confidently that I could, she nodded and reassigned me to a different class, a class in which there proved to be no black students at all. Not only that, there was not a single face I recognized from ninth grade. Miss Apostalocus had leapfrogged me over the intermediate classes and set me down in an honors course for fast-track kids. Again I went crying to Mommy. Her answer this time was: "You asked for it. You got it. You'll just have to work harder to keep up."

From that time on, I practically lived in the library. As a black person who hadn't had much chance to absorb general knowledge about the world in a casual, everyday fashion from the talk and interests of people around me, I felt I was starting out about five hundred laps behind the other students. To pace myself, I looked around and identified a classmate who did not seem impossibly far ahead and said, "Let me see if I can catch up to this one."

Pat, the girl I'd singled out as a rabbit in grammar school, had become addlebrained over boys and no longer excelled, so now I chose a white male. When I caught up to this first rabbit and was doing as well on tests as he was, I traded him for a still brighter rabbit and set my sights on him, and in that way I kept going up in my grades until I was at the top of the class. The whole experience taught me that if you let other people hold low expectations for you or if you hold them for yourself, you will come to believe that is all you are capable of. But if you really set yourself to trying and keep going after higher and higher goals, there is no limit to what you can accomplish.

Because I was studying so hard, I had little time for extracurricular activities, but I volunteered for the school band. Jeanette was a senior and I got a kick out of the idea of playing "Pomp and Circumstance" at her graduation. The music the band practiced was banal and I hated having to march up and down football fields at halftime in the freezing cold with my fingers and lips going numb, but I drudged away through the whole fall, winter, and spring of marching and practicing, looking forward to the moment when it would be my sister up there getting her diploma. Graduation day came. Mommy and Daddy were there. Donna and Linda and Rita were there. I was there blasting away in the band. The only person who was not at Jeanette's graduation was Jeanette. She was still sewing on her dress, or she had mistaken the time, or she was put out because she had not been selected for the National Honor Society. Whatever her reason, the rest of us were disappointed but not surprised—Jeanette was Jeanette and danced to her own music.

One other extracurricular activity I tried out for was a high school production of *The Music Man*. To my way of thinking, I was a professional musician, I had a terrific singing voice, and the least I could do was to offer to undertake the leading role of Marian, the librarian.

"The lead?" Daddy said.

"Don't you always tell us to go for the top?"

He didn't say anything more, but he was not nearly as startled as I was when I wasn't cast in the part. "It's because you're black," Daddy said matter-of-factly. He never believed in blinking at reality. "At the end the music man kisses the librarian. They're not going to have a white guy kissing a black girl. The parents would be taking their kids out of school so fast the kids wouldn't know what hit 'em."

I sat and pondered and I said to myself, "Daddy's right, so let me just get on with studying because becoming a doctor is the only chance this ugly duckling has of turning into a swan."

In the late fall of that year, the Princeton student called, as he had said he would, and made a date for us to play at the Cap and Gown—February 16, 1963, a date all of the Thornton sisters remember, for it marked the first time we played at Princeton, and playing at Princeton was the start of so much for us.

When we arrived on campus, crammed into an old white van Daddy had bought to transport us and our instruments, we were awed by the massive yet graceful Gothic buildings. We had not seen a university before, and Princeton's air of serenity, benevolent lordliness, *rightness*, reduced us to silence. The students, too, as they crisscrossed the campus, seemed wrapped in that same air of unquestioned right. They belonged. They moved with ease among the grandeur. They looked comfortable and at home.

But they weren't wearing socks. "How come?" we whispered to Daddy. "Aren't you supposed to wear socks with loafers?"

"They're down-to-earth folks," Daddy improvised. "See, they're accustomed to having so much money, it's just not a big thing with them."

We later learned that what is called "Princeton socks" refers to the Princeton custom of wearing no socks at all.

When we pulled up at the Cap and Gown, the social chairman was waiting to greet us and shake hands with Daddy to thank us for coming. He didn't say, as we half-expected: "Go to the back door and wait till we call you." Instead, he enthused, "You were so great in Brooklyn that I know you're going to give us a wonderful show." He even offered to help us carry in our instruments, but Daddy said his girls were used to doing it themselves. He wasn't going to have a boy hanging around even if he was a white college boy and just being polite.

That night we gave them rock, rhythm and blues, and James Brown–type music, raunchy, really tight stuff, and the students loved it. We played our hearts out, forty minutes on, twenty off. We were not jaded musicians rolling off a bus for a one-night stand and smoking joints out back between sets. We were kids, close in age to the students, and it was as though we were all having a party. The Princeton guys had dates from Radcliffe and Vassar and Bryn Mawr, and the girls began coming up to Daddy to ask if the band could play at their colleges. He said sure and handed out our telephone number to anyone who asked.

Word-of-mouth about the band spread fast, and almost before we realized what was happening, we were booked for Friday night at one college, Saturday afternoon and evening at another, and Sunday afternoon at another. It was as though all these years we had worked along in the dark, taking one step at a time, never knowing whether there would be a payoff, when it might come, what it might be, and suddenly here it was: Fate had clued us in to the perfect way of making money with the band. Our schedule was the same as the students'—study during the week, play on weekends and during vacations. The only difference was that they played for fun while we had fun playing for money.

Our success brought agents buzzing around with their blandishments: "I can get you more bookings. I can handle the paperwork for you. I can get you more money." Daddy gave one of them, a sharp-nosed, thin-faced fellow, a try, until he discovered the ferret was charging a third more than he was telling Daddy and pocketing the difference. "We don't need no middleman like that," Daddy decided. "We can get cards made ourselves and hand them out."

The cards had "The Thornton Sisters—You Never Heard It So Good" on the front, and our telephone number on the back. When someone called, Daddy yelled to me, "Cookie, can we get to Hamilton College on the same weekend we're playin' at the University of Pennsylvania?" I was elected to look these places up on a map and estimate the distances between them because Donna was working at her job and Jeanette, the social one of us, was usually somewhere else. It became a given that I figured out routes and travel times and how to book in clusters so that we played, for instance, Trinity, Wesleyan, and Amherst on one weekend, and Cornell, Rensselaer, and Colgate on another.

Knowing nothing about contracts, in the beginning Daddy just said, "Okay, the band'll be there," but once or twice, after we'd played a date, he was told, "Oh, gee, Mr. Thornton, we thought there'd be more people at the mixer. We just don't have the money to pay you what we agreed." A few incidents like that and Daddy contacted the musicians' union and got hold of a standard contract. At the same time, he learned about something called a "binder," and after that, it was, "We'll send you a contract to sign, and when you send it back with a binder of $125, we'll reserve the date for you."

One social chairman called and said, "I didn't get your cover letter explaining the contract," which clued us in that we should be sending a letter with the contract saying, "This letter is to inform you of such and such." As we grew more experienced and more secure about stating terms, we began stipulating that we had to have a place to dress with a full-length mirror and a bathroom reserved for our use. We needed the latter because when we had to use the bathroom set aside for the guys' dates, they'd all have been drinking beer and the line would be a mile long and we only had twenty minutes between sets.

Often enough in those twenty-minute breaks, we used the time to write out reports or essays or other pieces of homework we had been working on while traveling in the van. We brought our workbooks and textbooks and clipboards with us in the van and studied as best we could by flashlight while Daddy drove and Mommy sat beside him in the front seat doing last-minute sewing on our costumes. But it was hard to write with all of us crowded in and the car jiggling, so we saved the writing until we arrived.

We knew our playing schedule, of course, and we tried to get our schoolwork done ahead of time, but often, leaving at three o'clock on Friday afternoon to drive to a far-off place like Virginia, we still had a lot of studying to do and we had to take the work with us. Mommy and Daddy would not tolerate any falling off in our grades. They wanted to see A's on our report cards, and how we got them was our business. Their standard reply to any excuse was: "Playing in the band on the weekends is the way it is. You know it; you plan for it."

Mommy and Daddy rode in the front of the van with their coffee and their cigarettes; then Donna and Jeanette; then Linda, Rita, and I, and behind us, our instruments and our clothes. When we first played Princeton, we were still wearing Peter Pan collars, but Donna and Jeanette quickly convinced Mommy that we needed flashier, dressier clothes if we were to look professional and put on a good show.

Without telling Daddy, she made us slinky outfits split up the side. Daddy's mouth fell open when we appeared in them and he saw how sexy we looked. Only the fact that the students obviously liked the change made him admit, "Well, maybe I am a little old-fashioned."

He saw that theatrical clothes enhanced the act, and later on it was his idea that we should change outfits between every set, coming out one time in fringe, another in satin, another in sequins; one time in blue, another in white, another in red. The students loved it. They would wait to see what we would appear in next, and even Daddy got a kick out of the changes. He would stand there like Mr. Clean, arms crossed over his chest, and beam at us as we whisked out and up on the bandstand.

It was his presence while the band played, off to the side next to the piano, that established a bit of distance between us and the students. We didn't mingle during the breaks. The fellows were white and we were black, but that did not stand in the way of their liking to kid around, particularly with Jeanette. She was slender and outgoing and ebullient, and the guys were drawn to her. They would say when we arrived, "Hey, great, here come the Thornton Sisters! Where's Jeanette?" relegating the rest of us to supporting cast.

Jeanette would have relished bantering with the boys, but Daddy, in a joking, cheerful way, kept a tight rein on us. He wasn't a tall man—five feet eight or nine inches—but he had biceps as bulging as Popeye's and he was stocky and solid, a rather formidable figure despite a face that was so pleasant that people just automatically smiled at him. Perhaps if he'd been more of a weakling, the guys would have tried an end run around him, but as it was, they accorded him the same respect they did their own fathers. Deferentially, they'd say, "Hello, Mr. Thornton. How are you tonight?" and even full of beer, they did not get up on the bandstand without his permission.

To us, he made the point again and again: "You're not here for socializing. You play and then you get back to school."

At Colgate, there was that rarity in the early 1960s, a black fellow, a gentleman named Bill whom Jeanette had eyes for. The song called "Don't Mess with Bill" was popular then, as was the

Fifth Dimension's "One Less Bell to Answer," and Jeanette sang them with particular feeling when Bill was around, which did not, of course, escape Daddy's attention. Bill was a light-skinned guy, prompting Daddy to one of his pronouncements: "You gotta watch out for those gray-eyed niggers."

"What're you talking about?" Jeanette demanded.

"Those light-skinned jokers who think they're white. They go 'round lookin' for stupid dark-skinned black women, not to marry, but to have a good time with, and then when they're finished, they move on to the next one."

The dire tone of Daddy's voice spoiled any romantic notions Jeanette had about Bill.

Jeanette was eighteen, Donna nineteen by this time, and they were growing increasingly restive under Daddy's oppressive thumb. Mommy tried to get Daddy to relax his strictness by arguing, "They're growing up, Donald. They want to do like other girls their age."

But his answer was always: "They'll do what the rules of this house say they'll do. As long as they're in my house, eatin' my food, suckin' up my heat, wearin' the nap off my rug, they'll listen to me, not to some pimply-faced, pinheaded rascal."

The bedroom that Donna and Jeanette shared at the back of the house had an outside door, and the two of them took to skipping out at night after Daddy had gone off to work. Because in her heart Mommy sympathized with their feeling that they were missing out on being young, on the parties and the fun and the laughter, she didn't stop them or tell on them, but she had a no-nonsense warning for them.

"If you have a baby, you're not bringing it back to this house. You have it, you take care of it. I'm not like one of those mothers that says, 'Oh, why don't you go with Johnny? He looks good. He'll give you pretty kids, and I'd love to have some grandkids.' If you're stupid enough to get pregnant, you're out of here, on your own."

Donna and Jeanette, slipping out at 10:00 P.M. and back in at

2:00 A.M., stopped pleading with Daddy to let them go out on dates, and this breaking-off of the argument aroused his suspicions. One night he left as usual but returned an hour later.

"It's awful quiet," he remarked to Mommy. "Where's Donna and Jeanette?"

She admitted they were not in the house and we all waited for the explosion. It did not come. Instead, Daddy went downstairs and came back with a hammer and a fistful of the longest nails I'd ever seen. I had a moment's wild vision of a crucifixion, but Daddy went outside and around to the back. With methodical, heavy blows, he drove those long nails into the back door and through the door frame, one after another, up and down both sides, until there was not the slightest chance that anyone could ever open that door again short of tearing the house down.

He reappeared in the living room. "Don't any of you let them in any other door either," he said, glowering, and left for work.

When he returned at six the next morning, Donna and Jeanette and Mommy were huddled in blankets on the front porch. Mommy had not dared let the girls in but neither had she felt safe having them stay outside alone.

The ensuing row might have been worse if it had not been that Donna and Jeanette, unbeknownst to Daddy, had been accepted at Howard University. It was midsummer and they figured there was no point in bucking him since they would soon be off to Washington, D.C., free and on their own.

Almost a year earlier, the two of them had applied to Howard with Daddy's knowledge and approval because he was determined to have his daughters go to college—whatever college was; he was none too clear about that and he hadn't given any thought to where Howard was or what it was like. But then came the Princeton date, other dates followed, the band was making money, and Donna and Jeanette were afraid that if Daddy got wind of the fact that they'd be leaving the band, he'd interfere with their plans.

They stopped talking about Howard, and when he asked, they said, "Well, we don't know, Daddy. Word hasn't come through yet." Donna had saved money from working all year and Jeanette had been awarded a scholarship, so they figured they could swing college on their own if, at the last minute, Daddy refused them tuition money. They bought new red Samsonite luggage, and in August, with their suitcases packed, they told him.

He stared at them. "You're not goin'," he announced flatly. "How you gonna play in the band if you're...where? Washington, D.C.?"

"We'll have to let the band go."

"You're gonna take what the band's made and leave your sisters with nothin' for them to become doctors on?"

"But, Daddy, you want us to go to college."

"The young ones is payin' for you now; you gotta be around to pay for them later. Anyway, Howard's a black college, ain't it? You go to a black college and people'll think it's because you're too dumb to get into a white one. The rest of your life you're gonna be apologizin' for goin' to a black college."

"Daddy, do you want us to get an education? Do you want us to be doctors?"

"Ain't I said that from the beginning?"

"Then we have to go to Howard. It's too late to get in anywhere else."

"Well, let me see about that," he said. "I'll just ask around."

Donna and Jeanette imagined they had won because a college that was closer, like Rutgers, would be certain not to accept them only two weeks before the fall term started. They were smiling and laughing and talking about the boys they were going to meet and how delicious the freedom of not having Mr. Clean stand over them would be. Even when Daddy came home with the news that there was a college right in West Long Branch, so close they could walk to it, they were not disconcerted.

"We know that," they said dismissively. "But Monmouth College is a teachers college."

"College is college," Daddy insisted, and they did not argue or bother to explain that a teachers college is not where you go to take a premed course because they knew acceptances had gone out and enrollment had been closed months before. "Don't worry about that," Daddy said. "I'll just go over and talk to the president."

"If he says no, can we go to Howard?"

"He ain't gonna tell me no."

"But if he does, can we?"

"I s'pose you'll have to," he admitted grudgingly.

Again, they thought they had won.

Daddy put on a white shirt and tie. He put on the one suit he owned, and when he went out the front door, Jeanette giggled. "The president of a college won't give him the time of day. Anyway, he'll probably end up at the Star Laundry. He doesn't know a college from a hole in the ground."

They should have known better than to underestimate Daddy. He drove through the massive iron gates of the college, up the winding drive to Shadow Lawn, the mansion that was the main building of the recently founded college, parked the van in front, and inquired the way to the president's office, where a secretary asked if he had come about some work or about payment of a bill.

"It's about two of my daughters," Daddy said. "I need them to go to college here."

There was something about Daddy—a solidity, a sincerity, a simplicity—that opened doors. He gave the impression of courteous determination: he would cause no trouble, raise no fuss, but he would remain until he saw the person he had come to see. In a surprisingly short time, the secretary showed him into the president's office. The president shook his hand and asked what he could do for him.

"I live in Long Branch, I work at Fort Monmouth, I'm a veteran, and I've got five daughters," Daddy offered calmly. "Now I see by the pictures on your desk that you're a family man, too. Am I right?"

The president agreed, and in response to Daddy's warm questions, he attached names and ages to the photographs of his children and mentioned something about their talents and interests.

Telling us about the interview later, Daddy said this was the moment when he knew he was going to win. "Now I got him. Now when I talk about my children, he's got to see hisself in me. When I tell him I want to keep my family together, he's got to understand my feeling. He can't help hisself. He knows he isn't talkin' to some kid that he can tell, 'Sorry but you didn't do whatever in time. You don't meet whatever you gotta meet to get into college here.' He's talkin' to another man about his children. He isn't behind his big desk anymore. I've brought him around to my side. I've put him in my shoes."

The acceptance letters admitting Donna and Jeanette to Monmouth College arrived two days later.

Jeanette screamed and raged. Donna wept and pleaded. They shut themselves in their room and moaned and hollered. Daddy admitted to feeling sorry for them. "But," he said, "God must have meant for it to be because if Monmouth College wasn't there, they'd have had to go to Howard."

Jeanette yelled through the door at him. "It's a· teachers college! I don't want to be a teacher!"

"I told the president I wanted my daughters to be doctors," Daddy answered complacently. "They have everything you need, he said. They have liberal arts courses..."

"Liberal arts isn't for being a doctor!"

"They got biology. They're a private college, but that's okay, we'll get the money up. I'll get a loan."

The answer was a long, despairing wail. Mommy was the one who finally persuaded Donna and Jeanette to open their door. "We understand," she told them. "Daddy and I understand, but it's the band that's going to pay for you going to college, and it's the band that has to pay so your sisters can go, too." She did not say that they were being selfish, but that was hidden in her words and Donna and Jeanette felt it. Donna admitted to me later, "We really did feel bad about leaving you kids and the band."

"Even though," Jeanette added bitterly, "it was going to be party time in Washington, D.C."

Donna and Jeanette started college, I was a junior in high

school, Linda was a freshman, and Rita was in the sixth grade. Late Friday afternoon Daddy would plunge through the front door yelling, "How come you're not ready? Where are your dresses? Why aren't the instruments out? Come on, we can't be operatin' on CPT." CPT—colored people's time, he called it, an hour behind everyone else's time. Even though he was hollering at us, he himself was the worst offender; he was always running late.

"Daddy," I'd say, "we aren't going to make Princeton by nine o'clock."

"Tell you what we'll do, Cookie. We tell them we're takin' our twenty-minute break first. Then we'll get set up and play until ten o'clock." Other bands started at nine, played for forty minutes, then broke for twenty, but we were usually doing it the other way around because of being on CPT.

Daddy never spoke about money to us, neither about what was coming in nor what was going out, but he did say that he often spent the money from a gig before we made it. The expenses were high: top-of-the-line instruments for all of us, such as Selmer Mark VI tenor and alto saxophones, a Fender "Jaguar" guitar, Rogers drums; material for the dresses Mommy made, which got to be a bigger and bigger item as we went to costume changes and ever more elegant material; six pairs of matching shoes for every outfit; the best amplifiers, plus speakers in case the college speakers shorted out—because, said Daddy, "When you're all set up and they turn on the P.A. system and nothin' comes out, man, that's a bad feelin'." We needed reeds and Otto Link mouthpieces for the saxophones, which were overhauled regularly by an expert in Asbury Park to keep them in tiptop condition. The drums frequently had to be reskinned. Electronic keyboards were just coming out, and we carried an extra one of those for backup. It all added up.

"We can't go to colleges lookin' raggedy," Daddy said. "These are kids from wealthy families. They're used to things lookin' good, and we're there to give them a show, so everything's gotta be first class."

With our clothes, the instruments, the amplifiers, and seven hefty people in the car, the weight in the old white van was almost more than it could manage. Blowouts were so frequent that we were forbidden to open a can of soda without telling Daddy that we were about to pull a pop-top because the sound of *pssssssst* made him fearful that yet another tire had burst.

One time in the winter we were headed up to New Haven. An agent had called and asked us to substitute at a Yale weekend for Jerry Lee Lewis, who had come down with the flu. It was snowing, and the car was making a funny sound, like a rhythmic *flub, flub, flub*. "Oh, God," Daddy kept saying, "we got to make it. We can't miss this money."

He knew every sound the car made; he knew if a spark plug misfired, so he knew something was wrong. Finally he couldn't stand the anxiety of fearing the car was going to break down any minute. He got out, lay down on his back in the snow, and slid under the car. He looked and looked. Finally he spotted the trouble. All it was, was that a piece of the recap on a tire had come loose and was thumping against the fender. "Oh, I'm so glad, so glad," he kept saying as he took his knife and cut it off. And after we played at Yale and were headed for home, he exulted, "I don't care if all the tires blow out now. We got the money."

The loaded van couldn't make any speed, and when trucks thundered past us, it rocked and swayed and vibrated so much, especially on the narrow mountain roads in West Virginia, that we would be saying, "Oh, Daddy, we're going to die trying to get some money."

"Yeah," he agreed, "one of these days we got to get us something more streamlined that cuts through the wind."

But what really made him decide to buy a new car was a time we were heading for a date at the University of North Carolina. It was late at night and I was dozing when I heard Daddy whisper to Mommy, "There's somebody followin' us." That brought me wide awake, and I soon saw what he meant. When we turned left, the big pickup truck behind us turned left, right, and it turned right. Daddy tried to speed up and the pickup passed us as though we were standing still. When it zoomed by us, we saw the Confederate flag in its cab window and a rack full of guns behind the front seat.

The truck slowed to a crawl. Daddy put the pedal to the floor and passed it. It lazed up behind us and rode on our tail. Daddy said, "Kids, if anything happens, stay cool, stay calm." Was he thinking as we were, rape, lynching, bodies thrown in a swamp, Emmett Till and Viola Liuzzo...?

We went on through the darkness, rabbits being toyed with by hunting dogs, woods black on either side of us, no other cars, just a wheezing white van and a growling pickup with a rack of guns. Daddy warned us not to turn and look at the guys in the truck; he didn't want the whites of our eyes flashing our fear to them. With our heads held rigidly front, our ears were like radar screens to pick up the instant when the truck swooped around us to cut us off, the instant when the short, violent third act of our lives would begin. The script was a racial memory in us. We did not know our lines but, oh, we were familiar with the plot.

Daddy strained over the wheel as though if he willed it hard enough, he could make the van go faster. In the glare of the truck's headlights, I could see beads of sweat standing up on his arms like condensation on a glass of ice water.

Mommy whispered, "There's lights ahead."

"Streetlights?"

"Brighter than that."

"Please, God, please."

Suddenly there it was: a truck stop. Daddy waited until the last minute to turn in. The pickup truck hesitated, then went on down the road. We pulled in between two eighteen-wheelers. First we were silent, then we started to laugh and cry with nervous relief.

"We're stayin' right here till the morning and it's light," Daddy decreed. "We'll be late for the gig. We'll have to charge 'em less, but that's all right. I like money, but not that much."

When we arrived back home after that weekend, he ordered a new car from Detroit, a Chevrolet station wagon to be cut in half and stretched to the length of a limousine.

The Band's Wagon

THE NEXT MORNING, awakened by the dawn from a night of fitful sleep, we were on the road early. But even the reassuring daylight did not quite free us from the fright of the previous night. Daddy must have been carrying a picture of the gun rack slung across the pickup's back window in his mind, for he suddenly began talking about his days in a construction battalion in the navy in World War II, describing to us how blacks were not given guns until they were out of the United States.

"We went through all that marchin' and drillin' and all like that, but we never got a real gun. A lot of guys was comin' into Great Lakes from the South when I was comin' in from New York. A lot of 'em didn't have no shoes on. Big feet, toes as big as your fist. I thought I was uneducated but those guys couldn't read, couldn't write, couldn't hardly talk. Some of them had never seen lights before. I don't know where the navy got them. They must have wrapped them up and threw them on trucks and brought them on in. They wasn't gonna give these guys guns. We was drillin' with dummy guns, with broomsticks.

"When we got overseas, they had these big old wooden crates with rifles in them. All the black guys lined up and they started handing us these guns with thick grease on them. I said to myself, 'Here we are within shoutin' distance of the enemy, and this is the first time I get a rifle. I don't even know where the bullet comes out at. Three-quarters of these guys are gonna get killed 'cause they don't know what to do. This ain't right. I and the rest should at least be taught how to shoot the thing.'

"If we'd had guns, though, down at Jackson Barracks in Louisiana before we went overseas, some people would've got killed. Townies down there sneaked into the mess hall for the blacks and poisoned the food. A few of the men died. They had to get us out of there in a hurry 'cause some of the guys, if they coulda got hold of a gun, there was folks that was gonna get their heads shot off."

It was the first time Daddy had ever told us any of this, about how he had been too frightened in Louisiana to leave the camp to go into town, about fights in which black sailors had had their eyes gouged out, about being sent overseas and finding they weren't allowed to fight—they could only man the kitchens behind the lines and drive the trucks carrying ammunition to the white guys in the front lines. "But, hey, they were dyin' and we were livin'," Daddy said, "so we wasn't gonna argue about that."

Clearly, fighting, shooting, killing were on Daddy's mind that morning, and I imagine he was trying to think what he could have done if that pickup truck had forced us off the road the night before. Very little, but they would have had to kill him before they harmed his girls.

He spent a huge sum of money for those days buying the limousine, but we all felt safer because of its speed. Fully loaded, the new car weighed three and a half tons and the tires blew out just as regularly as they had on the old van, so Daddy had the wheels in the back replaced with split rims and truck tires. The car was so heavy that in the winter he would swing out and go ahead of snowplows opening the roads. Daddy drove with every bit of care and caution he could muster, but we always went steadily on. If, on the way home, Mommy suggested it might be better to stop somewhere and wait out the storm, Daddy replied, "We can't let the music make us lose nothin' on education. We can't lose no time or the purpose will be lost. The kids have to get to school, and I have to get back to work or I'll lose a day's pay. We'll make it."

Jeanette said that one of her boyfriends had offered to help with the driving. "He'd drive and set up and you wouldn't have to go with us all the time, Daddy."

"Sometimes," Daddy said slowly, "I don't believe what I'm hearin'. Here I'm bustin' my back and you're tellin' me your boyfriend can take over and drive the rest of my children. A little bit of money's comin' in and everybody wants to take over. Your boyfriend should've took over when you all were five years old and paid for the lessons and the instruments. What're you tryin' to do—cut my legs off?"

"It was just a suggestion, Daddy," she said soothingly. "You needn't get so upset."

When we stayed longer than just the four-hour stint at a college, we often strolled around the campus and sampled the ease of being in an academic setting where people used proper grammar and dressed in tweed jackets and carried books under their arms. Mommy reminded us that what we saw at the dances was only a small part of being a college student. "A skewed aspect," she called it. "The partying is only a little bit of it. Monday morning comes for them just like it comes for you."

As we continued to play and to return many times to the same fraternities, we encountered seniors who had graduated and they would tell us they were now in medical or law or business school. "Boy, you people just keep going to school," we marveled, and we asked questions. We knew we were going to be doctors, but we didn't know the steps to getting there. We didn't realize that you went through high school, college, and medical school, and then you were an intern in a hospital and after that a resident. When we found this out and spoke in awe of the long road that still lay ahead, Daddy simply said, "You can do it," and launched into one of his talks.

"Right now, you're written off because you're black, you're women, you're dark-skinned. Whatever the heck a totem pole is, you're about as low as anyone gets on it. Now, you can choose to go along with that. You can lay back and open your legs and get pregnant. But if you choose *not* to go along with it, your mother and I are showing you the way. You got to study. You got to always act like a lady. You got to not go around with a chip on your shoulder, like, You owe me 'cause I'm black and I come over on a slave ship. Nobody don't owe you a thing. You owe yourself the best you can do for yourself.

"A lot of black people don't want to work," he went on. "They'd rather party and say studyin' ain't gonna help, that it don't do no good to work hard. When someone says that to me, I say, 'Have you *ever* worked hard?' It's like gravity. It's a basic law. You work hard, you'll make it. Like, you girls are gonna be doctors. People say it can't be done. People say a lot of things can't be done. But then somebody does it. It just took somebody makin' his mind up to do it. All you girls got to have is made-up minds. Five doctors—now, isn't that gonna be a great thing?"

Linda, Rita, and I listened to these talks solemnly and avidly and were filled with fresh resolve, but I suspect at this time his words were primarily directed at Donna, to encourage her, and at Jeanette, to discourage her.

Donna was struggling at Monmouth College. In the year she had been out of school and working, she loved collecting her own paycheck, being able to buy beautiful clothes and have shoes made to match her dresses, and she did not enjoy having to study again, particularly since work that Jeanette sailed through was often heavy going for her. "I'm not cut out for this, Daddy," she kept saying.

Daddy tried to encourage her. "You're doin' the work, Donna. You're not failin'."

"Daddy, I'm not college material. The guidance counselor at high school said..."

"No other person's got a right to tell you what you can or cannot do."

"She said I'm good with my hands. I'm good at typing."

"You got a B on this test."

"But, Daddy, I studied for it for three days, and Jeanette studied one hour and got an A."

"Don't compare yourself with Jeanette. You got this far, you can keep goin'. You'll get through."

Jeanette, having a much easier time academically, was taking advantage of every bit of freedom she could wangle away from Daddy, making friends, running with a crowd, getting caught up in the ideas of the 1960s that were beginning to be bandied about on campuses. Daddy sensed this, and it was one of his reasons for emphasizing the importance of the band. We thought it was just the money, but years later, when we were grown and it was clear how it had all turned out, I heard him talking to a friend who was excusing the performance of his own children by saying, "Well, it was easy for you, educatin' your kids, 'cause the band was payin' for it."

"Put it this way," Daddy told him. "If it wasn't that the band was gonna make money, I was gonna get by. I never had depended on the band to actually do the whole thing. I wanted the band for the reason of givin' my girls something in that so-called age of boys and the lipstick, something to continue to keep my family together. I knew it had to be other than just the lessons and the studyin' and goin' to school, where the other girls would be lookin' for boyfriends, pickin' them up, the huggin' and the kissin'. In order to take something away from your child, you got to replace it with something. If you don't want them partyin', then you got to give them something else."

With the band making money, he gave us cars because he believed in girls having their own transportation. "I don't want no man or boy sayin', I'll give you a lift 'cause you don't have a car. From that lift he could take you someplace. He could rape you." The year Donna worked before going to college, he bought her a new Chevy Monza, a turquoise convertible, with the stipulation that she never let a fellow so much as hang his elbows on the open window.

One day he came home and asked her, "Well, did you have a great day today?"

"Oh, yes, Daddy, it was fine."

"Any problems?"

"No, no problems."

"You know, I saw a car in Asbury Park looked just like your car." All of a sudden Donna started sweating. "But I knew it wasn't you because there was a guy sitting right next to this woman who was driving."

"Oh, Daddy, didn't I tell you...?"

"No, you didn't tell me!" he roared. "And I ain't havin' some pinhead ride around on my gasoline and my car insurance that I'm payin' for!"

When Daddy got through yelling, Donna went to wash the tears off her face and Daddy went out to the Chevy, lifted the hood, and removed the distributor cap. Donna, having had a bit of time to think, came out of the house defiantly.

"I'm eighteen. I'm working. I have a job. I'll do what I want." She threw herself into the driver's seat and turned the key, intending to spin the wheels in Daddy's face. Nothing happened.

"Walk," Daddy said, turning on his heel. "You think you're so darned independent, you can just walk."

When Donna and Jeanette went to college, they had different class schedules and each needed her own transportation, so Daddy bought them matching Volkswagen Beetles and I fell heir to the Chevy. It was fun to have any sort of car, but then I got to be a senior in high school, I was working hard, playing and studying, and I decided that for graduation I wanted a car of my own choosing. I went to Daddy.

"Daddy, I've never had anything that wasn't a hand-me-down. I'm always the third one. I'd like to have the car I want."

"I understand what you're sayin', Cookie. What kind of car you want?"

"I know exactly. A 1965 Thunderbird convertible with sequential turn signals."

"What! You know how much one of them costs?"

"You got Donna and Jeanette what they wanted."

"A Beetle is not the same as a Thunderbird."

"Daddy, I'm getting all A's. I'm the first black girl in Long Branch High School ever to make the National Honor Society..."

"Okay, Cookie, you've earned it, I guess."

The Thunderbird was white with a black top, a hardtop convertible, motorized so that the trunk opened up and the top came down and folded into it. Sequential turn signals and all, it was gorgeous, and driving around in it made me feel like a million dollars. That is, until the sleeting day I was to pick Linda up at school and the car in front of me stopped suddenly and I put on the brakes and skidded into it, smashing the Thunderbird's beautiful grille.

"Oh, geez, Daddy is going to kill me," I moaned to Mommy when I got home. I suggested that she might like to call him at work to warn him about the accident so he wouldn't go through the roof when he saw the crumpled grille, but she said no, that I had to do it. I had never called him at work before, so he knew that something serious was the matter.

"Daddy, I had an accident."

"Are you okay?" The question burst from him. Not a word about the beautiful new car.

Oh, my gosh, I thought, *he really loves me.*

"Are you okay? Is Linda okay? Fine, then don't worry about the car, Cookie. We'll get it fixed."

What a generous man he was—except when you asked for two dollars and he'd come up with $1.98, but that was to teach you a lesson. When we wanted something, he never said he didn't have enough money to get it. His philosophy was: "Money you can always get. Don't limit yourself to whether you have money or don't have money. If you really think you need something, you pay a little down and then just work around and find a way to pay for it."

Daddy's mistrust of boys was such that he never did relax his rule against allowing them in our cars, nor did he come around to letting college students help us load or unload our instruments and amplifiers, which weighed a ton, and our suitcases of clothes. Daddy would thank the fellows kindly and say, "Me and my daughters know just how to take care of things, so you just show us where to go and we'll be fine."

We would set up on the bandstand, Linda in back with the drums, Mommy on the bass next to her, Donna and I with our saxophones in the front on the left, Jeanette on guitar, and Rita on piano on the right. When we started to play, Daddy would stand off to the side, with his soft drink on the piano and a stack of our business cards ready to hand out to anyone who asked for one. He rarely sat down, and just by catching our eye, he could somehow convey that we were doing fine or that we needed to pick up the tempo a bit or slow it down or whatever.

Even after he had said no any number of times, guys would still come up to him and ask, "Mr. Thornton, can I dance with one of your daughters?"

"They're playin'. How can they dance?" he always answered, but the guys were persistent, and finally he sensed that they suspected we wouldn't dance because we were the band and thought we were better than they were and didn't want to get down and boogie with them. At that point he began to ease off.

A song like "Shotgun," a hit for Junior Walker and the All Stars, didn't need all the instrumentation all the time. I'd be playing and Donna would be free, so that when Daddy nodded that it was all right, she'd jump down and dance. Or we would play the Rolling Stones' "Satisfaction," and I'd have sixteen bars free and jump down and start doing the bugaloo or whatever. When it was a place like Princeton where we played many, many weekends and came to know the fellows well, sometimes, with Daddy's permission, a couple of the guys would join us on the bandstand, and they'd be saying, "Hey, look at me! I'm dancing with the Thornton Sisters!"

After playing all evening, swinging, stomping, belting out the songs—I'd compare Linda's singing to Aretha Franklin's and take an oath that she'd not come out second best—we would be starved at one o'clock in the morning. Just outside of Princeton was a place called Mom's Pepper Mill and we would pile in there, everybody in high spirits. We'd had a great time, the music had soared, we'd sung, danced, and gotten paid for it. To top off the evening, we'd order whole dinners—veal Parmigiana and spaghetti and ice cream sundaes—and then we'd ask for cheeseburgers to go. Daddy claimed it cost more to feed us than to clothe us, even with all our costume changes and Mommy buying brocade at forty and eighty dollars a yard, but he remembered the oatmeal when he was a kid and never told us we couldn't have anything on the menu we wanted. Along about Wednesday every week, we would have to start dieting so we could get into our dresses by the weekend.

When we went on long trips, to Virginia or South Carolina or Kentucky, we brought food from home because Daddy, like most men, hated to stop once he was on the road. We would plead with him for a bathroom stop, but it was zoom, zoom, past every service station, I suppose because with six women waiting their turn, a half hour or more could be lost.

Heading back home after a gig in the South, we often drove all night. We would pile into the car, talking and laughing about different things that had happened, comments dancers had made to us, bits of byplay noticed, then after a while there would be silence as we dropped off to sleep. Mommy would doze off, too, because she was just as tired as we were from the hours of singing and playing, and Daddy, driving on and on through the dark, would begin to long for hot black coffee to keep him awake. But as soon as he spotted a lighted diner and pulled in, one of us would wake up and call out the window, "Daddy, bring me a cheeseburger," and then we'd all be yelling for sandwiches and drinks and another half hour would be wasted and Daddy would be fifty or sixty dollars poorer.

After that happened a few times, he tried cutting the motor and rolling silently to a stop down the street from a diner, but our bodies were so attuned to the vibration of the car that as soon as it stopped, we woke up. So then he left the motor running, and that worked pretty well. We would sleep through the stop, he would get his coffee, and we would roll on again through the night.

One morning when we arrived back home, I brushed against him and discovered his pants leg was wet. I looked closer. "Daddy, you're bleeding."

"Yeah, well, Cookie, I had to pinch myself awful hard to stay awake. The hurtin' kept my eyes open."

His eyes would be open, but he'd get over the line into New

Jersey and say to himself, "Geez, I don't remember comin' through Washington." Driving in that automatic way, he pulled up one night at the entrance to the Chesapeake Bay Bridge, which was miles and miles of two-lane roadway just skimming the waters of the bay. He had a sudden vision of being tipped just a bit further over into semiconsciousness by the hypnotic unrolling of the center line and, drawn by lights reflected on the bay, steering the car into the black water. It was the only time Daddy gave up, parked the car, folded his arms on the steering wheel, and went to sleep until the first light of morning.

Because this was still the early 1960s, sometimes when Daddy stopped for coffee, he was told, "You can't get served here. You'll have to go around back." This happened in the South, of course, but more often it was in a border state like Maryland or Virginia, where racial prejudice seemed to be more intense and racial coexistence less worked out than in the Deep South. It was in a diner in Virginia that four men at the counter talked loudly about "niggers."

One of the men said, "Fella asked where the niggers hang out around here and I told him, 'On that oak tree in the center of town.'"

Daddy went to the cash register to pay the check so we could get out of there. The four men strolled out, and as they walked by the booth where we were sitting, one of them spat in Rita's cup of tea. Daddy didn't see it happen—luckily, or there would have been a fight despite the four against one odds because, as he said, "I can stand being Uncle Tom but don't do nothin' to my kids."

"It hurts," he ruminated when we were back on the road and we told him what happened. "Spittin' in a little girl's tea is way beyond forgiveness." He was silent, studying the road, then he commented: "Why he done it was nothin' but hate that was taught him. Because if he had been taught love, he'd have been like that nice fellow at South Carolina."

We had arrived to play that weekend at one of the fraternities at the University of South Carolina, and when we pulled in, a fellow sneered, "Look at the carload of niggers." The social chairman grabbed the man by the collar and hissed, "If you ever call Mr. Thornton and his girls that again, I'll kill you myself." Daddy was remembering that occasion, and another at Salem, Virginia, when a student called Daddy a nigger and another grabbed the fellow, told him he was a son of a bitch, and threatened, "If I hear you call anybody, especially Mr. Thornton, other than his name, I'll bash you in the mouth."

"It made me feel good to hear that," Daddy said. "Like I say, there's a lotta good white people. Let me tell you about a woman lived in Deal, next to Asbury Park, where all them big houses and rich folks from New York is. It was winter and I was workin' my second job, pickin' up garbage at night, from eleven to seven. I had to go around to the back of the houses. They didn't put no garbage cans out on the street. I had to enter the yards to pick up the garbage and not make no noise.

"Like I said, it was winter and this particular night it was cold. I guess I wasn't dressed warm enough. It got around three o'clock in the morning and I couldn't move my fingers no more. Another five minutes I knew I was going to freeze to death, that's how cold I had got. There was a light in this house and I could see a lady in the kitchen. I said I got to ask this white lady just to please let me sit in the garage. I knocked on the door. She looked at me—I mean, I was the garbage man, dressed like a garbage man—she looked at me and said, 'Come on in.' She gave me hot coffee. She let me stay right there in the kitchen and get warm. I mean, this was the wee hours. She could have said, 'You black ape, how dare you knock on my door?' When I left, I kept lookin' back at that house. I said, 'Jesus Christ, there's some wonderful people in the world.'

"That's what you got to remember, kids. You're glad for the good people, and when you meet up with the ones that wasn't brought up to love, you keep on goin' past them 'cause you know the road you're followin'."

It was his talking to us like this that made us philosophical about the prejudice we encountered. One night we arrived at a motel where we had made reservations weeks before, only to have the clerk stare at us and say stupidly, "But this reservation came from New Jersey," as though we had somehow purposely misled him. He then claimed that the reservation was so old it couldn't be honored, and anyway it had been lost and the motel was full up because there was a convention in town.

"It's the Chevy motel again tonight," we joked as we piled back into the limousine.

These were blips on the screen of what was essentially a happy time, a time I think of now as Camelot, when we were all pulling together, close and directed, caring and covering for each other, a family that was making it all work. By this time, 1965 and thereabouts, colleges were booking the band as much as a year and a half ahead for their dances. What made us such a success was that we played all the big hits, the songs that the artists who made the records couldn't play themselves because so much had been dubbed in the studio, or if they did play that one song, they didn't have the songs by other artists that were currently popular. But we had them all.

At first, when a new hit came out, we would buy the sheet music for each instrument, but then, even though Daddy had never wanted us to play by ear and we didn't, we said why pay all this money for the sheet music when we can pick it up from the record. I'd hear what the sax was playing, Rita would get what the piano was doing, Linda would pin down the beat, and Jeanette would hear where the guitar came in. Every one of us could sing solo, with the others singing backup, or we could all sing together, and because of the variety of instruments, woodwinds as well as strings and drums and piano, there wasn't a song we couldn't do. The dancing kids claimed our version of something like the Isley Brothers' "Shout" was even better than the original.

"You women are hot!" the students raved. "You sound like men."

"Because we were taught by men to play like men," we told them.

At Princeton on big weekends, every eating club would hire its own band, and often when we were performing, people left other clubs to come to hear us. The Cap and Gown fellows would protest: "Look, we're paying the band, you're not paying, yet you want to come in and enjoy the music." Eventually they had to have bouncers to keep the people from sneaking in.

Daddy would hiss at us, "They're diving through the windows, kids! Give it some more juice. You're really, really hot now." And it was true: the students literally broke windows to get in.

In 1966, for Spring Weekend at Princeton, two top Motown groups—the Temptations and Martha and the Vandellas—were booked, and the Thornton Sisters, all to play at the Dillon gym. The Motown groups were on the main floor and we were to play in a corner up on the second tier. "Oh, wow," we said, "we've got to play extra good tonight. We're up against these famous groups."

We kept our cool. We didn't do anything gauche like ask the stars for their autographs even though we were fans just as much as any of the kids there. But we were undeniably pumped up. We went for that little something special in the music, singing extra loud and cutting up. People started to drift off the main floor, up the stairs to where we were.

We winked at each other. "We got them. They want to hear us." The group downstairs was getting smaller; upstairs it was getting larger and larger. We were really tearing it up. "This is it! We got them right where we want them!"

Between sets, back in the changing area, Martha and the Vandellas looked right through us, not a word, no answer to our hello. The Temptations did the same, except for one musician. He said, "You girls are *good*. You're giving us a heck of a run for our money."

"That's a nice person," Daddy said. "He's got a good heart. He'll last." Daddy made predictions like that: "He'll be dead in three years." "Her voice'll be lost in a few years." The funny thing is, he was often right. The lead singer of the Temptations, David Ruffin, died of an overdose; Eddie Kendrick died of cancer; another one committed suicide. Only two of the original Temptations are left, and one of them, Melvin Franklin, is the sweet guy who was generous enough to tell us we were good on that wonderful night when we played our best against the best.

Having found we could hold our own against big-time competition, we again proposed to Daddy that we go after big-time money. He shook his head. "We're in the right place," he said. "You get famous like them, you get the spotlight on you, you're up there only to come down. Us, we'll occupy the middle. That's where you stay out of trouble."

One Friday afternoon the limo was packed, we were set to go, but Donna was missing. The telephone rang, Daddy answered, and a man's voice said, "Donna ain't goin' with the band this weekend."

"Who's this?" Daddy demanded. The fellow hung up.

Daddy was, briefly, in shock, then he began to steam. "Where is she? What's she doin'? She's afraid to call on her own. She has this guy call—this young buck callin' the old buck to say he's stealin' his doe." He turned on us. "If you're gonna be a woman, be a woman. If you're gonna do somethin' against your father, be woman enough to come and talk to me. Don't have some sneakpot comin' on the telephone sayin', 'Donna ain't gonna be there'!"

We waited...down to the very last minute we could wait if we were going to make the gig. We couldn't wait any longer. Daddy started backing out of the driveway. At that moment Donna turned the corner and half-walked, half-ran to the car. Daddy said nothing. Donna said nothing, just snatched open the car door, jumped in, and we were off. We waited for Daddy to say, "I'm gonna break your head if you ever do that again," but he was silent, perhaps letting her sin against the family grow ever heavier in her mind or perhaps gloating in his own mind that whoever the young buck was, he had not been strong enough to take her away from the old buck after all.

The only time he might have been referring to the incident was one morning the following week when, at the round table over coffee, he said to all of us, with peculiar emphasis: "Do anything you want to do as long as you, and you alone, are willin' to pay. If I make a bad decision, I've got to pay and I don't mind payin'. If I've got to work another couple of hours or another couple of days to cover my mistake, I know I'm gonna do it. But I'm not gonna work extra to cover nobody else's mistake."

Was this one more warning: Don't come home pregnant? Perhaps so. I think he knew his oldest girls were slipping away from him, that the young bucks were going to win in the end. He referred wistfully to a time when Donna was so small he could hang her up on the back of the door from a coat hook and first have her squeal with delight and then kick and scream to be let down. "I wish all you girls were that young again."

"But, Daddy..."

"Yeah, I know, kids grow up. You gotta think about this, though. You can have two or three husbands but only one mother and father. Four or five husbands but you ain't never gonna have but one mother and father."

He wanted us to continue to listen to him as we had when we were small, to accept his strictures on the right way to go, and we three youngest did. But Jeanette, in particular, more and more often said, "I'll just have to find out for myself, Daddy. I can't just accept what you say."

One day she announced that she was taking the coffeepot to college because she and some fellow students intended to stage a sit-in in the dean's office: for Black Power, for equality, for African studies on campus, for blacks being admitted to off-campus housing.

"The dean's office!" Daddy fumed. "The guy I went to and begged, 'Please let my daughters in'?"

"That was the president."

"Whatever, they let you in and now you're gonna make trouble? I'm sendin' you there to learn. I'm not sendin' you there to be one of those radical Black Panther people!"

"Daddy, this is the way it is. I need to express myself."

"I don't care what you need to do! You're gonna spoil it for your sisters! Cookie's fixin' to go to college and you're listenin' to some black rat from upstate New York who comes rollin' down here and is gonna make your own father look bad and spoil it for your sisters."

"I'm a woman now. I have to declare myself."

"You can't be burnin' your bridges."

"I don't care. It's for a cause."

He couldn't dissuade her but he had the last word. "Yeah, well, you're not takin' my coffeepot!"

The sit-in ended when the administration threatened to expel the striking students, and the black rat, as Daddy referred to him, got kicked out of college a couple of months later.

I hadn't been concerned about Jeanette spoiling things for me because by then I knew that Monmouth College was not where you went to be prepared for medicine: You went there if you were a kid who needed to age four years before going into your father's construction or dry cleaning business, or if you were interested in elementary or secondary school education. I wanted to go to a more prestigious school, some place with a name, and I thought if I could get a scholarship at a nearby college that was really good, Daddy might let me go there instead of Monmouth.

Miss Apostalocus, the guidance counselor whom I had made a believer of, suggested Barnard College. I applied, was accepted and awarded a scholarship. Daddy said no.

"New York City is too far away. Anything more than eighteen minutes away, where Monmouth College is at, you're not goin' to."

"Daddy, if you want us to become doctors, we have to go to medical school, and no medical school in the country has ever heard of this dinky little college in West Long Branch, New Jersey."

"It's a college."

"I'm trying to tell you, it doesn't have a reputation."

"It don't matter. You get A's in college, you can go anyplace."

When I tried to argue with him further, he walked away. I said to myself, Well, maybe Daddy knows something I don't know. I'm going to do it the way he tells me to, and if I don't get accepted into medical school, it'll be his fault and I'll have something to hang over his head the rest of his life.

The truth was that he wanted it all to stay family—nobody going out of the circle, nobody breaking into it. But it is the natural order of things for children to grow up and move out and move on. Sooner or later there was bound to be a break.

♦ 8 ♦

The Break

FOR THREE YEARS, from the time I entered high school, I fantasized about my senior prom, the first time I would have a date with a boy. I didn't know which boy. I figured Daddy would hire a soldier for me as he had for Donna and would have for Jeanette, except that she had said no, thanks, she could get her own dude. I just knew I was going to that dance. I found a picture in a magazine of the gown I wanted and badgered Mommy to make it for me.

"Cookie, the prom is a year away."

"I know, Mom, but this is such a special dress and I just have to have it." It was pastel blue satin, with a bodice of blue sequins, an Empire waist, and an overskirt of draped chiffon. The material cost four hundred dollars, money I had saved from the ten or twenty dollars Daddy gave each of us after we played a gig, except for Donna and Jeanette, who got one hundred dollars because, being in college, they needed more. I planned to wear the gown with a fox stole and perfume I had sent away to France for, and as the day approached and Mom put the finishing touches on the gown, all I lacked was an escort. Daddy turned the problem over to Donna.

"Find somebody on campus to take Cookie to the prom," he ordered.

Donna thought about it. "Well, I know one boy. He's in my class in biology, and he's really nice."

"I'll take him," I said.

His name was Jimmy Hutcheson, and he was tall and good-looking, polite and gallant, a smooth dancer, and I was in seventh heaven. All I could think of as we danced was: *Is this what it's like to be in love? Maybe I'll know when he kisses me goodnight.* I had the keys to every door in the house, plus the garage, and Rita and Linda had promised to make sure that Daddy didn't drink any coffee that evening so that he would be certain to be asleep and I could get my first kiss.

Jimmy had his hand under my elbow as we went up the front walk at three in the morning. According to my scenario, when we arrived at the front door, I'd unlock it, then turn appealingly to thank him for the lovely evening, lifting my face to his so that the light from the street lamp fell on it, at which moment he would bend and, breathing in the fragrance from my French perfume, place his lips passionately on mine. My heart was pounding. This was the moment when my whole life was about to change, the moment I was to be initiated into the mysteries. Key ready, I reached for the screen door, which always came open at a touch. I touched. I tugged. I pulled.

The hall light blazed on, and in a replay of Donna's experience, here came Daddy padding down the hall, barefoot, barechested, in boxer shorts, rubbing the sleep from his eyes. "I'll get it, Cookie," he called. "Come on in, Jim. Sit down and have a soda."

"No, thank you, Mr. Thornton. I had a lovely evening with your daughter. I'll just say goodnight and go on."

I shook Linda and Rita awake to flay them alive for not checking the screen door, but they swore it had been unlatched when they went to bed. Not wanting Daddy to hear me cry, I buried my face in my pillow and wept until Linda and Rita complained that my sobs were shaking the bed. Such a bittersweet evening—I'd had a perfect time at the dance but I missed out on the kiss that I had ached for all through high school.

Years later, when we sat at the round table talking about old times, laughing about it but still with a trace of tender pain, I would remind Daddy of that night, and of another night when I was in college and came home at 12:30 instead of midnight as promised. I rang the bell and Daddy came to the door.

"Hello?"

"Daddy, it's me. Let me in."

"My daughter was home at twelve. I don't know who you are." He switched off the light and walked away.

I begged, I pleaded, I wept, I promised, promised, promised never to be late again. And I wasn't. If Daddy said 9:00, I was there at 8:55; 10:00, I was there at 9:30. All the rebelliousness in the family had gone to Donna and Jeanette; there was none left when it came to me.

"If you'd done that to Jeanette," I remarked to Daddy, "she'd have said, Fine, Dad, I'll just go party until tomorrow morning."

"Of course," he agreed. "I had to do something different for each one of you. I remember once with Donna, she's like nineteen and it's 1:00, 1:30 in the mornin', I'm lying on the couch and I see her try the door and then look through the window. She thinks I'm asleep, so she figures to sneak in the kitchen 'cause you girls was always schemin' together and somebody had slipped it off the latch for her. I jump up and run downstairs and stand behind the door and she comes in. She tiptoes through the kitchen, headin' for the stairs, and I cut the light on. I jus' look at her and walk past her and up the stairs."

One time I said to him, "Dad, we're laughing about it now, but it wasn't so funny then. Why were you so hard on us?"

He answered honestly. "Bein' out there, bein' a man and hearin' how boys talk about girls, I knew that the weak girls would be the ones to end up with the turned-over shoes. When I see a woman who looks bad, I don't see her as a woman but as someone's baby, a little child who was given a bottle or nursed to health, her diaper changed, and now she's bein' beaten, knocked around by some man. I just couldn't see that happenin' to one of my daughters." He summed up: "Why I was the way I was, I wanted to make sure my daughters could take care of themselves. I didn't want them never to have to put up with a man who mistreated them."

Forewarned is forearmed, Daddy believed, so he didn't pull any punches when he talked to us about men. "When they're hard, they're soft," he told us, "and when they're soft, they're hard."

We younger ones didn't know what he was talking about. "What does that mean, Daddy?" we asked.

"It means men will promise you anything if they want to get

you in bed. First the guy says, 'Oh, honey, I love you. I'll buy you a mink coat.' And she says, 'Oh, will you, honey?' He says, 'Just come on over here to the bedroom.' She says, 'But what I really want is a diamond ring.' He says, 'A diamond ring? I'll get you a diamond ring. Tomorrow we'll go get the ring and the mink coat. Just for tonight, just go over to that bedroom.' And she says, 'Okay.'

"Now the guy's got the woman where he wants her, and after he's been satisfied, the next morning she reminds him, 'Honey, what about my diamond ring?' And he says, 'Are you kiddin'? You got to be crazy.' That's what I'm tellin' you about men and that's what you got to remember: When they're hard, they're soft; when they're soft, they're hard."

He explained, "It's just human nature. That's how we keep the human population goin'. I raised you girls to be tough, but no matter how tough I try to teach your brains to be, nature is bigger than both of us. So, like I say, you got to choose the moment to be weak, not just let some guy talk you into it."

In the summer, although the colleges were closed for vacation, the band was nevertheless in demand to play at debutante balls and sweet sixteen parties. When wealthy people hire musicians, they are inclined to treat them like any other hired help: "You're just the entertainment for my daughter. Go around to the back door. Wait until everyone else has been served. Don't mingle with the guests." They assume that musicians are their intellectual inferiors, and they also assume, with greater reason, that at least some of them are on drugs.

When we arrived at a country club or an estate or a Sutton Place triplex and were unloading our instruments and setting up, we wore Monmouth College blazers so that the parents would be on notice that their sons and daughters weren't the only ones going to college. We further confounded the parents' expectations by being a family—a mother and father and daughters, well dressed, well groomed, and well mannered. That didn't always make parents change their minds about treating us as hired help, but often enough it did, and we were welcomed as part of the whole festive occasion.

At a coming-out party in Virginia for the daughter of the head of a pharmaceutical company, the members of the Glenn Miller orchestra, who were to play for the adults, were consigned to the servants' quarters, but we had the run of the place. The debutante's mother, when we were introduced, said, "Why, you're a family. How very nice," (which translated as "reassuring") and the daughter, who knew us from college dances, welcomed us as old friends with, "Come on, kids, come see the house. Let me show you my room. Daddy won't let me drive the Rolls, but we can sit in it and feel the lovely leather."

In the fall of 1965, I entered Monmouth College as a freshman and Donna and Jeanette began their junior year. As science majors on the road to becoming doctors, this was the year they had to take organic chemistry, the course with the reputation of being the toughest in college. A few weeks into the fall, Daddy was trimming the hedge in back of the house when Donna came around the side.

"What you doin' home, Sugar?"

"Daddy, I've got something to tell you."

He looked at her face and carefully put his clippers down. "You want we should go in the house so your mother hears too?"

"She already knows, Daddy." Donna took a shuddering breath. "Daddy, I'm going to drop out of college...."

"Naw, you ain't."

"Daddy, I've tried to tell you time and again I'm not college material...."

"Just because that old guidance counselor said..."

"Because I can't do the work!"

"You're doin' it."

"There's no way I'm gonna pass organic chemistry. And don't tell me I just have to study harder! I've studied as hard as I know how."

"Honey, you've made two years. If you can do two, you can do four."

"Daddy, organic chemistry is a course you have to pass if you're a science major, and you have to major in science to go to

Aunt Ellie and Mommy auditioning at the Apollo Theatre in New York, 1934

Daddy, age 18, seaman second class, United States Navy, during World War II, 1943

Mommy and Daddy when Daddy was in the United States Navy, 1944

Family picnic in Lakewood, New Jersey. *Front:* Donna. *Next row:* Mommy, Linda (*on her lap*), Cookie. *Back row:* Daddy, Uncle Reggie, Betty, and Jeanette. 1950

The Thornettes. *Back, left to right:* Donna, 12, tenor sax; Yvonne, 9, alto sax; Jeanette, 11, guitar. *Front:* Linda, 7, on drums. 1956

Linda, age 9, drum solo on "Ted Mack and the Original Amateur Hour," 1959 (Library of Congress)

"Ted Mack and the Original Amateur Hour," Donna and Yvonne on sax, 1959 (Library of Congress)

The Thornton Sisters on stage at the Apollo Theatre. *Upper frames, left to right:* Donna, Jeanette, and Yvonne. *Center and lower frames:* Yvonne, 13, solo on alto sax. 1961

A Week With the Stars, the Thornton Sisters on center stage at the
Apollo Theatre, 1961

Our business card, 1963

The Thornton Sisters. *Back row:* Jeanette, Donna, Mommy, Yvonne.
Front: Rita and Linda. 1965 (J. J. Kriegsmann)

Daddy with social
chairman Terry Trovato
at Antebellum Weekend,
University of Kentucky,
1964

The Thornton Sisters
performing at an
Amherst College
fraternity party, 1965

Dr. Yvonne Thornton, graduation day, Columbia University College of Physicians and Surgeons, 1973

Graduation day, Columbia University College of Physicians and Surgeons. Mommy, Yvonne, and Daddy. 1973

Dr. and Mrs. Shearwood J. McClelland, in front of
Riverside Church, 1974

Family of the bride. *Left to right:*
Linda, Rita, Mommy, Yvonne,
Daddy, Donna, Jeanette, and Betty.
1974

Ringbearer and flower girl,
Yvonne's wedding, 1974

Shearwood and Yvonne, lieutenant commanders, United States Navy
National Naval Medical Center, Bethesda, Maryland, 1982

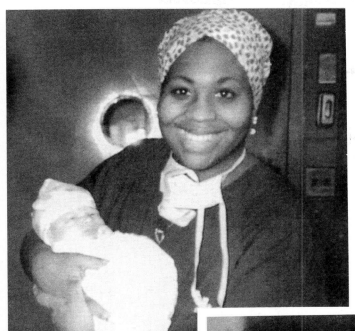

Yvonne and Daniel Hastings, delivered March 26, 1986, New York Hospital

Yvonne S. Thornton, associate professor of obstetrics and gynecology, Cornell University Medical School, 1989

Cruise on the *Queen Elizabeth II.*
Front row, left to right: Yvonne,
Kimberly. *Back:* Shearwood,
Woody. 1992

Daddy (Donald E. Thornton),
1977 (William E. Sauro/New York
Times)

Dr. Yvonne Thornton,
director of the Perinatal
Diagnostic Testing
Center, Morristown
Memorial Hospital, 1993

The Thornton family. *Left to right:* Yvonne, Mommy, Rita (*on her lap*), Donna, Linda in front, Daddy, Jeanette. 1952

On the porch of the house that Daddy and Mommy built. *Left to right:* Donald, Donna, Linda, Rita, Betty (*sitting*), Yvonne (*standing*), and Jeanette (*sitting*). 1977

medical school, and I'll never make it. I can't make it. I don't *want* to make it. I *like* being a secretary. That's what I want to do. I don't want to be a doctor."

The sentences landed hard and heavy, as heavy as the shovels of dirt Daddy had tossed as a ditchdigger. The sentences were burying his master plan. He lifted his hands, then let them fall despairingly to his sides. "Seems like you ain't gonna let me guide you no more."

"Daddy, I tried." Looking for a bright side, she said, "I'll get a job. I'll help you pay for Cookie going to college."

"You can help me pay two hundred and eighty-five dollars a month on the loan I took for your tuition," he snapped.

The fact that he still had to pay off the loan even though Donna was leaving college rankled him, perhaps even more than Donna's decision, because I think he knew in his heart she was right, that she had studied as hard as anyone could be asked to and that she probably was not cut out for college. His dream had been for all five daughters to become doctors, but he could revise it in the certainty that the next daughter was going to make it— Jeanette, the star of the family, the brilliant one, the one who had started Future Doctors of America when she was in high school.

After landing a job as an executive secretary at the Bendix Corporation, Donna began going out with a guy named Danny, a light-skinned guy, one of Daddy's "gray-eyed niggers." Light color and "good" hair had always been important to Donna despite Daddy's making fun of women who cared about such things. They were more important to her than the fact that Danny was a freeloader.

At Christmas, Donna turned up with a large box, and when we asked what it was, she said it was a present for Danny, a new suit. "He's such a good-looking guy," she said, "I want him to have nice clothes."

"Oh, geez," we groaned, "don't you remember what Daddy said?"

One of Daddy's roundtable soliloquies had featured women who get involved with men who are too stupid or too lazy to make enough money to buy their own suits. "The woman doesn't want to be escorted by a guy with turned-over shoes, by a guy who don't look good next to her, so she says, 'Honey, I can't be seen with you looking like that,' and she goes and buys him a suit. Women are like that. They'll give and give and give. And the guys keep takin' and takin' and takin'."

When Donna realized she was living out Daddy's prediction, she hid the box under the sofa so Daddy wouldn't know about it. But Danny was wearing the suit one night when he came to pick Donna up for a date. Proudly revolving to show off the fit, he said to Daddy, "How do you like the new suit Donna give me for Christmas, Mr. Thornton? Pretty cool, eh?"

"Real cool," said Daddy with heavy irony and a glance of withering scorn at Donna. "Uh huh, uh huh, buying men suits," he taunted her the next morning and for many days thereafter, until Donna wished she had never heard of Danny or the suit.

It was shortly after Christmas that Jeanette announced, as calmly as though it were of no concern to anyone but herself, that she, too, was dropping organic chemistry. "I don't like it. I can't do it. I'm not interested in it," she said flatly. And then, as though her news was a grenade, she pulled the pin. She was, she said, switching her major from biology to psychology.

"I'll still be a doctor," she told a stunned and devastated Daddy. "It's just that I'll be a Ph.D. instead of an M.D. I'll be a doctor of philosophy instead of a doctor of medicine."

"You won't have a scripperscrap around your neck?" he said weakly.

"It's called a stethoscope, Daddy!" She was defensive under her calm, and it made her react irritably. "Aren't you ever going to learn that?"

She was destroying a family joke, and it made us all ache with sadness. So much was ending. Our castles in the air were being dynamited.

The veins in Daddy's temple swelled into ropes and he swung his head like a battered bull. "What does a doctor of philosophy mean? That don't mean nothin'! People don't need no philosophy!

They need somebody can make them well!" He was sick with rage and disappointment. Language he had never before used in our hearing came pouring out of him. Profanely, bitterly, he outlined the dimensions of the mistake she was making and how cruelly she was letting him down.

"Do you know how much I sacrificed for you greasy-assed kids! I didn't have to stay around here. Look at your friends, look at the black kids. How many of them have got fathers? I'm not askin' to have a medal, but I've done a lot of things in my life for you kids that I didn't have to do. And now it's time for you to sacrifice something and you don't want to do it. All I'm askin' of you is just to hold off whatever it is you want to do until we can get where we're goin'."

Jeanette, the only one of us who could stand unblinkingly toe-to-toe with Daddy, let his argument slide off her. "I'm not going to be what you want me to be," she informed him. "I'm going to be myself. I've found what I want to do. And if you don't like it, I'm outa here."

Donna, with her job at Bendix, had rented her own apartment, and now Jeanette joined her until she found a part-time job and moved into a place of her own. She and Donna continued with the band, and Daddy was fair about giving them their share of whatever the band earned, which meant they had money in their pockets and freedom, the heady, delectable freedom to go out on dates and get home at an hour of their own choosing.

What they left behind on Ludlow Street was a poisoned atmosphere, dark, roiled, rancorous. Daddy's disappointment needed a target, and he found it in Mommy. He snarled at her for having let Donna and Jeanette go out on dates when he was at work. He charged her with destroying everything he had planned and schemed and fought for. He accused her, wildly and harshly, of conniving behind his back to subvert his teachings, and when she, goaded into answering, defended herself by pointing out that Donna and Jeanette were twenty-one and twenty and could not always be kept from having some taste of fun and normal life, the quarrels would go on until two or three o'clock in the morning.

Never had we known our parents to fight before; now we knew nothing but. When there weren't fights, there was silence. Linda, Rita, and I fled the house as often as possible. Between classes, I studied in the library at college, and every evening I went back there and stayed until closing time at ten. I studied intensively, not only because it was preferable to going home, but because I was determined that Daddy was going to have at least one doctor and that it was going to be me. I did not say this to him, though, for fear he would merely answer harshly, "Yeah, just like Donna and Jeanette was gonna be doctors." And, too, I knew it would not console him for Jeanette, still the special daughter.

In biology class the professor said, "Look at the person on your right, look at the person on your left. By senior year they'll be gone. There are a hundred and fifty of you now who plan to major in science. By graduation, a handful of you will be left. I'm not saying anything about Monmouth College in general, but this is the biology department and I am chairman and I am tough. You'll do it my way and become scientists or you won't be here."

I'm listening, I hear you, I said to myself. *And I can tell you right now, Dr. Garner, when you look at me, you're looking at one of the people who's still going to be here when the four years are up. There's no way in the world I'm going to let Daddy down.*

I did wish, though, that the professor would call me by my rightful name. When I raised my hand to give an answer, he said, "Well, Jeanette?"

"No, sir, I'm Yvonne."

And the next time: "Well, Donna?"

"No, sir, my name is Yvonne."

I complained to Daddy: "See what happens because you made us all go to the same college." It didn't strike him as important, but it was to me because I did not want to be identified as one of the Thornton sisters who had not been able to survive organic chemistry.

Because Donna was working and Jeanette was now going for a B.A. rather than a B.S. and was on a different part of the campus, I didn't see them except on weekends when the band was playing, and then it was with some sense of estrangement. They had fractured the circle of the family, walked away into their own pleasures, leaving us, the younger daughters, with a father who no longer smiled, with scrapping parents who no longer pulled together, with a family that had lost its common goal. But when the band played, that was still good, still tight. We made music that grew ever freer and richer because we were older now, more knowing, more sophisticated. The number-one hits we played had a Thornton Sisters edge.

Linda, a quiet girl, a shy girl, an introverted girl, was that very rare thing in a female: a brilliant drummer. She was capable of coming out with a beat that made us all turn around and look at her in wonder. She would smile and ad lib like crazy, doing marvelous things, and later she'd say shyly, "I get going and I just can't help myself." The mood would infect Rita at the piano, then spread to the rest of us, and we'd carry the dancers with us, sailing into a different space, all one, all high, swept up in the music.

New Year's weekend in 1967, we played at Norfolk, Virginia, slept in the car from three o'clock in the morning until it was light, then drove to Charleston, West Virginia, 225 miles west of Washington, D.C. After a fabulously successful show that night, we were packing up to start the drive north to Saratoga Springs, New York, where we were to play the next night, New Year's Eve, at Skidmore College. When the instruments and amplifiers were in the limousine, Jeanette faced Daddy. "Listen, Donna and I'll meet you in Saratoga. We're driving up with a couple of fellows."

Daddy straightened and stared at her. "What's the matter with you? Get in the car. The band's got to stay together."

"We'll be there. Don't worry."

"Get your butts in this car!"

Jeanette emphasized each word. "Either we're going with Paul and his friend or we're not going at all." Daddy's fists clenched, the color surged into his face, but he knew he was defeated. Jeanette turned to me. "You want to come with us, Yvonne? The guys'll get a nice date for you."

"Unh-unh. Nothing doing."

Daddy made a last plea. "Listen, Jeanette, Donna, every time we got one of these long drives, I say to myself that if something happens, at least I got all the kids and I got the instruments. How do you think my heart's gonna go if we get there and we don't have a saxophone player, we don't have a guitar player?"

"We'll be there," they said jauntily, and walked away.

This was about three in the morning. At four in the morning, as we drove the mountain roads of West Virginia, it began to snow. In the best of circumstances, we were not fond of these roads because of sheer drops into valleys hundreds of feet below, with no shoulder on the roads and nothing between us and the drops but cement posts with cable strung between. Now, with snow slicking the road, we were doubly frightened. Twice the limousine went into a spin, sliding crazily across the road. Daddy confessed that at these moments his heart jumped so hard it hurt his arm. At the bottom of one mountain, a jackknifed tractor-trailer hung on the wire, its cab dangling over empty space. A few miles farther on, we inched around a tangle of wrecked cars, emergency vehicles, and bodies lying in the road.

The farther north we crawled, the harder the snow swirled and blew. Trucks threw up salt and slush, reducing visibility to near zero. Daddy cursed steadily, monotonously. The car Donna and Jeanette were riding in passed us on the road, a broken chain on a rear tire pounding the fender to bits. As if we didn't know, the radio told us we were in the midst of a major blizzard. But on we crept. We had never yet failed to show up for a gig.

About five o'clock in the afternoon, we arrived at the entrance of the New York State Thruway. Daddy let out a thankful sigh, almost as though we were safely there although we still had four or five more hours of driving. The man at the tollbooth warned us to take it very slow because the road was icy, but Daddy kept swinging around the snowplows, passing them because he needed to stay at a steady fifty miles an hour to make the gig on time. The drivers honked their horns repeatedly at us, we thought to warn us about the dangerous conditions. We waved, and on we went.

We were still forty miles from Saratoga when a state trooper pulled alongside. "You're on fire!" he shouted. "Your back wheel's on fire!"

Daddy pulled off the road. The wheel, when we stopped, wasn't on fire, but apparently, as we rolled along, it shot sparks.

"How could it be?" Daddy kept moaning as he drove the two miles to the service station the trooper told us was just ahead. "I took it to the garage, knowing we had all this drivin' this weekend. I told the guy to take the wheels off and pack the bearings with grease, that I didn't want no mess-up with all the weight this car's got to carry and the heat buildin' up in the wheels. That was the mistake: I shouldn'a let him fool with the wheels. He musta tightened them too much or forgot to put the grease back in."

The service station mechanic said nothing could be done until Monday morning and we'd be better off getting a tow truck to take us to the nearest town, so Daddy called Saratoga to tell them we had broken down in the blizzard and would not be making the date and to tell that to his two daughters who had, he learned, already arrived. As he was driving the car around in back of the station to wait for the tow truck, the wheel fell off. The car lurched and crashed to the pavement.

Daddy kicked himself later that it hadn't occurred to him to offer the tow truck operator extra to tow the car all the way to Saratoga. That way we could have made the gig. But he was so upset about the car and having to pay for hotel rooms and having to return the deposit to Skidmore and losing the thousand dollars for the night that it didn't cross his mind.

It was the first time the family hadn't arrived together for a gig and the first gig we had ever missed. "God's making us suffer for splitting up," Mommy whispered. Daddy, when we'd checked in at a hotel, muttered, "I'll be back," and went off by himself, either to cry or put his fist through a wall, or both.

The next day, carrying our suitcases but having to leave the costly instruments and amplifiers behind in the car, Mommy, Daddy, Linda, Rita, and I climbed on a bus for New York City, where we changed to another bus for Long Branch. That bus let us off a mile from Ludlow Street. The snow from the blizzard of the day before lay deep on the uncleared sidewalks, and we were dressed in light clothes—jeans, sweaters, and sneakers—no socks, no boots, no coats because it was warm in the car and all we ever did was jump out and run inside to change our clothes wherever we were playing. Mommy and Daddy marched ahead of us, their mood clearly etched in the rigidity of their backs.

The snow soaked our sneakers and chunks iced our ankles, the bottoms of our jeans dripped slush, the wind pierced our sweaters like frozen needles, the suitcases grew pounds heavier with every step. Our feet became numb. And then there was no feeling in them at all.

"We're frozen!" we called out. "Our feet are ice!"

"Keep walkin'," Mommy and Daddy ordered without turning.

We stumbled on, following those rigid backs. When we reached the house, we fell inside the front door, crawling on our hands and knees like survivors of an arctic crash. Mommy, who was wearing sturdier shoes, filled roasting pans with water and ice cubes, and as cold as the water was, it felt boiling to our frozen feet. The pain as circulation slowly returned was excruciating. We rocked and moaned as Daddy paced the room.

"God damn it, boys have destroyed what I've tried to do for this family! Jesus Christ! You see what happens when the family don't stay together? Now I have to go back up there to get the car, and it'll cost us all the money we made in West Virginia! Those two friggin' girls are sittin' somewhere sippin' on a cool one while the rest of you are gettin' frostbite! I'll kill 'em when I get my hands on them!"

"Donald, it wasn't their fault."

"God damn what boys have done to this family!" His eyes were red with surging blood and the veins in his neck were popping like a ship's hawser.

"It doesn't do any good to get so mad, Donald."

"Don't tell me not to get mad! Look at the money we lost 'cause of those damned kids!"

"Donald, they got there and we didn't."

"'Cause they split us up!"

Donna and Jeanette walked in the door, come to see if we had made it back and mad in their own right for our having made them look bad by not showing up. Daddy furiously accused them of letting boys come between them and their family and causing this trouble of the car's catching on fire and their sisters nearly freezing to death in the snow and having to leave the instruments behind—thousands and thousands of dollars' worth of instruments and who knows whether they'd still be there when he went back for the car.

Donna kept repeating helplessly, "But, Daddy, we were there. We were ready to play. If we'd been with you, we'd have gotten frostbite too."

Jeanette said nothing until Daddy ran down, just looked on, distant, controlled. Then she spoke evenly. "Daddy, if you're going to act like this, I don't want to be a part of it anymore. I don't want to be in the band anymore."

Daddy, who could break a brick with a blow of his bare hand, took a step toward her. But Jeanette did not flinch. She lifted her chin higher. "I'm tired of having you scream at us. I'm tired of having beer spilled on me. I'm tired of working when everybody else is playing."

Mommy moaned, "Jeanette…"

"I mean it. I want out."

"One monkey don't stop the show," Daddy ground out between clenched teeth. "You think the band can't go on without you? One monkey don't stop the show!" Now he was shouting.

"That's a good thing," Jeanette said, wheeling, "because I'm through."

And out she went, out of the front door and out of our lives for months to come.

◆ 9 ◆

One Monkey Don't Stop
the Show

ALL THE TIME WE WERE GROWING UP, Daddy had never cursed, or if he started to, Mommy said, "Not in front of the kids, Donald," and he acknowledged this with, "Oh, right, the kids," and shut up. But after Jeanette left, four-letter words came whipping out of his mouth as though he were a sailor. His tirades against Jeanette for leaving the band sometimes went on for an unbroken hour. Larded into them at intervals was the resolute, defiant phrase: "One monkey don't stop the show." I never knew its origin, whether it was a circus phrase or an army exhortation, but it summed up his angry determination not to be defeated by his ungrateful child.

The problem was, of course, that this child was the one most like him. She had all of his determination, drive, fortitude, independence, and energy, which meant that he admired her, loved her, and fought with her passionately. Where the rest of us were negative poles to his positive force, he and Jeanette were two positives and inevitably the sparks flew between them.

When he wasn't excoriating Jeanette, Daddy said over and over, "Where did I go wrong? I should have done something else, but what? Maybe if I'd done this…Maybe if I'd done that…"

When Mommy tried to say, "Donald, that's the way kids are, that's the way life is," he turned on her and heaped blame, sending her fleeing into silence, retreating far back into the cave of herself. Day after day her depression deepened until she almost ceased to function and spent much of the time when we were at school sitting in the dark with tears trickling down her cheeks.

In between his fulminating outbursts, Daddy was a broken man. When Jeanette left, so did his sense of purpose, his drive, his smile. Late at night, when I entered the pitch-black living room I would often be startled to see the lighted end of a cigarette suddenly glow in the dark and realize that Daddy was sitting there staring out of the picture window, staring silently at the ashes of his life. We didn't speak, but everything in me went out to him and I vowed in my heart that never would I let him down as Jeanette had done, never would I reduce him to such desolation because of something I had failed to do.

With Jeanette gone from the band, Daddy instructed Rita to play mostly chords on the piano and to play them louder to make up for the absence of the guitar, and he turned up the amplifiers to compensate, so the band still sounded great. But now it was becoming obvious that Mommy was not going to be able to continue, and he cast around for some way of substituting for the bass, because without the electric bass, which Mommy had switched to a couple of years before to keep from being drowned out by the drums, the band wouldn't have the solid backbeat we needed for the music to sound right.

Daddy tugged and pulled at the problem until he came up with the idea of having some sort of bass made that Rita could play with her feet, like the pedals on an organ. He went to Newark in search of someone to make it for him.

"It can't be done," was the answer at several places.

"Look," Daddy cajoled, "I'll pay for your time. Just try it."

"Naw, can't be done."

His bolstering belief that people always say something can't be done until one person goes ahead and does it kept him searching, and finally he found a man in Kearny willing to test out his idea. This fellow took the bass pedals from an organ, fashioned a keyboard with about thirty keys, and wired it into an amplifier. The sound this foot bass made replicated the sound of an electric bass played with the hands.

Daddy brought the contraption home, placed it on the floor under the keyboard, and told Rita to take off her shoes and play the pedals with her feet while she played the piano with her hands. Now it was her turn to say something couldn't be done.

"Just try it," Daddy urged. "Try, try, try."

Dutifully, each afternoon Rita practiced and practiced, attempting to master a workable technique. Daddy, when he came home from work, listened and announced the tempo had to be faster. He dropped to his hands and knees and beat out the tempo on the floor.

"Faster. Faster like this."

"Daddy, I can't go that fast."

"Sure, you can."

"Daddy, I've got cramps in my legs!"

"Okay, go put hot towels on them, then get back here."

Rita, kicking out to get at the pedals, time and again fell off the piano bench backwards. But driven by Daddy and by the determination she and Linda and I shared not to let Daddy down as Jeanette had done, she kept at it until she had not only mastered the foot bass but become wondrously good at it.

The sound was terrific. We could play all of our regular repertoire plus any of the hit songs that demanded a heavy bass. With Daddy working the controls on the amplifier, he would have the bass really pushing when the song called for that kind of kicking out. Not long ago, I ran into a fellow who had been at Princeton when we were playing, and he said, "You'd hear the music and you'd say, 'Wow! How many people are in that band?' Then you'd go inside and you'd see three women up there on the bandstand. You just couldn't believe it, the sound was so incredible."

Mommy did have to drop out of the band. Her depression, aggravated by the fact that she was menopausal, deepened so intolerably that she was hospitalized on the psychiatric service at Monmouth Medical Center. When she was released, she was on medication that so slowed her reactions that it was months before she could rejoin the band, and she never did get back to being the player she had been. She just more or less went through the motions, which was all right because by now Rita was so good on the foot bass that we didn't really need her.

Donna stuck with us, turning up some weekends because, in effect, the younger ones had played to pay for her college tuition and cars and clothes and now it was our turn. I was going into my junior year at Monmouth College and Linda was coming in as a freshman, and Monmouth, because it was a private college, was expensive even though both Linda and I had grants-in-aid and small scholarships.

Junior year meant that now it was my turn to come up against organic chemistry. By this time I had learned that it didn't make much difference what you majored in—it could be Chinese literature or English or mathematics—but you had to have organic chemistry to get into medical school. It was like a screening course—really tough. If you could make it through organic chemistry, everyone said, you could make it through anything.

The professor was a male chauvinist who announced on the first day of class, "All the girls sit in the front row, and you don't wear slacks in my class," which didn't mean that he liked women, only that he liked to look at their legs. He was, if anything, tougher on the women than on the men, and I prayed silently, "Just let me pass this course. Just let me get a C and I'll be happy."

"You're going to get these five unknowns," the professor told us, "five chemicals in test tubes, and it's your job to find out what these unknowns are. You have the entire semester to do it. You can be in the lab until midnight, until two in the morning, I don't care, but unless you get four out of the five, you're not going to pass the course even if you get A's on the tests."

I took him literally about being able to use the lab until two in the morning and searched out the night custodian, Willie Dee, who scratched his head and said nobody ever used the lab after ten o'clock. I told him there was a first time for everything and he'd be seeing a lot of me that semester.

Willie Dee became my guardian angel, and night after night

he'd stick his head in the lab door to check on me. "You sure you're okay in there?"

"I'm fine."

"Is anybody else comin'?"

"Not that I know of, but they can if they want to."

"I just want to know, are you waitin' for somebody?"

He had a hard time believing that a girl was in the lab until two in the morning looking, not for love, but for unknowns. I got one rather quickly, then a long time later two more, so I had three but I couldn't get the fourth, couldn't...couldn't...couldn't. A week before the end of the semester I faced the fact that I was never going to get the all-important fourth. I leafed through the books a last despairing time. All during the course, the professor had lectured about an alpha-phenol, never once mentioning that there was a beta-phenol with an entirely different chemical reaction from an alpha-phenol. I stumbled across mention of it in a textbook. "I wonder. I wonder," I said, and I began testing.

As the results came through, "I can't believe this," I kept saying out loud, all alone in that lab at two in the morning. "I can't believe he would try to trick me like this." But it was my fourth unknown and I passed organic chemistry. I got a B.

"How come you didn't get an A?" Daddy said.

When I answered, it was the first time in my life that I really hurt my father. I had studied so hard, worked so hard, other students had flunked the course right and left, and here he was criticizing me for not getting an A. I exploded.

"What do you know? You never even graduated from high school and you're telling me I should have gotten an A!"

He sank down in his chair, shriveling like a spider dropped in a candle flame. Instantly I longed to be able to take the words back. "Daddy, I'm sorry."

"Yeah, I didn't graduate from high school, but I'm puttin' your ass through college." He was trying to bluster, but his voice sounded hollow. "This old dumb father is gettin' you through college."

"Daddy, it's just that I worked so hard...." I knelt beside him but he wouldn't look at me.

"You work hard and your kids betray you." He buried his face in his hands, and I knew he was thinking about Jeanette and Donna. "That's the hurtin' part. You go in front of people with big ideas about what you want for your kids and then you have to go back and admit that your kids aren't going to be doin' that."

"I am, Daddy." I grabbed one of his hands and tried to turn his face toward me. "Daddy, listen to me. I'm going to be a doctor. I promise you, Daddy."

He was a long time in answering. Finally he said, as he had all those years ago when I'd asked for Donna's saxophone, "You, Cookie? You're too little."

"Daddy, I'm on the dean's list, I'm getting straight A's in my biology courses, and I've made it through organic chemistry, the one course you have to pass to get into medical school."

"The one that flummoxed Jeanette and Donna?"

"Yes."

"Really, Cookie? You really think you can do it?"

He never expected it to be me. In his mind it was going to be Jeanette, and when she swerved off the path to the goal, that was it. The dream was dead. Now he sat up straighter and a light came into his eyes. "You really think you can be a doctor?"

"If I can get accepted at a medical school, Daddy, which may not be possible because of applying from Monmouth College that nobody's ever heard of."

"College is college," he said automatically, and suddenly he was back to sounding like the old Daddy. "If there's a will, there's a way. If you can't get in the front door, go around the back. If you can't get in the back, try a window. Just don't give up, and you'll get in." He changed the pronoun confidently. "We'll get you in."

He was seeing himself putting on his suit and tie and sallying forth to seduce the dean of a medical school as he had seduced the president of the bank and the president of Monmouth College, luring them into stepping into his shoes and seeing things from his perspective. But I thought I had better try a more conventional approach first. I went to the chairman of the science department and asked his advice about applying to medical schools.

"It's really nice that you're coming to me for guidance, Yvonne," Dr. Garner said. "But, unfortunately, I can't give you any because we've never had anybody from Monmouth College go to medical school. I'll support you with letters of recommendation and whatever else you need, but all I can suggest is that you go to the library and see what you can find out."

This I did, and began making out a list of schools that were near enough for me to continue to play in the band; schools in New York, New Jersey, and Pennsylvania, except that I left out Cornell because I knew from the band playing there that Ithaca was too cold and too far away, never noticing that the medical school was not in Ithaca but in New York City.

In a handbook put out by the American Association of Medical Colleges, I went through the listings of over one hundred medical colleges. My eye was caught by one that did not term itself a medical school or school of medicine. Unlike Harvard Medical School or Yale School of Medicine, this one was called the College of Physicians and Surgeons. "Oh, what a pretty name," I said to myself. It sounded professional, imposing. Where is it? Columbia University, New York City, Presbyterian Hospital, where I was born. That seemed a good omen. It had, according to the handbook, an early-bird admission policy—if granted an interview, the prospective candidate would be notified within a few days whether he or she had been accepted or rejected rather than having to wait until the following spring to find out. "That's it," I said. "That's the one I want."

To be on the safe side, I picked out twelve other schools to apply to, thirteen in all, and went to Daddy for money for the application fees.

"Just tell me what you need, Cookie. However much money you need, I'll get it for you."

The only college he objected to on my list was the University of Michigan, and I knew he was thinking about my staying with the band. But Michigan was my ace-in-the-hole, I explained, because the medical school had spelled out that they were actively seeking women and minorities. If all else failed, maybe Michigan would take me, not despite my being female and black but because of it.

There was one more thing I told him. "If I get to be a doctor, Daddy, even if I get married, I'm never going to change my name. I'll always be Dr. Thornton, in honor of you."

Did I want to be a doctor or did I want to make my father happy? I think it was both, and I think I needed both. One motive without the other might not have been enough to see me through the tough times, times when I wondered if it was worth it to have to work so hard, times when I felt so far behind the pack because I didn't have educated parents, I didn't have the background to compete head-to-head with the other kids. People have asked why I didn't become a midwife. But my father didn't talk about midwives. He said *doctors,* and a doctor who delivered babies was an obstetrician, so that is all I ever was going to be—a doctor for him, an obstetrician for me. Plus, I had one more motive: after Donna and Jeanette left the family, I knew that if I screwed up, that would be the end of things for Linda and Rita, too. If three of us couldn't make it, what hope did the last two have? I had to keep going.

Around the house now Daddy seemed reborn. His eyes danced. He cracked jokes. He was gentle with Mommy, and Jeanette's name could once again be mentioned. Jeanette herself began to show up occasionally. It was, "Hi, Mommy, fix up my dresses. I think I'll play with the band this weekend." And Mommy and Daddy welcomed the prodigal's return: "Wow, Jeanette's coming! Let's make a cake!"

"Daddy...!" we protested.

"She's your sister. You guys love each other."

We wanted to answer, "Yeah, but she doesn't love us. She abandoned us. She's got her own apartment and is living her own life. She goes off on skiing weekends and we never even learned to ride a bicycle. She's got guys who bring her flowers and candy. She only goes to college part-time. We're here breaking our butts studying and playing in the band and she's hanging out."

We did say some of this, but Daddy didn't want to hear it. When she telephoned, it was like, "Oh, I love everybody the same, but Jeanette might be coming tonight to play!" And he laid down the law. "If she wants to come back, she's welcome here and there's not going to be any screaming and yelling and 'Jeanette did this, Jeanette did that.'"

We respected what Daddy said, but the Jeanette who turned up now and again was like a stranger to Linda and me—Rita was too young to feel strongly one way or another—which was not really too different from the way it had always been because she and Donna had been so close that the rest of us felt excluded from their pairing. We were polite and didn't object that Jeanette showed up when she pleased—or when she needed money—but we resented that she didn't practice and did little more than fumble around on the bandstand. We wished that Daddy would pull her up short on the music, tell her we didn't need her. But what Mommy and Daddy were seeing was that all the kids were there. We could tell by the look in their eyes how much it meant to them. At whatever price, they felt it was okay for Jeanette to come back when she felt like it just so we would all be together again.

We heard that Jeanette was seeing a lot of her ski instructor, but she didn't bring him around to meet us, unlike Donna, who asked Daddy if she could bring her friend Willis along on weekends to help with the instruments. Daddy didn't allow it too often, until Donna and Willis got engaged, and then he let Willis come along every so often to hear the band play.

Willis was Catholic and Donna converted, which didn't go down well with Mommy, but Daddy said, "What the hell, it's the same thing. Baptist, Catholic, they're all a bunch of crooks."

To Donna he said, "You see what you're doin' for this man? He's just a husband. He can leave you at any time. He could leave you with a couple of kids. He could just walk away from you. Where are you gonna be then?"

"Daddy, I have two years of college and I'm a stenographer and a court reporter, I'll be all right. Besides, Willis loves me. He isn't going to leave me."

Daddy snorted. I think the only man whose faithfulness he ever really believed in was himself. But in the long run Donna was right and he was wrong. The marriage lasted.

The one he might have done well to warn was Jeanette, for she married her ski instructor even before Donna married Willis. Unlike Donna, who was married in church on Valentine's Day, 1970, with all of us as bridesmaids in pink satin dresses that Mommy made, Jeanette and her ski instructor, whose name I barely knew at the time and have long since forgotten, were married in her apartment. Jeanette made her own gown of white satin. The two of them knelt on pillows, the vows were said, and that was that. The marriage ended a year later.

Donna and Jeanette were having dates, going away on weekends, and getting married, but when I asked permission to go to a boy's house, Daddy's eyes narrowed. "Charlie Sands' place? What for?"

"To study biology, Daddy. There'll be other kids there. It's a study session. You go over to somebody's house and you study from seven till midnight."

"Unh, unh, you tell Charlie Sands to come over here."

Necessarily, our house became the study house for Charlie Sands, George Kimball, David Larkin, and me. The Four Horsemen of the Apocalypse we called ourselves: two blacks and two whites, three fellows and a girl. Dr. Garner had been right: people to the right and left of us had fallen by the wayside; there were eight of us left out of the 150 students who had started out to be biology majors. And we four stuck together to get each other through.

When the fellows were there, Daddy kept peeking in, especially if he thought it had grown too quiet in the back room. "How ya doin? You doin' okay?"

"Great, Daddy."

The guys loved him because he made buckets of fried

chicken for us and kidded around with them, especially with George Kimball. George was a white guy, tall, thin, with little buck teeth, a lighthearted fellow, a jokester. He'd say, "Okay, time for a break," and he'd make up names for rock groups from the things we were studying, like Hassall and His Corpuscles, or Graafian and Her Follicles, or Zymogen and the Granules.

Daddy talked to David Larkin, the other black, a lot and really liked him, but he warned me, "Watch David. He's a climber."

"You mean, he's ambitious? What's wrong with that?"

"Naw, I mean he'll climb all over you if you give him a chance. If you two ever get together and you're having sex..."

"Daddy!"

"I'm just warnin' you."

When I told David my father said to watch out for him, he laughed. "Unh, unh, I know your father. I'm not getting myself killed for messin' with his daughter." After we graduated from Monmouth, David taught science in a high school in Princeton. Years later, successful, married with five children and practicing medicine in California, he told me: "While I was teaching in Princeton, I thought and thought and thought about your Dad and things he had said, like, 'If you're down, you'll come back up again if you just don't lose sight of your goal,' and I realized I was letting my goal of becoming a doctor slip away. I quit my teaching job and went to medical school and now I'm a urological surgeon, and I wouldn't have done it if it hadn't been for your father."

David, George, Charlie, and I were a study group through physiology, comparative vertebrate anatomy, embryology, and histology; studying hours and hours and hours at a time, testing each other, helping each other along; asking, "Did you get that?" And if one of us said, "I'm not sure," we all agreed, "Let's go over it again."

I had thought, contemplating having to go to Monmouth College instead of Barnard, that Monmouth was really no better than a fifth year of high school, but in the science department it was far from that. Bell Labs, which was nearby, had beefed up the department with money so that they could send workers there for higher-level training in chemistry and physics, and we under-graduate students benefited from that.

Professor Gimble, who had wanted to be an M.D. but for some reason had not gone on to medical school, was in charge of the more advanced courses in the biological sciences, such as embryology, histology, and physiology, and Harvard could not have had a better professor. In his course in histology, the study of tissues, the college supplied a box of slides—if you lost them, you had to reimburse the college several hundred dollars—and we bought our own microscopes. The slides were in groups: muscle tissue, thyroid, kidney, etc., and we had to memorize the distinguishing features in each. In class, Mr. Gimble allowed us one minute to identify the slide under a microscope, then we'd have to move to the next microscope and identify that slide, and so on. We protested about having only a minute, but he said, "Either you know it or you don't. By the end of the semester I'll give you just fifteen seconds with each slide." Our group drilled each other, and by the end of the year, ten seconds was plenty of time. The four of us aced the course.

I worked and worked and worked, following the curriculum and hoping that it was going to lead to where I wanted to go. I didn't have parents who could guide me, no uncle or cousin who was a doctor and could advise me, but I told myself, "Don't envy somebody else what they've got. Don't start comparing yourself to other people. That way lies trouble. Just do what needs to be done. Do your best and let it speak for itself." I knew that once you start saying, "His uncle knows this. His aunt's got pull there," right away you're trying to use somebody else to cover for your inadequacies when really what you should be doing is using your energy to shore up the assets you've got, like the capacity to work hard.

Mommy was a help to me there. I'd say something about needing to get up at three o'clock in the morning to finish my physics, and at three o'clock she'd be shaking me quietly until I said, "Okay, Mom, I'm awake." I look back now and wonder at the person who would get up at three in the morning to wake her child to study, but anything to do with education, Mommy was there. She'd go down to the kitchen and make hot chocolate for me and linger until she was sure I was wide awake and studying before she went back to bed.

In the spring semester of my junior year, when I was still struggling with organic chemistry, I had to take the MCATs, the medical college aptitude test. It was given in May, at the same time as final exams at Monmouth, and to add to my woes, the band was booked to play at Princeton that weekend. I figured it was a prescription for failure, whether it was the MCATs or my exams, but I said to myself, "Let's see if I can get it all together," and I arranged to take the MCATs at Princeton.

I had one final exam at Monmouth on Friday afternoon. When I came out of that, the family was in the limousine waiting for me outside the college and we drove to Princeton. From nine. until one o'clock in the morning, we played at the Quadrangle Club. The sounds were really grooving, and the fellows were yelling and screaming for encores. Finally I said, "Hey, look, I got to get some sleep. I'm taking my MCATs tomorrow."

"Yeah. Right," the guys laughed. To them, it was like Tina Turner was going to step off the stage and turn into Mother Superior. They thought it was a big joke.

At eight o'clock the next morning I was at McCosh Hall. I sat down next to a guy who stared at me in sort of a puzzled way and said, "You look familiar." I didn't say anything, just got out my pencils and started in and didn't look up until four hours later. It was one o'clock when I finished, and I was so tired from the night before that I fell going down the steps. Guys rushed to pick me up and offered to take me to the infirmary, but I asked them just to please take me to the Cap and Gown Club because I had to play there that afternoon.

"Hey, it's one of the Thornton Sisters," somebody said and they all started applauding and offering to escort me.

We played that afternoon at Cap and Gown, and that evening at the Campus Club. Sunday afternoon we played at Stevenson Hall, and when that was over, we headed for home, with me studying all the way because Monday morning was my final exam in organic chemistry and Monday afternoon my final in vertebrate embryology.

At home I slept until midnight, then I got up and studied through until exam time the next morning.

I came out of the last exam so tired that I was disoriented and with the certainty that I had failed everything. I made it to my car, got the door open, climbed in, and sprawled on the front seat. The next thing I knew, Daddy was tapping on the window and it was dark outside. He'd come looking for me.

"It's okay, Daddy, I can make it home."

"No, honeybun, you move over. I'll drive you."

When my MCAT scores came back, they were high and I knew I was blessed, that God was in my corner. And when my college grades came out, it was the same; I had made the dean's list again.

The fall of 1968 was a special time. I was to have my twenty-first birthday in November, and all thirteen of the medical schools I had applied to had granted me a personal interview, which meant that I was at least getting my foot in the door. The first of the interviews was at the University of Michigan in Ann Arbor, Michigan. I bought a plane ticket for an 11:00 A.M. flight. Daddy volunteered to drive me to the airport, and because he was working on a masonry job that had to be finished, he was, in typical Daddy fashion, late. We arrived at the airport at five minutes to eleven. The clerk at the check-in counter told us the gate was at the other end of the terminal and the plane had already boarded; we'd never make it.

"Just give me the ticket," Daddy said, snatching it from her hand. "Come on, Cookie, run!"

We got there as they were closing the gate. Panting, Daddy shoved the ticket in my hand. "This is just to teach you, don't ever let anybody tell you you can't do something."

When the plane was in the air and I had begun to breathe normally again, my stomach hit its own private air pocket. I had forgotten to ask Daddy for money. My wallet held a single dollar bill. Scraping around in the bottom of my pocketbook yielded another dollar in change, and that was it. I was about to land in Michigan with two dollars. "Don't let anybody say you can't make it," I repeated over and over to ratchet up my courage.

Bus fare to the medical school, I discovered at the airport, was $1.70 round trip, so I was okay, except that I was just going to have to forget about being hungry. At the dean's office, a couple of people were waiting to be interviewed and I started talking to the fellow next to me, a blond, blue-eyed guy who said his name was Raymond Gonzalez.

"Who're you kidding?" I said. "Raymond Gonzalez?"

"My mother and father come from Spain," he said. "I really am Spanish."

"I don't believe it," I kidded him. "You're just trying to cash in on this affirmative action stuff."

We joked around until he went in for his interview. After he came out, I was summoned. There was a clock on the wall, and during the interview, out of the corner of my eye, I could see the minutes ticking away, up to and then on past the time of the last bus back to the airport. There was no hope for it; I would be sitting on a park bench all night until the buses started running again in the morning.

I came out of the dean's office and Ray Gonzalez was still there in the anteroom. I was surprised. "Does he want to see you again?"

"You were telling me you didn't have any money to get back home, so I thought I'd hang around and buy you dinner."

I could hear Daddy's voice: *He'll get you outside where it's dark. He'll ask you for some pleasurin'. He's plannin' to rape you.* But I was so hungry. "That'd be lovely, Raymond," I said. After dinner, he put me in a cab and handed the driver the fare to the airport. "Raymond, you don't have to do this," I protested.

"Good luck in medical school, Yvonne," he said with a grin and stepped back and waved goodbye.

When Daddy heard this, he demanded, "And he didn't do nothin' to you?"

"You're always saying there are nice people willing to help along the way."

"Well, I'm right, aren't I."

My next interview was at the Columbia University College of Physicians and Surgeons, on October 22, 1968, with a Dr. Lamb. This was the school I wanted, and I boarded the bus to New York City with high hopes. The bus broke down on the New Jersey Turnpike. On that day of all days. I was frantic. I was delayed an hour and a half. The minute I got to the Port Authority bus terminal I called the medical school and told a secretary what had happened, trembling with fear that they would reject me then and there for being late. But the woman was very nice and told me that because I was late, Dr. Lamb wouldn't be available to interview me but that Dr. Perera was free, adding, "Dr. Perera is dean of admissions."

At four o'clock I was shown into the office of a distinguished-looking gray-haired gentleman who was seated at one end of a long, long desk. I apologized for missing the earlier appointment as he waved me to a seat at the opposite end of the desk. "These things happen, my dear," he said. "So you're Miss Thornton." He peered at me through the smoke from his cigarette. "Somehow I expected there to be a halo around your head after reading the letters from your biology and chemistry teachers."

"Really?" I hadn't seen the letters so I didn't know what my professors had said. "That's very nice."

"Monmouth College. Is that accredited?"

"I think it is," I replied, not having the faintest idea if it was or not.

He passed a list down the long desk. "This is a roster of the colleges our applicants are attending." I ran my eye down it: Harvard, Yale, Radcliffe, Barnard... *See, Daddy, I should have gone to a good school.* "I've never heard of Monmouth College," he said. "How do you think you could hold your own with students coming from such high-powered schools?"

I was raging against Daddy in my mind. *All the work, all the A's, and it's all going down the drain, your dream and mine, because this man has never heard of Monmouth College.* "Not one of them wants to be a doctor more than I do," I told Dr. Perera, "and not one of them can work harder than I can."

He nodded noncommittally and went on to ask: "What do you do for an avocation? We have chess masters and students who are interested in Chinese art, for example."

"I play in a band with my sisters on the weekends."

"What kind of a band?"

"A college band. We've been the number-one band on the Princeton campus since 1963."

"Oh? My son goes to Princeton."

"Then he must know the Thornton Sisters."

We talked some more about the band and my playing with it, and then he said, "You know, Miss Thornton, we're trying to enroll more women at P & S and we're finding they make good physicians, but our concern is their getting married, raising a family, and not utilizing the knowledge they have gained here. What if you find Mr. Right?"

"If I do, he's just going to have to wait until I finish medical school and become a doctor."

"And what if he doesn't want to wait?"

"Then he's not Mr. Right."

"Hmm."

Dr. Perera thanked me politely for coming and showed me out. I cried all the way home on the bus.

"What's the matter, Cookie?" Daddy demanded.

"He never heard of Monmouth College!" I wailed. "I told you I should have gone to Barnard! He wanted to know how I expected to hold my own with people from the high-powered places."

"What's the matter with him? Don't he realize you're a good person?"

"He doesn't care about that! He cares about a track record, and Monmouth doesn't have a track record."

"You're makin' the record for Monmouth. Why'd you let this man intimidate you?"

"Oh, Daddy, you don't understand. I told him how long I've

wanted to be a doctor. I told him why I had to go to Monmouth. That's all I could say."

"Well, I don't like any man who makes my baby cry."

Three days later I had an interview at the Woman's Medical College of Pennsylvania in Philadelphia. This time Mommy and Daddy went with me, one on the right, one on the left, both determined that nobody was going to make their baby cry again. The interview went well enough, except that Daddy didn't like the sound of off-campus housing and muttered against a school that didn't look out for girls better than that.

When we arrived back home that evening, there was an ivory-colored envelope addressed to me from Columbia University, College of Physicians and Surgeons. They had kept their promise of prompt notification. It was a thin envelope and I knew what that meant—rejection—because if you have been accepted, they send a fat envelope full of all kinds of information. I snatched up the envelope and headed for the bathroom, the only room with a lock on the door, because I knew I was going to start crying all over again and I didn't want Mommy and Daddy to know how desperately my heart had been set on the wonderful-sounding College of Physicians and Surgeons. I slit the envelope and began reading.

I can no longer quote it exactly but the letter said something like this: Dear Miss Thornton: Even though the history of the College of Physicians and Surgeons is an illustrious one, and even though we are unacquainted with the college you are presently attending, your college record and recommendations are outstanding and your interview with me suggests that you are a person on whom we should take a chance. Therefore, we are happy and proud to offer you admission as a first-year student at Columbia P & S, class of 1973.

Wow! Whoopee! I almost ran through the door getting out of the bathroom. "I'm accepted! I'm accepted! I'm going to medical school!" I hugged and swung Mommy, Daddy, Linda, and Rita. I was laughing and dancing and crying and waving the letter. "I'm accepted! I'm accepted!"

Daddy said very calmly, "Is that the medical school that made you cry? You ain't goin' there."

"Daddy, it's *Columbia*! It's *Presbyterian Hospital* where I was born!"

"I don't care what it is. You're not goin' to any school that don't appreciate you."

He was serious, I could see that. I didn't say anything then but I did a lot of intense thinking. Daddy went with me to all the remaining interviews, and I made sure to ask very specifically about the housing arrangements. "You don't have dormitories for the medical students?" I'd say. "Not even for the female medical students?"

"You sure?" Daddy persisted when we were talking to the dean at the New Jersey College of Medicine and Dentistry.

"Mr. Thornton, people coming to medical school at twenty-one, twenty-two years of age prefer to make their own living arrangements, we've found."

"I can relate to that," I said. "It must be fun to have your own pad off campus." Daddy frowned. I went serenely on. "Come and go as you please, have people over, have fellows come to study."

I expected Daddy to cross this school off the list as soon as we got outside. Instead he said, "This is where you're goin', Cookie."

"You don't mind my having to live off campus?"

"I got it figured out. You don't have to. You can commute from home. It ain't that far."

I thought fast. "That's true, but I'd still have to have an apartment for those nights I'd be working late at the lab or be on duty at the hospital. I'm going to have to have an apartment wherever I go. Except at P & S. They have a dormitory for women."

"They do?"

"Right there in the medical school."

"Okay, that's where you're goin'."

And that's why I went to Columbia University, College of Physicians and Surgeons, at least as far as Daddy was concerned—

not because it was one of the top medical schools in the country but because it had a dormitory for its women students. Looking back, I think that I was accepted *because* the bus broke down on the New Jersey Turnpike. It was another of those bits of magic, like Daddy finding the extra five dollars in his pocket when he went to fetch Mommy and me home from the hospital. If I had been on time for the interview, I wouldn't have been seen by the dean of admissions who had the authority to admit me on the basis of his own impression despite my having gone to a college he had never heard of.

I don't believe there is a doctor in the country who can't tell you the day, the hour even, he or she got accepted to medical school. It is a red-letter day in one's life. Having been granted early acceptance in October of my senior year at Monmouth College, it was as though I was walking on air from then on, through my twenty-first birthday in November right through to graduation in May. At Monmouth, because of the number of students graduating, only the top person in each discipline goes up to collect the diplomas, and I said to myself that it had to be me going up on-stage because Mommy and Daddy would be taking pictures and bursting with pride. I calculated the grades I would have to get: A's in these courses, not less than a B in this. I just made it.

Dr. Garner called me in. "Yvonne, in your biology major you came out with a 3.76 average. Would you be ready to do the honors for your fellow students?"

He didn't have to ask twice. When they called off the names on graduation day, no peacock could have strutted more than I as I headed up on that stage. And when the president made a special announcement: "Miss Thornton has been accepted at Columbia University, College of Physicians and Surgeons, the first person to go on to medical school from Monmouth College," my day was complete.

◆ 10 ◆
P & S

I MIGHT BE FROM MONMOUTH COLLEGE, not Radcliffe or Wellesley or Bryn Mawr, but I didn't intend to arrive at medical school looking like a yokel, like I couldn't hold my own in the big time. Mommy and I went shopping and I bought the snappiest outfits in the stores, everything matching, color-coordinated—miniskirts, frilly blouses, high heels, the right purse for each ensemble. I was going to be the best turned-out person ever to walk through the portals of P & S, right down to my eye makeup, which, on account of being in the band, I used a lot of. I really felt good about myself, ready to take on Columbia, New York City, the world.

Mommy and Daddy drove me to the city and to Bard Hall where I was to room. "Yvonne," Daddy said, which marked it as a solemn occasion since he seldom called me anything but Cookie, "this is as far as your mother and I go. We can only take you to the door, hon. From now on, you're on your own." I was twenty-one, going on twenty-two, an adult, and I was finally getting away from home, which is what I thought I wanted, but all of a sudden tears were tumbling down my cheeks.

Daddy reached in his pocket and brought out a glass ashtray. "Just in case someone tries to get in your room," he said, pressing it into my hand. "This is New York. You gotta be careful."

"What am I supposed to do with an ashtray, Daddy?"

"You put it on top of your door, and then when somebody opens the door, it falls down, which wakes you up and you can grab something to hit him over the head with. Okay?"

"Okay." I never put it on top of the door because I knew perfectly well that I'd forget it was there, go rushing out, and I'd be the one to get hit on the head, but I still have that ashtray.

I hugged my parents, kissed them goodbye, watched them drive away, and went up to my room to stare through swimming eyes at the George Washington Bridge as though it were my last link with home. For the first time in my life I was alone: no mother, no father, no sisters; just me. I felt as though an elevator cable had snapped and I was in free fall—all but my stomach, which I had left several stories behind. I cried off and on for the next three days.

In the dining room that first evening, the main course was fried chicken. I was reaching for the leg on my plate when I noticed the person across from me pick up his knife and fork. I swerved my hand and closed it around a glass of water, and while I sat back pretending to take a long drink, I watched the other diners over the rim of my glass. They were actually cutting their chicken with a knife and fork. It struck me as a foolish way to attack something that was clearly designed to be eaten with the fingers, but I picked up my utensils and went to work. They weren't going to catch me looking like I didn't have the right table manners.

I've often thought since those early days that the reason black people drop out of white colleges in disproportionate numbers is because the culture shock is so intense. The necessity of learning new ways, the fear of making a mistake, and the despair over differentness is such a heavy strain on top of the academic work that it sinks students who otherwise could make it. As a black, you think you know the white world because you have spent so much time looking on at it, but *looking on* is very different from *living in*, as I realized almost immediately with the discovery that my table manners needed to be considerably more formal and my clothes considerably less.

The next day, at a tea given to welcome the incoming students, I quietly drifted into a corner, trying to make myself as inconspicuous as possible. I was pretty certain that, above the eyes, there was nobody better than I and that I could outstudy anybody. With regard to presence and decorum, however, I might as well have come from the Deep South. It was one thing to perform for the kids at Harvard, Yale, and Princeton; they loved me in that context. It was quite another to be in a situation where I had to live and work with these kids as a peer. I stood in the corner and prayed, "Oh, God, please don't let me do anything stupid or awful."

I was watching the people from Harvard and Yale, trying to identify the moves that made them look so smooth and suave and utterly at ease, when a guy from Princeton came over and said, "Aren't you one of the Thornton Sisters?" More guys from other places where the band had played joined us, and soon I was the center of a group reminiscing about the dances and the music. Somebody said it was great I was in medical school but sad that the band would be breaking up now.

"Absolutely not," I told them, explaining that we would still be playing weekends because Linda and Rita were coming along and there was a lot of education to be paid for yet.

"But how are you going to do that," the guys asked, "—take the courses, study, and travel every weekend?"

"It's what I've been doing since 1963," I said. "I'll make it."

The group was joined by a huge fellow, six feet five or six, an African-American with hands like a lumberjack's. "Hi. How ya doin'?" he said, folding my right hand inside his. "I'm Shearwood McClelland. They call me Wood."

A bell went off in my mind. That past summer, David Larkin, moving to Princeton to teach in the high school there, had rented an apartment over Miss Burrell's beauty salon, and Miss Burrell mentioned that the guy who previously had the apartment, and who left a lot of his records behind when he graduated from Princeton, was going to medical school in the fall. "He's going to be at P & S," David told me over the phone during the summer, "and his name is Wood. Look him up and ask him if he's ever coming back for his records."

With my hand still in his, I told the guy hello and then asked, "Did you used to live at 21 Leigh Avenue in Princeton?"

He looked at me with the disgruntled astonishment of someone confronted by a psychic. Muttering, "The woman's getting into my business," Shearwood McClelland turned and stalked away.

Dr. Perera, who knew all of the incoming students by name because he had had the final say on each acceptance, spoke at the tea. The gist of what he said made us all stand taller: "This institution was the first medical school in the American colonies to award the M.D. degree. It is the oldest four-year college of medical training in the country. Because we have a strong tradition to maintain, each of you has been handpicked. You will become a doctor—there is no doubt about that. The only question is what kind of a doctor you will become. We don't want you to be technicians; we want you to be physicians. We can teach a chimpanzee to do surgery, but you're here to develop into that very special kind of physician who is a P & S graduate."

He was referring to the P & S tradition of blending being a doctor with being a nice person, of being bright but also interested in people, of not talking over the patient's head or pontificating, but of saying, "Hi, Mrs. Jones, it's nice to see you," and touching her and listening to her and doing a thoughtful physical examination. "When you go forth from here," Dr. Perera summed up, "just from the way you speak, your attitude toward the patient, the way you arrive at a conclusion about the patient's illness, everyone will immediately recognize that you are a graduate of P & S."

It was heady stuff and I was thrilled by his words, feeling myself infinitely lucky to be at this very special school. But I couldn't shake the consciousness that I was coming from Long Branch, New Jersey. In class, I was very, very quiet. Professors began to chide me: "Yvonne, whenever I ask you a question, you have a great answer. Why don't you volunteer?" I didn't because I wasn't sure of the proper way to say things. I kept remembering a T-shirt I'd once seen: NOBODY KNOWS YOU'RE IGNORANT IF YOU KEEP YOUR MOUTH SHUT, BUT IF YOU OPEN IT, YOU REMOVE ALL DOUBT. So I kept my mouth shut and put my answers down on paper. A wonderful thing about science is that you don't have to know the grammatically correct way of stating something. In organic chemistry the answer is yes or no, aldehyde or ester. You don't have to know the graces and cultural arts to excel, and I was grateful for that.

One of the first classes I had was in histology. The professor was a woman, Dr. Sara Luce, a female doctor of the old school, mousy graying hair, wire eyeglasses, bitter corners to her mouth. She looked me up and down and said, "Who are you? Are you a first-year student?"

"Yes, ma'am, I'm Yvonne Thornton."

"Well, Miss Thornton, what are you doing with all that makeup on your face?"

"I play in a band with my sisters and we wear a lot of makeup when we're performing."

"Well, you're not performing here, Miss Thornton. You look like Cleopatra. Where did you go to school?"

"Monmouth College in New Jersey."

"Never heard of it."

By now, I was thinking, Oh, gosh, I'm in for it. This is one wicked witch.

The routine was the same as it had been in the histology course at Monmouth: microscopes with slides in them lined up on tables around the room. The professor said, "You have just two minutes to look at each slide and attempt to identify it before moving on to the next one."

I raised my hand. "May I go first, Dr. Luce?"

"Why not, you from Monmouth College with the makeup and the miniskirt?" She may not have quite said that, but that's what her withering look conveyed.

I was through in fifteen minutes. Dr. Luce looked at me almost with pity, as though saying to herself, Poor thing doesn't know anything, coming from that Monmouth College. She clearly thought that I was one of the affirmative-action people allowed into medical school on sufferance. Most of the professors looked at me that way at first: *"Oh, she's black. Okay, we're going back to remedial reading now."*

I got a perfect score on the lab test. Dr. Luce called me in and, believing that I had somehow managed to cheat, ordered me to take the test again by myself. Again I identified every slide correctly.

"I'd be happy to take it a third time," I volunteered.

"No. No, that's all right," she replied, somewhat baffled.

I told her then about my histology professor and our study group where we had drilled each other so hard and so long that finally we didn't even need a microscope to identify the slides; just by holding them up to the light, we could recognize the type of tissue.

"Hmmm," said Dr. Luce. "I need a teaching assistant in the lab. Would you be interested in the job?"

I accepted happily and called Dr. Gimble at Monmouth College to thank him for the way he had trained me. It had made an enormous difference to me to come out of that first test so well. There were students in the class who were the sons and daughters of physicians, some of them the third or fourth generation in their families to go into medicine: Bob West, son of a P & S graduate; Ed Leahey, son of an orthopedic surgeon on the faculty at Columbia; Bob Santulli, son of a surgeon on the staff at Presbyterian Hospital; Doug Halstead, descendant of the surgeon who invented the Halstead clamp used in thyroid surgery. How could I compete with a tradition like that? But I could, I decided, after that first histology test: *I'm here and I'm well trained, and it's one-on-one just like at Monmouth.*

Usually the first two years of medical school are didactic years: lectures, labs, textbooks to study, course work. However, beginning with our incoming class, the medical college instituted a new concept known as the "core curriculum"—one and a half years for the basic sciences and two and a half years for clinical work. That meant the time allotted for each basic science course was abbreviated and the subject matter condensed to allow the students more time for clinical experience. Over and over again the various professors would say: "Last year I had eight weeks to cover this subject but I have only two weeks this year. Nevertheless, you are responsible for knowing the entire subject and you will be tested on all the material, whether we have covered it or not."

It wasn't easy but I managed to get the work done and still travel with the band. My tuition was twenty-five hundred dollars a year, which doesn't sound like much now but at the time was one of the highest in the country. Rutgers, by way of contrast, was about half as much. Linda and Rita were both at Monmouth College, with Linda aiming for dental school and Rita for medical school. Tuition ate up the money as fast as the band made it.

The three of us kept looking at each other, wondering if one of us was going to falter. Linda and Rita assumed it would be me because of the demands of medical school, but I said over and over, "Look, I'll hang in if you'll hang in. I'm not going to pull a Jeanette." Sometimes I was so tired, I didn't know if I could stay on my feet, but I believed, as my father believed, as my mother believed, get the job done. *Get the job done.* If your job is to be part of a team, and if by leaving you're going to weaken that team, then you don't leave. You stick around until the job is finished.

This is the way Mommy and Daddy looked at marriage along with everything else: *Whatever it is, we're here, good or bad, that's it.* Because I'm black, people sometimes say to me in surprise, "You had a father?" Yes, I had a father. He stayed to raise us. He stayed to get the job done. So, when Linda said, "You're gonna leave, Cookie," I said, following Daddy's example, "No, we're here together. I'm here as long as it takes to get the job done."

The band was the three of us, plus Mommy occasionally, by the time I was in medical school. Donna had developed epilepsy and was on considerable amounts of medication to control her seizures. Also, she had a baby, a little girl named Heather. Daddy told her, "It's okay, honey, we can go on without you. You stay home with your baby." Donna's leaving the band was a different breaking away than Jeanette's had been. Daddy had known it was coming, and he appreciated that Donna had made an effort to keep on and wasn't just listening to her own imperatives, which meant that he wasn't traumatized by Donna's dropping out as he had been by Jeanette's.

The aftermath of Jeanette's leaving had been so horrendous and seemed to me so directly the fault of men and dates that I had taken little interest in either since. At Monmouth College, I had met up again with the nice Jimmy Hutcheson who had taken me to my senior prom and we became friends. He played folk guitar and I sometimes went to hear him at a club in Sea Bright. I bought a guitar, paying for it myself so Daddy wouldn't have anything to say about it, and Jimmy taught me to play, but we never had anything like a formal date.

In medical school, there was a fellow named Larry Johnson I'd met when we played at Brown University. I told Mommy, "He's six-one and he's really sharp." She raised her eyebrows. Then I said, "There's this other boy at medical school. He's so quiet, he's like country, and he's not pleasing to look at because he's so huge, so I can't get hot over him. But he's very nice."

I was talking about Shearwood McClelland, whose name was pronounced *Sherwood* and who had finally gotten over thinking I was psychic and asked me to go to the movies with him, which I couldn't do because I was either buried in my books or off on weekends with the band. But we did study together sometimes, and we talked. We talked about life and philosophy and psychology. Shearwood wanted to be a psychiatrist, which was a mistake, to my mind.

"You're too tall and your hands are too big. Besides, no white person'll come to you because you're black, and no black person'll come to you because black people are not going to say they're crazy, so you're going to be poor, you're going to starve to death. If you ask me, you should be in orthopedics because you've got big hands. People are always going to break their bones, so you could be sure of having work."

"Hmmm," he said, and went on talking about the philosophy he read in his books. I quoted Daddy to him, which was everything I knew about life and living, and it convinced Shear-wood that I was a deep thinker with a knack of putting things simply.

Shearwood kept coming on, not like gangbusters, but quiet and steady and always so *nice*. Meanwhile I was running after Larry Johnson. Finally it occurred to me that I was being stupid. I told myself: Larry Johnson obviously has other things to do, so why don't I just turn around and reciprocate a little here with Wood, at least by going to the movies? I decided that about April of our first year in medical school. In May, Shearwood's mother died, and that's when we became really close.

Like my father, Shearwood's father worked at two jobs. In Gary, Indiana, where the family lived, he was a laborer in a steel mill, and when not needed there, he drove an eighteen-wheeler, which meant that he was away from home a great deal. It was Shearwood's mother who had been the great influence in his life. She was preaching the same doctrine in Indiana that my parents were in New Jersey: study, study, study. My mother used to talk about "barrelhouse niggers," people who were always dancing and drinking. "In twenty years," she said, "they'll be just the same as they are today, or they'll be dead." Shearwood's mother said, "My son is going to be a doctor. *He's going to be a doctor.* He's no barrelhouse nigger." Shearwood and I used to laugh and say, "Did your mother know my mother?"

When Shearwood was accepted at Princeton, it was such a foreign idea that his friends in Gary thought he was going to Princeton, Indiana. His father wanted him to go to Purdue and become an engineer, but his mother spoke of his becoming a doctor as though it were the natural order of things, and perhaps for the same reason as Daddy did: because being a physician gives an individual a place and a stature in the world that can never afterward be denied him.

When Shearwood's mother died that spring of our first year, the life went out of Shearwood. He stopped eating and lost a startling amount of weight. He gave up studying because, however long he stared at a book, the words refused to swim into focus and make sense. Nothing I said could pull him out of the dark depths where he wandered lost, but my presence was a bit of comfort and I spent what time with him I could until he decided to leave medical school without taking final exams and start over again as a first-year student in the fall.

It was another year after that before he began to get back to being his old self. Saying he wanted to meet my parents, Shearwood came down to Long Branch with me one weekend, and afterward Daddy, who had no use for any man who came around one of his daughters, grunted his approval of Shearwood. Daddy loved honesty. When he encountered anyone, he was always thinking: *Yes, but what do you really want?* And later he'd say, "I know what that joker really wanted." The honesty with which Shearwood approached Daddy was what won him.

Shearwood said, "Look, Mr. Thornton, I know how much you love your daughter. If I had a daughter, I'd love her that much, too. Now, what I want to say is this. Yvonne and I, we're in New York, we could sneak around, but I think it's better to come and ask you if I can take her out, and if you say no, I'll understand."

My father sort of said, "Oh." Then, "Sure." And later to me, "That's a nice boy, Cookie. That's a really nice boy."

He didn't fail, however, to start talking about "Samsonite weddings," as he called them. "She says: 'I want to live with him to find out how we are with each other. We don't want to get married; we just want to live together.' It's shack up; if you don't like it, pack up. Except the next thing you know she's pregnant and her life is over. That's what happens. Women are to have kids. Men are to run around. It's the natural order of things."

He had always drilled into us that women can do anything, that they are brighter than men, but when he was talking about sex, he changed his tune. "You stupid women! Emotionally you're stupid. You can't help yourselves because God made you that way." Then he'd repeat his dictum about the three seconds in an hour that a woman is weak, and then the six seconds in the second hour, and how in the third hour the six seconds become nine, and, "He can zoom right in and get you. It's just hormones. Even if he doesn't kiss you in the ear, you'll decide you want to kiss him in the ear. You get weak. You're stupid."

At P & S, Shearwood and I would sit talking by the hour about C. S. Lewis, Nietzsche, Rollo May, and an art-of-living book Shearwood called his bible, *Advice from a Failure.* It was during these long intellectual discussions that I'd think: *Shearwood would never do anything.* Two hours would go by, then three, and I'd find myself looking at him and thinking: *He's so sweet. He's got a lovely smile....* And all of a sudden I'd catch myself. If Daddy hadn't warned me about the three-second rule so often, maybe it would have been shack up and pack up and all my plans would have gone out the window, a lifetime's goal sabotaged in three seconds. Instead, I'd remember Daddy's voice saying, "But...*but* I'm here to tell you that you can select the time you're gonna be stupid," and I knew this wasn't the time.

One day Mom and I were talking and, to my surprise, she remarked, "If you're going to get married, the best thing is to marry somebody who loves you. It's not necessary that you love him."

I said, "Can we go around on that again, Mom?"

"What I'm saying is that if you have a choice, it's better to marry a guy who cares more for you than you care for him. In a relationship, one person always loves more than the other; it's never equal; and a woman's a lot better off if she's the one who's loved rather than the one doing most of the loving."

I asked Daddy what he thought about this, and he said: "Your mother's right. She's absolutely right. You know how I love your mother. I'd go through fire for her. And that's the good way for it to be. Women have the capacity to love anybody, but men are dogs. It's in their nature to run around. But if a man latches on to somebody he truly loves, if the sun rises and sets in that one woman, if she is all he ever wants, then he'll stick by her. On the other hand, if he doesn't feel that strong, then things are tilted in his favor; he has the power, and he abuses the woman. I see that a lot of times," Daddy said. "The guy gets into the relationship, he likes her, but that fades after a while, and then she's in a pickle."

I was in the third year of medical school when Shearwood asked me to marry him. "Unh, unh," I told him. "I'm not marrying anybody until I finish medical school and that M.D. is behind my name and I have at least a year of obstetrical training. And if I marry anybody then, I won't change my name. I'm always going to be Dr. Thornton, in honor of my father."

Shearwood said calmly, "I know that. If I have to wait five years, I will. I'll wait however long I have to because you are the only woman I will ever love."

"Shearwood," I said, "you're too serious about this. Lighten up."

"Now we can lighten up," he answered. "I just wanted to let you know my intentions."

Before this, in one of our times of long talks, I had mentioned that I didn't ever expect to get married but that if I did, my dream was of a three-carat, marquis-cut diamond for an engagement ring. One of my college professors had worn a two-carat, emerald-cut diamond that glistened in the sun and was so beautiful that it got me interested in diamonds, and I'd looked them up in a book and decided that what I liked was the marquis cut.

When I described it to Mommy, she said I was too materialistic and I said it didn't make any difference if I was because I'd never find a black guy with that much money, but one thing was sure: I wasn't going to settle for what she'd settled for—going to Woolworth's and paying $1.50 and I love you dearly and love is better than anything else and you don't need a ring.

Shearwood asked me, if we were to become engaged, what I wanted for an engagement ring, and I said, "You know what I want."

"Yvonne, my father is a steelworker, not the chairman of the board."

"I didn't say that's what I had to have. I said that's what I wanted."

"Then that's what you're going to get."

Medical students could earn extra money by following surgeons around and assisting on appendectomies and such.

Shearwood went to work in the emergency room at Harlem Hospital during the summer and on nights and weekends and holidays to save up for my ring. He was cracking chests and sewing up people, and more and more he began to say, "Hey, I like doing this stuff!" Eventually he changed his mind about becoming a psychiatrist in favor of being an orthopedic surgeon.

My mother said, "If he can do this for you, work so hard to show you that he loves you, that's a good man. There are times when you really need a man—when you're pregnant, when you're incapacitated—and you know Shearwood'll be there for you. He'll take care of you because he loves you."

Daddy commented: "The Bible says the man is supposed to work by the sweat of his brow and the woman's supposed to go forth and be fertile, go forth and procreate. What's happening now is that women are having babies and working by the sweat of their own brow and doing everything else, too. Why? Because the guy doesn't love her enough to get two jobs and she doesn't want to lose him, so she's doing all this stuff. But Shearwood gets the job to get you the ring, so you know he's gonna look after you, you know he's gonna be there when you need him."

I saw what they meant, but it was all somewhat theoretical until the day I did poorly on an exam in biochemistry, the first time I had ever done badly on a test, and I went to pieces. Shearwood was there for me, holding me, comforting me, talking to me with the voice of reason; not once saying, Aw, don't worry about it, like another man might have. Other men I knew, when it was a crisis situation, they fell apart, they had no depth to their being, but "steady as she goes," that was Shearwood.

Now I was beginning to understand why Mommy and Daddy claimed there was no such thing as easy love. "The word is used so often," they said. "It's such an overused word. People say *love,* but what they usually mean is *lust.*"

Mommy explained, "There is such a thing as responsibility, companionability, working together. You have to develop love. You don't even know what the man is when you've only known him a couple of months or a couple of years. He's gotta show his love. He can't just say it."

"Look at your mom and me," Daddy said. "We were young kids. Yeah, we liked each other, but it's working together, it's sacrificing together, it's doing the same things, caring for each other when one's sick, doin' something you maybe don't want to do—when you've done all that, then you can start talkin' about love."

I felt lucky that Mommy and Daddy had talked like that to us when we were kids because when I was twenty-one and got in the situation of having to make choices, their words came back to me. I listened to other women saying, "Oh, look at that hunk. Look at those buns." I watched them fall head over heels for somebody who was cute and flashy, which is what the culture says you're supposed to want. And then I'd look at Shearwood. He was no Rudolph Valentino. What he was, was my best friend. Our love affair, if such it was, wasn't exciting, wasn't romantic. But when I looked five years, ten years down the road, as Daddy had always taught us to do—"Size up the situation first. Try to see to the end of it. If it looks okay to the end of it, take that path. But if there's any problem with it, don't even bother wasting your time"—I looked, and as far as I looked, there was Shearwood: intelligent, gentle, generous, caring. Yes, he was the man for me.

Even if he didn't have cute buns. As Daddy said, "For such a big guy, he doesn't have enough butt to last him until tomorrow morning. But," Daddy added, "don't even think of getting him on a diet. He'll be a big man all his life. He'll be heavy. Don't try to slim him down. Nobody can buck what he's made to be."

Daddy believed that a person's attributes are God-given. "If God didn't want you to be the way you are," he said, "you wouldn't be that way." In his opinion, if you're happy-go-lucky, that's the way you are. If you're calm and deliberate, you're that type of person. You can't change no matter how much you try. Nor can you be changed. He admitted that he'd tried to make Jeanette helpful and loving and generous. He'd tried to make

Donna outgoing and worldly like Jeanette. He'd tried to make Linda stand up for herself. But, as he said when we were grown, "I've got five of you guys, and I couldn't change one of you into something God didn't make you to be. All I could do finally was to try to steer you toward a path that was going to protect you when you got older."

For me as the middle child, it was finding someone to be, acquiring an identity of my own, which translated into becoming a physician. It still happens these days that people, when I come into a room, look at me with that little frown on their forehead, which means, *What's that black woman doing here?* Then we're introduced and it's, "Oh, *Dr.* Thornton," and I look up to heaven and silently say, *Thank you, Mommy. Thank you, Daddy*.

For Linda it was to be dentistry, and for Rita, like me, it was to be medicine. Linda, having seen how hard I had to study to make it as a biology major, gave some thought to switching to a major in the Russian language. Daddy was skeptical.

"What're you gonna do with that?" he demanded.

"Become an interpreter," Linda told him. "Maybe at the United Nations."

"I'll tell you this," Daddy said, "a Russian fellow is going to have a lot easier time learnin' English than you're gonna have learnin' Russian, so he's gonna be the one that gets the job at the United Nations and you're gonna be on a long line at the unemployment office."

Linda nevertheless persisted—for a while. Then one day she said, "Daddy, I'm dropping Russian. I've decided I'm going back to the original idea of being a dentist."

Ever hardheaded, Daddy did not applaud her decision but instead underlined her mistake. "Look how much time you lost. You took the Russian and then you dropped it. If you had started off with what you're supposed to start off with, you would have been that much time ahead. You're not going to catch it up. It's lost. So, whenever you go out to do something, make sure you're going right straight ahead because you can't go ahead and then back up. That time is down the drain."

Linda was accepted at New York University College of Dentistry in 1971, Rita was about to take organic chemistry at Monmouth College, and I was entering the third year of medical school. Because Linda and I were in New York City, Daddy and Mommy and Rita would drive to the city on Friday afternoons and pick us up to head out to wherever the band was playing on the weekend.

By now the music was changing. Rhythm and blues and the Motown sound had gone out, and psychedelic sound was in. James Brown had been replaced by the flower child. Our band could play Janis Joplin and Jimmy Hendrix, and we played some of the old music that was still good, but instead of dancing, the kids would just sit there and look and listen. They were into LSD and other drugs.

"What happened to good old beer?" we said to Daddy. "What is that smell?"

"Probably something out of the kitchen," he kept saying, until we finally figured out it was marijuana, a smell that was becoming pervasive on campuses. The type of student had changed. They were no longer getting out on the dance floor and having a great time. As Daddy said, "They're like sitting and...pondering."

Yale was the worst for that. The students would smoke a joint and listen and say, "Hm-m-m." I really hated to play there because the most difficult thing for an entertainer is to be up onstage singing her heart out or blowing her lungs out and the only reaction she gets is, "That's interesting, isn't it, Martha? Quite pleasant, really."

But Linda and Rita and I were still saying to each other, "If you'll hang in, I'll hang in," and that's what we did, even though I was now on call every other weekend and Daddy had to book our gigs around my schedule. The last two years of medical school are people. You're on the wards, and you start learning to apply the things you've learned from books and in the lab to the pathology of patients. You're called a clinical clerk, and you rotate through the different clinical disciplines: three months of medicine; three months of surgery and its surgical subspecialties, such as urology and orthopedics; six weeks each of obstetrics/gynecology and pediatrics; three months of neurology and psychiatry.

When you've been immersed in biochemistry and the lab, confronting patients for the first time is daunting. Many of my fellow students had had occasion to observe an operation and be present at a delivery, and were less intimidated than I. I finally had to say to myself, "Okay, Thorn, just take it one step at a time," and plunge in.

We could choose where to start our rotation, whether to begin with medicine and end up with psychiatry or to begin with surgery and end up with medicine. Once you chose your starting point, you had to go through the sequence in order. Medicine, I was told, was the most difficult service; nobody wanted to take that first. That made up my mind for me. "Let me take that first," I said to myself. "Then maybe the rest of the year will seem easier by comparison." I asked around, to check out my instinct that this was the best thing to do, and got it confirmed: "If you take medicine first, that'll give you a good basis for getting to the patient, then surgery allows you really to work with your hands, then the rest of the rotation is easy."

When you go on the wards, you're braced to hear a patient say: "I don't want any medical student touching me! I'm not going to be a guinea pig. I want a *real* doctor." But it turned out that patients are really very kind when you say you're a student. My first assignment was to draw blood. Along with my fellow students, I'd been practicing on oranges and a little bit on each other, although none of us was enthusiastic about getting stuck with a needle. Now I was face-to-face with a real live patient, and I was perspiring with nervousness.

"Hello, Mr. Carroway," I said. "I'm a medical student, and I'm here to draw your blood."

"Are you, dear? Sit right down here."

I put the tourniquet on. "This might be tight, but if it hurts, just let me know."

"No problem, dear. I've been here three weeks and I have

diabetes and they've been drawing blood all the time. Take your time."

Mr. Carroway had veins as big as Arnold Schwarzenegger's. I put the needle in, drew back the plunger—nothing; I'd missed the vein. I put a Band-Aid over the needle mark and asked Mr. Carroway if I could try his other arm.

"Sure, dear."

I tried again. Missed again. After the third try, I said, "Mr. Carroway, you're becoming a pincushion."

"That's all right, dear. You have to learn."

On the fourth try, blood came through the needle and into the test tube. I felt as though I had struck gold! *I am hot now*, I thought. *I am brave.* The chief resident came by and saw all the Band-Aids. "Yvonne, you think you can do a little better next time?"

Mr. Carroway consoled me. "You did fine, dear. If you need to take some more blood tomorrow, I'll be here."

As a clerk, I was assigned to an intern. When he was on call, I was on call. My intern would say, "Yvonne, we've got an admission coming in from the emergency room." Okay, fine, I'm right behind you. He'd say, "Get the blood pressure, get this, get that," and I would do whatever he said. That's how medical students learn. It is basically an apprenticeship.

When a patient came in—say, with gastrointestinal bleeding—we stayed with her until she was stabilized, which might take a few hours or it might take all night. Being on call means you can't go to a movie, can't go to a party, can't say, "I'm going out to dinner. I'll be back in two hours." There's no going home to your own bed. I'd find an empty bed and grab a few winks until a nurse would come in and say, "This patient needs her medication" or "That patient needs blood drawn." You get up and do what you have to do, and that's when you really become a doctor. You have to sacrifice, you have to be inconvenienced, because taking care of patients is more important than your sleep or your dinner, more important than any plans you've made.

You and your intern work together as a team, so when I was told, "Stick to this intern, Yvonne," I'd be like a stamp on a letter. I didn't intend to miss a thing, not one bit of experience or learning that I could possibly grab hold of. I was following so close on my intern's heels one day that when he came to a sudden stop and said, "You can't come in here, Yvonne," I banged right into him.

"Why not?" I demanded.

"Look at the door."

It was the men's room.

What a fascinating time those two years were. I came out of them feeling like no training anywhere was the equal of the training at P & S. I came out of them knowing I was not too insignificant, not too black, not too ugly—knowing now that I was not a person to be written off. I was a graduate of the College of Physicians and Surgeons. *I was a doctor.*

◆ 11 ◆

Dr. Thornton, Dr. Thornton...

"I CAN'T STAND DOCTORS," said Daddy. This was when we were teenagers. "I mean, they'll find something and they'll go in there and cut you up...."

We'd interrupt. "But, Daddy, you want us to be doctors."

"Yeah, that's different. That's good for you kids."

Good for the prestige it conferred, for the income it provided, for the chance it offered to be of value to other people. But for Daddy to go see a doctor himself? He would have had to be at death's door with his hand turning the knob. And Mommy had not been to a gynecologist since Rita was born in 1952.

When I was on the obstetrics/gynecology rotation in medical school and becoming aware of the deadly toll of ovarian and uterine cancer, I asked Mommy when she had last had a Pap smear.

"After you kids were born, I swore I wasn't going back to a gynecologist ever again if I could help it."

"Mommy, please don't embarrass me. I'm in medical school. I'm going to be a gynecologist"—I'd found out by now that it was a dual specialty, that in order to be an obstetrician, I had to become a gynecologist as well. "How's it going to look if my own mother dies of cancer because she won't go for a pelvic exam?"

"You're right," she agreed. "I should go. I'll get around to it one of these days."

But before she got around to it, something else happened. I was home on a weekend from medical school and followed Mommy into the bathroom while she was washing her hands and before she had flushed the toilet. The bowl was full of blood.

"Mommy!"

"Oh, yeah. That's okay."

"Okay? That's blood! That's gross hematuria! It is *not* okay."

"Sure, it is, honey. That's been happening for a long time. When I was carrying you kids, you lay on my right kidney. That's all it is. If it was anything else…

"Like kidney stones. Like nephritis."

"Those things are painful, aren't they?"

"Yes."

"So, nothing hurts, so I can't have anything or I'd feel some pain."

She did have a great deal of pain, but in her face. Called *tic douloureux,* this excruciating pain on the left side of her face often froze her to the spot for several seconds when it struck. Over a period of many years she had been taking Tylenol for it, and since this allowed her to tolerate the pain and we were all used to her sudden winces, we had long since ceased urging her to consult a doctor. I might have been equally casual in my reaction to the hematuria had I not learned in my pathology course about the seriousness of the symptom. After the weekend, when I returned to New York, I called Mommy daily to insist she make a doctor's appointment.

She grew impatient with me. "Yvonne, you're still in school. You're not a doctor yet."

"But, Mommy, you don't just graduate from medical school and suddenly you know everything where before you knew nothing. For four years you're studying, and I already know more than enough to be positive you've got to have that diagnosed."

"Well, I'm not going to, so you can just stop nagging me."

Since Daddy was a nonbeliever too, there was no use in appealing to him. I called a doctor in Long Branch who had been involved in hospitalizing Mommy for depression, explained the situation, and asked him to call Mommy. He did, and succeeded in persuading her to come in for tests. Her hematocrit, which should have been forty, was down to twenty-five; she needed an immediate blood transfusion; and one kidney, seriously damaged, apparently in an idiosyncratic reaction to prolonged use of the Tylenol, had ceased to function and had to be removed. After she recovered from the operation, Mommy felt better than she had for a very long time; she had been half-sick without realizing it and without imagining that there was a remedy available. For the first time, all of us became aware that there was a practical, personal benefit to my becoming a doctor. If I hadn't been studying medicine, I would have accepted Mommy's reasoning that no pain meant no problem.

I became a doctor—that is, I was awarded my M.D. degree—on a brilliant spring day in 1973. There were two graduation ceremonies for the medical students. One was for all Columbia University graduates and was held on the main campus at 116th Street, while the second, at Presbyterian Hospital, was just for the medical students. Rita and Linda, Mommy and Daddy, and Donna with her husband Willis and little Heather were there to cheer—everyone except Jeanette, who had something else to do that day.

Mommy, beaming but bemused as though she couldn't quite believe this moment had arrived, radiated happiness, while Daddy's chest was so puffed with pride that I teased him that he was going to have to go through doors sideways. Mommy told me later that he grabbed the elbows of perfect strangers to point to me and whisper loudly, "That's my daughter up there. She's graduatin' from medical school." At the second ceremony at Presbyterian Hospital, he added, wanting everyone to share his awed delight, "She was born right here at this hospital and now she's graduatin'. Ain't that somethin'!"

In a quiet moment between the two ceremonies, he turned to Mommy. "Remember when you said all those years back about wanting our children to be educated?"

"And you said, 'Tass, if that's what you want, I'll go along with you.' Yes, Donald, I remember."

"Well, we did it!"

"A ditchdigger and a day worker."

"That's our daughter up there, and she's a *doctor*." They looked at each other in wonder, marveling that it had happened.

"Why've you got tears in your eyes, Tass?"

"Same reason you have, Donald."

They were thrilled and touched when the Thornton Sisters Band came in for a mention in the course of the ceremony at the hospital. The College of Physicians and Surgeons prides itself on its graduates being versatile and accomplished human beings with interests extending beyond the narrow confines of medicine. The graduate who best typifies this well-roundedness, by vote of the entire class, is given the Joseph Garrison Parker award. For the class of 1973, there was a three-way tie: the award went to Sharon Grundfest, who was a concert pianist; to Ed Leahey, who was a gifted actor; and to Yvonne Thornton of the Thornton Sisters Band. I swear I could pick out Daddy's double-time clapping in the applause that followed the announcement. It sounded like the time he was beating on the floor trying to coach Rita to speed up on the foot bass.

He was only a little less jubilant at the awarding of an honorary degree to Duke Ellington. "This Columbia's cool, man!" he kept saying, with his ear-to-ear grin.

At the Columbia University ceremony, every college was presented to the president of the university: graduates of the medical school were in one section, of the law school in another, Teachers College graduates in a third, and so on. The president acknowledged the colleges, then said, "Those graduates of the medical school, please stand." The dean of the medical school stepped forward.

"Bow your heads in accession," he directed, for thus would we signify our assent to the Hippocratic oath, which he began to read out: "I swear by Apollo the physician..." It was a solemn and impressive moment as 126 newly minted doctors vowed to "follow that method of treatment which, according to my ability and judgment, I consider for the benefit of my patients.... With purity and holiness I will pass my life and practice my art."

"How come we don't have something like that?" the law students and the teachers lamented afterward, envying the oath by which we medical students dedicated ourselves as doctors.

I wasn't the only Negro woman graduate of the medical

school. A light-skinned girl of Jamaican heritage, who had grown up in this country and attended Manhattanville College, was my classmate throughout the four years. We had not, however, become close friends because, as I had quickly become aware, she was somewhat snobbish about American blacks. No matter what their status in the islands, when Caribbean natives come here, it's: Oh, you're an American black. You're not as good as we are.

I wanted to say to my West Indian classmate, Look, you wouldn't be getting this opportunity if there hadn't been black-skinned Americans who were lynched or shot or had dogs and fire hoses turned on them fighting for the chance to get into decent schools. But I knew she would counter by saying that Caribbean blacks have a work ethic that American blacks are deficient in and back up her argument by citing all the Islanders who have made it in the United States. If there is truth in this, perhaps it is because the Caribbean blacks, even though they were slaves on the sugar plantations, were allowed plots of land to raise their own food, the surplus of which they could sell if they wished, which gave them business experience, while American blacks, during slavery, were kept in such a dependent position that they never learned how to look after themselves. In honesty, I have to admit that an American black all too often will whine, "You owe me this, you owe me that," while a Caribbean black will turn to and get the job done. But I didn't relish having my nose rubbed in this sad fact by my Jamaican classmate.

How many prejudices am I going to get hit with in my life, I wondered when I realized that even she looked down on me. Talk about being on the bottom of the heap. Black. And not just black but a *dark-skinned* black. And not just a dark-skinned black but a dark-skinned black *woman*. And not just a dark-skinned black woman but a dark-skinned black *American* woman. It did seem like a very large eight-ball for just one person to be behind.

As of graduation day, however, I had something to weigh in with on the other side of the scales. I was now Yvonne Thornton, M.D. Was it going to be enough?

The wave of change making things easier for blacks had

inched up through the high schools, colleges, and medical schools by the 1970s, but it had not necessarily influenced minds and hearts at the postgraduate level, as I discovered when I applied for an OB/GYN residency at Mount Sinai Hospital in New York.

"What are you doing here?" the interviewer demanded when I walked into his office. "We don't accept black people. You wouldn't fit in with our other residents."

"Thank you for telling me," I replied, without knowing whether I meant to be sarcastic or not; my mouth was functioning but my head was blank with shock. "If that's the case, why did you schedule me for an interview?"

"Obviously we didn't know you were black."

I left Mount Sinai wondering how many other directors of training programs were going to react in exactly the same way, although I would have been surprised if they were all quite so blunt about it. Was I going to end up having to train at a black hospital because no other hospital would have me? There is nothing wrong with Harlem Hospital in New York, or Metropolitan, or Lincoln in the South Bronx—the training is fine— except that they are dead ends. In private hospitals, where the attending physicians also have private practices, if you have been there as a resident, when you graduate and become a member of the attending staff, the patients you saw as a resident now come to you and you can set up your own private practice. That same opportunity does not exist if you've done your residency in a black city hospital.

Telling myself to approach the problem with Daddy-type thinking, I reasoned in this fashion: I was at P & S with the smartest guys. I graduated with honors. Clearly, I could hold my own with the best. I didn't want to be shunted off to Harlem Hospital, but somehow that's where all the black P & S medical students seemed to end up if they stayed in New York. Why? Because when they submitted a list of hospitals where they wished to be considered for an internship, they included Harlem Hospital as their fail-safe choice, figuring that if all the other hospitals turned them down, Harlem would take them. And sure enough, all the private hospitals did turn them down once they knew the student had ranked Harlem. I said to myself that if I put a black hospital on my list, even just as a safety valve, that's where I was sure to end up, so I took a chance and only listed private hospitals, none of the city ones.

After you graduate from medical school, if you know what you want to specialize in, you apply for either a medical or a surgical internship. But if you're very sure, as I was absolutely certain I intended to be an obstetrician, and if your grades and your medical school performance demonstrate that you are capable of advanced work, the hospital will sometimes allow you to skip the internship and sign on as a resident. At least that was true in those days, and it was what I wanted to do because as an intern, you're at the very bottom of the hierarchy; you're harried, chivied, and bullied by everybody from the chief resident on down. You survive a year of that, only to go into your first-year residency in neurology or internal medicine or whatever and again find yourself on the lowest rung of the ladder, with everyone teeing off on you. If I could manage it, I decided, I would prefer to get knocked around for only one year instead of two, so I put down an OB/GYN residency for all my choices except the last. This was my fail-safe choice: a medical internship at Presbyterian, which I was almost certain I could get.

When I applied for an OB/GYN residency in the early 1970s, few women wanted to go into obstetrics and gynecology because the training program was, and still is, one of the most intense and demanding of all the specialties, plus the nature of the practice is disruptive to family life since babies are born at their convenience, not yours. Most women either went into internal medicine or into one of the four P's: pathology, pediatrics, psychiatry, or public health. But I had wanted to be an obstetrician for so long that I never hesitated.

At Roosevelt Hospital, I was interviewed by the chairman of the OB/GYN department, Dr. Thomas F. Dillon. He seemed impressed that I had published a scientific paper based on the independent research I had done with Drs. Anthony Cerami and

Joseph Graziano in the hematology laboratory at Rockefeller University during my fourth-year elective and that I had two more papers in the works.

"You're a P & S student and your recommendations are excellent," Dr. Dillon said. "Our program will be ranking you very high for a first-year residency position."

I was then given a tour of the hospital and, liking what I saw, I in turn put Roosevelt first on my matching list. Three days later it was settled: my postgraduate training would be at Roosevelt Hospital. My Jamaican classmate, who had listed Harlem Hospital last, went to Harlem Hospital.

One of my P & S professors, a distinguished surgeon who had trained at Bellevue Hospital and who was black himself, stopped me in the hall one day. "I hear you're going to Roosevelt."

"Yes, sir."

"Congratulations." He added thoughtfully, "You know, there's not too many black people at Roosevelt."

"I didn't know, but that's okay. I've been trained well here so it shouldn't be a problem." He was suggesting that blacks tend to feel uncomfortable when they're the odd man out, but I'd been the only black in so many situations that it didn't bother me in the least. "Actually," I told him smilingly, "I don't think of myself as black. I think of my skin as being just one large freckle."

He laughed. "Is that why you didn't list Harlem Hospital?"

"I imagine I didn't list it for the same reason you probably didn't list it when you graduated," I answered.

He said nothing more. He knew how the system worked.

A year later, when Shearwood was graduating, he did as I had done: avoided playing it safe and was accepted for his surgical training at St. Luke's, a private hospital. Interestingly enough, now, two decades later, he is Chief of Orthopedic Surgery at Harlem Hospital, but that is by choice, not because he was shunted off there because of his color.

At Shearwood's graduation, I was his family because his father had also died by then and his brother, who was living in Indiana, was unable to be there. As Shearwood took the Hippocratic oath with his class, I lifted my eyes to heaven in the hope that his mother was looking down, and in my heart I murmured, *Your boy made it, too. Be proud. Be proud of him and be proud of yourself that you gave him the vision.*

Shearwood was Dr. McClelland now. I was Dr. Thornton. We could talk about getting married.

In my early days at P & S, I had mentioned to a black nurse that I was a Baptist and was looking for a church, a quiet one, a dignified one, not one where the sermons started late and went on for hours and people rolled on the floor shouting, "I got the spirit, Lord!"

The nurse said, "You'd like Riverside."

"Where's that?"

"Come over to the window and I'll show you."

"That's a Baptist church? It can't be." From what I could see of the spire, the building was as lofty and massive as a cathedral. But the nurse assured me that it was indeed a Baptist church. The next Sunday I took the bus there and walked in—diffidently because I was awed by the soaring space and the echoing silence—and sat in the last pew. The singing of the choir was so fine, it made me feel as though I were at the Metropolitan Opera, and when it came time for the sermon, the senior minister, Dr. Ernest T. Campbell, spoke simply and eloquently about the presence of God in everyday life. The congregation listened quietly; no one interrupted with shouts about the Holy Spirit. At the end of the service, another minister said, "Those of you who wish to become members of Riverside Church..." and I knew he was speaking to me, that I had found the religious home I was seeking.

When Shearwood first asked me to marry him in 1971, I had wondered whether we could be married in Riverside Church. I inquired of the pastor, who said that since I was a member, of course I could be, and did I want the wedding to take place in the Christ chapel or the nave?

"The nave?" That spiraling, soaring, gorgeously generous space? Suddenly, in my mind's eye, I was starring in a rerun of *The*

Sound of Music—Maria in her wedding dress and floating veil walking down the long, long center aisle, that was me. "I want the nave, yes. For June 8, 1974."

"But that's three years away."

"I want to get in early here."

"How do you know that you and your fiancé will be feeling the same way in 1974? You do understand that once I put you down for that date, I have to turn away anyone else who might want it?"

"This is real love, sir. We're not 'in love.' We love each other. That's not going to go away."

In my first year of residency, I stopped in at Scribner's bookstore on Fifth Avenue and bought a book called *It's Your Wedding*, which, to all intents and purposes, I proceeded to commit to memory: the proper this, the correct that—when the announcement goes in the newspaper, the wording of the invitations and their mailing date, the bridesmaids, the ushers, the ring bearer, the reception…everything. I intended to have an impeccable, dazzling wedding, and I was going to pay for it myself so nobody could order me to put the brakes on. My salary as a first-year resident was twelve thousand dollars for the year, and I saved it all, which wasn't difficult since I was working far too hard to socialize. I was on call every other night and every other weekend, and on the off weekends I traveled with the band.

We still needed the money the band made because Linda and Rita were both studying dentistry at New York University—Rita had decided to follow Linda into dentistry rather than me into medicine. Daddy lined up gigs that we could fit around our schedules, but they were necessarily fewer and tuition costs were high. Linda, who was in her second year, had to apply to NYU for a loan. She was told that it would not be granted without two cosigners and she called Daddy in despair. He could sign, of course, but where in the world would they find a second person to sign?

"Sugar, calm down. We'll work it out. I'll come up and talk to them." Daddy counted on his customary approach: good suit, white shirt, no challenge, no argument. It worked, as it always had. "I told the man that I took care of my kids all my life. I asked nothin' from nobody, and if I could go this far without askin' anyone to cosign, I could surely carry the weight the rest of the way. I told him, 'I'll sign, and I will pay,' and he says, 'Talkin' like that, Mr. Thornton, your signature is all we need.'"

Linda, still quiet and shy and painfully conscious of how overweight she was at five-foot-three and 298 pounds, did not have an easy time of it at NYU. Several times a week she called Daddy, often in tears because of problems with the work. "I just can't get it, Daddy. The other kids get it, but I just can't."

"Sure, you can, honey," he'd tell her. "You got this far. You can make it."

"I'm dumb. I'm stupid."

"No, you're not. It's just that you get upset. Look, honey, stop cryin'. Take it easy, you're gettin' me all upset too. I'll tell you what you do. If there is something you're not gettin,' you go to the library and go back to the elementary part of what you're studyin', then gradually move up again. If you're not understandin' everything the professor is talkin' about, you go back and you learn back up to where he is."

A day or two later, another phone call would come. "Thanks, Daddy. I did what you said, and it worked." As he himself said, "I can't do none of this myself, but I can give my kids good advice."

To Rita, who had the youngest child's psychology of competing for attention and was infinitely feistier than Linda, he offered quite different advice. "Rita, don't be brilliant. Keep how smart you are to yourself until you're off by yourself somewheres. When you're around teachers, play dumb. You learn more when you play dumb, and that way you don't challenge them so they got to prove themselves."

We were together one weekend, traveling to a gig, when Rita admitted to Daddy that he was right. "The other day," she said, "I was practicing cleaning teeth and I wanted the teacher to check my work, but he passed me up. The next time I blocked the aisle so he couldn't get by and I said, 'Would you mind seeing if I did this right?' He was kind of irritated but he took a look. 'You didn't scrape that surface,' he said. 'We weren't told to scrape there,' I answered him back.

"The minute I said it," Rita went on, "I knew it was the wrong thing. Like you're always telling me, I had hollered him a challenge and right away he got determined to be the winner, like 'Who are you to be telling me?' He was like a dog with his ruff going up, and I knew I was in trouble if I didn't do something quick.

"I said, 'I'm sorry, sir, I'm mistaken. You're right, you're absolutely right, I did do it wrong.' And the minute I said that, he changed completely. He'd been going to part my hair for me, cut me off at the knees, but I hollered 'no challenge, no contest' and the fight went right out of him. He said, 'That's okay. Maybe your class was taught to do it some other way.'"

"That's what I'm always tellin' you," Daddy said. "You challenge a person, he'll fight you. He's got to prove he's right. You're not makin' his paycheck no bigger by tryin' to get him to admit he's wrong. You're just makin' him give you a hard time. If you know you're right, after you leave, you can go on down the steps and holler 'the big dummy!' if that makes you feel better."

Daddy may have been uneducated in a formal sense but he understood personalities and human interactions and communicated this understanding to us so clearly that he was our prophetic educator in the ways of the world. It was because of him and exchanges like this that I knew better than to make the mistake an intern at Roosevelt Hospital made the very next week. The chief resident made a statement, and the intern, fresh from medical school and immersion in textbooks, volunteered, "Actually, you're wrong about that." Indeed, the chief was wrong, but that only increased his anger at being shown up, and from then on, throughout the rest of the year, the intern was picked on unmercifully.

I wondered if I was about to be singled out for an unusually hard time when I first presented myself in the doctors' scrub room at Roosevelt. "I'm here to scrub with Dr. Bartsich," I said to the man sitting there reading a newspaper.

"I'm Dr. Bartsich," he said in a thick German accent. "Who are you?"

"Yvonne Thornton, your first-year resident."

He rustled the newspaper ominously. "We'll be going in ten minutes," he barked and jerked the newspaper up in front of his face. I knew what he was thinking: *She's one of those affirmative action people.* I said to myself, *Oh, boy, I'm in for it now.* But he was a fair man and gave me a chance to prove myself. When I showed him I was eager to learn and willing to put in any amount of time, that I never failed to be there when he needed me and never went off duty if there was anything more to be done, he lost his doubts and poured his knowledge into me. He had the most skillful hands I've ever seen in a surgeon, and because I was determined to emulate him, I too became a more than competent surgeon.

Occasionally, when I entered a patient's room, even though I was wearing white garb and had a stethoscope around my neck, the patient would glance up and say, "The wastebasket's over there."

"I'm not here to empty the wastebasket, Mrs. Jones. I'm here to do your preoperative evaluation. I'll be assisting Dr. Bartsich in the operating room."

The little furrow in the middle of Mrs. Jones's forehead would tell me the woman was thinking: Are you skilled enough to touch my body? Are you trained enough to be here in the first place? Often the patient would ask, "Did you go to Meharry?"

"No, I didn't. How many children do you have, Mrs. Jones?"

"Did you go to Howard?"

"No. Are you allergic to any medication?" I never offered the information of where I had gone to school because Daddy always said, "Keep your credentials in your back pocket. That way you don't sound like you're braggin', and it'll really take people by surprise when they do find out."

"You're scrubbing for Dr. Bartsich?"

"With. *With* Dr. Bartsich. He cannot operate alone. It takes a team."

A Mrs. Jones I remember well was silent while I listened to her lungs and heart, then suddenly said, "Are you a racist?"

I laughed. "Mrs. Jones," I said, "if I were, your chances of getting off the operating table wouldn't be very good. But I'm not, so don't worry."

I would tell Daddy stories like this when we were driving to a gig, and all he'd say was, "Builds character, Cookie. Builds character."

When I went to Roosevelt Hospital, I was the only black and the only American woman in the OB/GYN residency program. The chief resident, whether or not he was prejudiced against blacks, which he didn't reveal, was openly and avowedly prejudiced against women because he believed we "hen-medics" were taking up spaces that should have gone to men. "You women," he'd rant, "you'll get pregnant and have babies and all this training I'm giving you, it's going to be totally lost." Grumpily, as though in retaliation for what he foresaw happening, he piled work on the women and looked for opportunities to show us up. I recollect one instance vividly.

Every week in a teaching hospital there are grand rounds at which residents present cases to the attending physicians, giving details of a patient's presenting problems and how the case was managed. What was done, and why, is discussed, and the appropriateness of the management is thrashed out so that everyone—attending physicians, residents, and interns alike—can learn from the experience.

At P & S, I'd had the experience of presenting in front of an attending physician who railed at students who used index cards to jot down the facts of the case. "Do you know the patient or don't you?" he'd hiss. "Why do you read from those damn cards? Either you know the patient or you don't."

Being in show business, besides being blessed with a photographic memory, when it was my turn to present a case, I would make notes but then memorize the cards and give the facts and answer any questions without referring to them. The first time I did this, the attending physician said, "Residents, did you see that presentation? That's exactly the way I expect it to be done every time." With that experience behind me, I was never nervous about my ability to present a case, and perhaps it was just this poise that riled the chief resident enough to look for a chance to show me up.

He thought he had found it when a really bad case came in at ten o'clock one night: a botched abortion on a woman who was much too far along in pregnancy to have had an abortion at all. An instrument had been inserted into her uterus and had gone right through the thinned-out wall, rupturing veins and an artery and causing massive hemorrhaging. The woman's uterus was all ripped and she had lost over half of her blood volume by the time she got to us. It was a terrible case. Several of us went without sleep all night to save her. At five in the morning, with grand rounds scheduled for 8:00 A.M., the chief resident said, "Yvonne, you're presenting this case."

"Good heavens, Steve, why didn't you tell me that last night so I could have made notes of her lab results and the progress reports from the intensive care unit?"

"Tough," he said, smirking because he knew full well I wasn't going to be prepared. I had only three hours, I had another delivery to go to, and I was dead on my feet so I would certainly fall asleep if I had a free moment between now and then.

"Oh, no, you don't," I said to myself. "You're not going to make a fool out of me." I checked on the patient in labor and found I wasn't needed quite yet, so I ran over to the ICU and quickly reviewed the patient's chart and the many pages of lab results. I then went to a conference room and found pieces of blue, yellow, and pink chalk. In the amphitheater where the grand rounds were held was a free-standing, two-sided blackboard. With the colored chalk, I diagrammed the uterus with its veins and arteries and the exact path of the perforating instrument to make it clear to the audience the situation we had been confronted with. Then I turned the blackboard around so that when everyone gathered in the amphitheater at eight, it was seemingly blank. Then I ran back and delivered the baby.

As people filed into the amphitheater, the chief resident walked past me and said slyly, "Are you ready?"

"I'll do my best," I answered meekly. While two other presentations were being made, I memorized the facts I had gotten down on cards. Then it was my turn. I stood at the front of the room and described the emergency situation we'd been confronted with.

"In order to make it easier to conceptualize the situation..." I said, and moved to the blackboard and swung it around. Out of the corner of my eye, I could see the chief resident come bolt upright in his chair. "This shows the angle at which the instrument perforated the uterine myometrium...."

Afterward the other residents grabbed me. "How did you find time to do that?"

"My mother always said you don't find time, you make time." I didn't add that my father had worked two eight-hour jobs for twenty-five years so I'd had plenty of evidence that it is possible to keep going when you have to.

The chief resident's only comment was: "Show-off." But after that he left me alone, perhaps sensing that that kind of testing only made me stronger and more determined. That reaction had started way back when all of us were little kids and Daddy had said, "You're already being written off because you're black and female." And had been reinforced with the band when he said, "They don't think girls can make great music come out of these instruments." Each time we were tested, we showed what we could do, and when we did, we were allowed to progress to the next step. This is why, if I may be forgiven a digression, I believe it is time for the black race to forget about rhetoric and instead show what we are capable of doing. The testing will surely go on for the next generation and the next, but each time we meet the test, we'll climb another rung of the ladder until finally we arrive at parity, having earned our place rather than pleading or demanding that it be given to us.

I was just going off duty one day when I heard myself being paged: "Dr. Thornton, Dr. Thornton, line five, line five." I picked up a phone and was told I was wanted at the front desk. In my whites and with my stethoscope around my neck, I went striding down the hall. From the distance I saw Daddy. He was standing with his head cocked, his eyes on a corner of the ceiling, a rapt expression on his face that I couldn't read.

"Daddy! Has something happened to Mommy? Is she all right?"

"Your mother's okay." He still hadn't looked at me. I followed his gaze to the far corner. He was staring at a loudspeaker for the paging system. "Could they do that again?"

"Do what?"

"Call your name."

I went to a phone and asked the operator to repeat the page. As I walked back to Daddy, the words came over the system: "Dr. Thornton, Dr. Thornton..."

Daddy turned an ecstatic face to me. "Did you ever hear anything sound so great, Cookie?" He mimicked the paging system: "Dr. Thornton, Dr. Thornton..."

"Better than music from a horn, Daddy?" I teased.

"Oh, sweeter, much sweeter," he murmured. "You're Dr. Thornton. With a scripperscrap around your neck."

"I could be a green monkey..."

"And still the richest man in the world would grab your hand and say, 'Please help me, Doctor.'"

"I remember you saying that every time we drove around Asbury Park."

"Was I right, Cookie?"

"You were right, Daddy."

"Sometimes you'd want to give up—you'd get tired or the work was too hard—and I'd say, 'Come on, Cookie, do it for Daddy.' Remember that?"

"You said it often."

He turned to me and took my hands. "Cookie, I wasn't askin' you to do it for me."

"I know that now. It was for me, Daddy, wasn't it?"

"Yes, Dr. Thornton, it was for you."

◆ 12 ◆

Till Death Do Us Part

JUNE 8. JUNE 8. JUNE 8. A laborer digging the Panama Canal single-handedly couldn't have worked any harder than I did that first year of my residency, hard and conscientiously and as creatively as I could, honing my skills as a physician. But running on a parallel track in my mind was the countdown to June 8, the day in 1974 when Shearwood and I were to be married at Riverside Church—at 12:00 because the book on weddings said that formal weddings took place at high noon and I was determined to have a formal wedding, not one of those slipshod affairs, which is all I'd ever been to, where the bride is late, the minister is late, the guests are late, and the reception is punch and cookies in the church meeting room.

Two years earlier President Nixon's daughters had been married in wedding gowns designed by Priscilla of Boston, which was recommendation enough to send me to that shop for my gown. I told the bridal consultant that I wanted a train like Maria's in *The Sound of Music,* that is to say, about eighty feet long. "Impossible," the designer said. "The longer the train, the wider it gets, and it would end by spreading over the whole church." We compromised on the maximum feasible length for the train—detachable so I could dance at the reception—and a cathedral-length veil. I was doing some nervous eating and a lot of snacking because of the odd and long hours I was putting in at the hospital, which meant that every time I showed up for a fitting, the seams of the wedding dress had to be let out a little more, until finally a decree was issued that I was not to gain another ounce lest the sides split when I walked down the aisle.

In reconfirming the date for the nave, the church secretary

asked how many people would be at the wedding. "About a hundred," I told her, then rethought the figure. "No, probably about fifty."

"Fifty? Then we have to reschedule you from the nave to the chapel. For the nave you have to have at least two hundred people. That huge space is really for, like, dignitaries' daughters when lots of people have to be invited to the ceremony."

"Wait a minute," I said, thinking of my glorious train and the walk down that center aisle. "Let me get back to you. I haven't checked my mother's list yet." An hour later I called her. "I sure was wrong," I said cheerily. "There'll be at least two hundred and fifty people. It turns out my mother has her heart set on inviting all her friends and my dad's determined to invite everyone in his office, so it's going to add up."

Daddy didn't have an office and Mommy didn't have three friends to her name, but I was going to have two hundred and fifty people at my wedding if I had to sweep strangers in off the street. I planned to invite practically everyone I had ever known, including fellow students, interns, residents, doctors, and professors, and I told my relatives, all the aunts and uncles on both sides, to ask anyone they wanted to. Because it struck me as chintzy to invite people to witness a wedding without wining and dining them in return, all two hundred and fifty people were to be invited to the reception as well, which was to be held at the Tavern on the Green, a restaurant with a magical atmosphere on the edge of Central Park. I had made the reservation years before, at the same time I reserved the church, so there wouldn't be any hitch. Except that there was. A letter arrived saying the restaurant was being closed down for six months for renovations and my deposit was being returned.

I was frantic. June weddings are myriad; the good places to have receptions were certain to be booked. I was bemoaning my luck loud and long when one of the hospital clerks interrupted to remark that she had attended a firemen's ball the night before at a fabulous place. "Where?" I pounced.

"Terrace on the Park in Queens. You know that building left

over from the World's Fair? It's got this fantastic restaurant on top."

"Queens? I don't even know where Queens is!"

"Dr. Thornton, let me tell you, if you're looking for the perfect place, this is it. I promise. Go see it."

I rented a car, found my way across the East River to Queens, got on Grand Central Parkway as directed, and in the distance saw a building in the shape of a T. "T for Thornton," I said to myself. "Maybe it's a good sign." The restaurant was in the crossbar of the T and had a spectacular view of the New York skyline. The banquet manager described a band playing, hors d'oeuvres circulating, an open bar, then a set of doors folding back to reveal a sit-down, prime rib, champagne dinner for two hundred and fifty.

"That's it!" I said. "Do it all. Everything but the band. That I want to choose myself." At the headquarters of Local 802 in the city, I listened to tapes, picking out several bands that sounded first-rate but finally settling on the Steven Scott orchestra because I was assured that it had played at the society wedding of an elegant, much-written-about debutante earlier in the season. I used the same reasoning to choose a wedding photographer, settling on one who had pictures of Jackie Kennedy all over his studio.

Shearwood said, "The way you're going, Yvonne, all I have to do is, like, show up, right?"

"Right," I laughed. "And if you don't show up after all this, let me tell you, Shearwood McClelland, you are dead meat."

The wedding book alerted me to the fact that having the organ burst into "Here Comes the Bride" was passé, gauche even, news which I passed on to the choirmaster at the church and asked if he could suggest a substitute. "Well, at Queen Elizabeth's wedding they played the "Trumpet Voluntary."

"That's good enough for me! That's what it'll be."

After I bought a record to hear what it sounded like, I went back to Local 802 and interviewed trumpet players, making each one play for me "because there's a high note I don't want you to mess up on." I ended by hiring not one but several players: the Festival Brass Players of New York. They were in addition to the Riverside organist and the full church choir. The wife of the minister who was to perform the wedding ceremony was a member of the choir and told me later that her fellow singers kept saying at rehearsals, "Who are these people?" All they knew was that the music, all of which I selected, was for the wedding of Drs. Thornton and McClelland, and they kept speculating, "Boy, they must really be *somebody*."

Because the maid of honor has various responsibilities and Linda's time was taken up with dental school, she asked to trade roles with Rita and be one of the bridesmaids while Rita became maid of honor. The book said that for a formal wedding there had to be at least five bridal attendants, which was fine; I had five sisters. But again there was a hitch: Jeanette kept not showing up for a fitting of her dress.

I called her on a weekend when I was down in Long Branch. "Jeanette, come on, you've got to give me a time when you can come to New York."

"I can't make it."

"What do you mean, you can't make it? It's already April. The wedding's in June. We're running out of time here."

"I can't make the wedding. I have the flu."

"For two months! You aren't going to make my wedding because you're having the flu for two months?" I was steaming, but my eye was caught by Daddy shaking his head at me. I took a deep breath, said as calmly as I could, "Okay, Jeanette," and hung up.

"One monkey don't stop the show, Cookie," Daddy reminded me. "There's other people."

That was the trouble; there weren't other people. As it was for my mother and father, my life had been the family and work. I hadn't had time for friends. I asked Rita to get someone she knew to be a bridesmaid, and as it turned out, she had to produce two of her friends for me because Donna worried that she might possibly have an epileptic attack during the ceremony and spoil my wedding.

Shearwood had seven groomsmen—the book said they weren't to be called ushers anymore—and he had written vows that he would pronounce during the ceremony, as had I. The night before the wedding, the wedding party was at the Holiday Inn across from Roosevelt Hospital. "Shearwood, have you memorized your vows?"

"Don't worry, Yvonne, I'll get to it."

"If you mess up, I'm going to be awfully upset."

"I won't mess up."

"Maybe you'd better read them to me." I wanted to make sure all the grammar was right and proper.

"Yvonne, you don't have to review my vows. I'll tell them to you in the church."

"Everything's got to be perfect!" I wailed.

Afterward people commented on how nice it was that we had written our own vows rather than just echoing the minister. The book had suggested it, but with the caveat that most people were too nervous to pull it off. We managed fine, with just one little glitch that I can hear on the tape we have of the ceremony. I smile now when I play the tape and hear how earnest and sweet we sounded.

Something old—a diamond and sapphire pinky ring Daddy had given me when I graduated from Monmouth College. *Something new*—my wedding gown and a heart-shaped diamond necklace. *Something borrowed*—hosiery from Rita. *Something blue*—a blue satin and lace garter. *With a sixpence in her shoe*—a real sixpence given to me by Ed Leahey, my P & S classmate.

At 11:55 on June 8, the organ was playing, 250 guests were assembled in the church, the limousines were waiting outside to transport everyone to Queens, I and my bridesmaids carrying our wedding bouquets were in place at the back of the nave ready to walk down the aisle. There was only one thing wrong: Daddy hadn't appeared.

I'd told him repeatedly that this wedding was not going to be on CPT. I was in a state. "Rita, go out there. Get Uncle Kenny. Get somebody! In three minutes they're going to play the 'Trumpet Voluntary' and I'm walking down the aisle if I have to walk alone!"

"Okay, Yvonne, but stop crying. Your mascara's running."

At two minutes of twelve, Daddy came through the door. I greeted him hysterically. "Daddy, can't you even be on time for my wedding!"

"You're not married yet, are you?" He looked handsome in a silk Hickey Freeman suit—he had drawn the line at wearing a morning coat. The "Trumpet Voluntary" sounded. "Ready, Cookie?"

I took a deep breath to get my heart back in my chest and laid my hand on his arm. "Ready, Daddy."

Scarcely thirty minutes later it was over. Reverend Dr. Robert L. Polk pronounced us man and wife. Shearwood and I were married. I said to myself as he and I walked back down the aisle together: "Three years of preparation and already it's over? It can't be!"

But it was, and it had been perfect, an elegant wedding, the wedding of my dreams.

"You're Cecil B. DeMille," Linda whispered. "I was expecting doves."

"I was thinking of doves," I admitted, "but I was worried they wouldn't be housebroken."

I'd wanted something out of the ordinary for Shearwood and me to travel to the reception in, and when I'd seen an ad that urged, "Have your wedding in a Rolls-Royce," I knew that was the answer and had taken myself off to the Rolls-Royce agency.

"You'll never regret it," the salesman said.

"Right. Where's the car? I want to see it."

"It's being used in the filming of *The Great Gatsby*, but I promise you, it's white, it's elegant, it's big."

In front of the church it was white, elegant, and big. It also had a prominent dent in the front fender, which came close to ruining my wedding, except that, as we were driven across

Manhattan on 125th Street, little kids stopped playing and ran to the curb to watch the sleek Rolls glide by and I waved graciously, benevolently, charmingly—queen for a day.

Even all these years later, one of the doctors who was at the reception introduces me to people by saying, "You should have been at her wedding. Best wedding I ever went to." As one of the residents described it, "The waiters were coming in with these big platters of hors d'oeuvres, and the plates they gave us to put them on were so huge that I figured this was it and I'm just going to tank up on all this great food. Then they opened up the doors for the real dinner! I couldn't believe it!"

Every wedding I'd ever been to had been done on the cheap. Not mine, I was determined about that. "Give them as much as they can eat and drink," I had told the caterers, "and then offer them more." I had no chance to eat and drink myself: I was too excited and I was too busy. First it was the picture-taking, which went on and on in various permutations and combinations: bride and groom, bride and groom and attendants, bride and parents, groom and brother, bride and sisters. Jeanette walked. into the reception dressed in a brashly colored dashiki, hair cut in an Afro, and Mommy wanted her to be in the picture of the bridal party.

"Mommy," I objected, "she wasn't in the bridal party. She didn't want to be."

"She's your sister."

"She's dressed Nairobi out of Kenya and I'm dressed Priscilla of Boston."

"She's your own sister."

"All right, so we'll have a family portrait, you and Daddy and the six of us."

The most charming of all the wedding pictures was one of the flower girl and the ring bearer. The book had said the children should be about five years old, so when I began planning the wedding so long in advance, I asked Aunt Dollbaby Joy, who had eight or nine kids, if she would lend me the two youngest, who would be the right age at the time of the wedding, and I would see to their outfitting.

"Okay, that's wonderful, Yvonne," she said two years before the wedding. Two *weeks* before the wedding, she said, "I can't come, Yvonne, and I can't allow my children to come because we're Jehovah's Witnesses now."

My flower girl scattering rose petals. My ring bearer with the little satin pillow. "Mommy, Mommy, Aunt Joy's screwed me up!"

Daddy said, "Cookie, what did I tell you? These people are gonna come up lame. They're not dependable."

Uncle Kenny's wife, the only aunt that I remembered being kind to Mommy, volunteered her daughter. The little girl was only three and I was afraid she would cry and mess up my wedding, but Aunt Thalia promised she wouldn't and offered to make her dress herself. Now I had the flower girl, and Mommy often baby-sat for a little boy who was as cute as a shiny button, so she asked his mother if we could borrow him. Both children carried off their roles beautifully, and when the photographer took their picture, she in her frilly dress and he in his little white tuxedo, they looked heartbreakingly innocent. Weeks later, when I stopped by the photography studio, their portrait had joined Jackie Kennedy's on the wall.

After the picture-taking, Shearwood and I went around to all the tables and thanked the guests for coming because the book said that was the gracious and proper thing to do. We carried our glasses of champagne and picked up an hors d'oeuvre here and there, but we never sat down to dinner because when we weren't laughing and chatting with our guests, we were dancing—first Shearwood and I, then Daddy and I. It was the first time Daddy and I had danced because always before we were the band making the music, not the people swinging to it. "Your daddy was a dancing fool," his sister had said, and she was right. Even all these years later, Daddy moved to the music like water taking on the shape of a glass.

Because Shearwood and I weren't leaving on our honeymoon until the next day, we had made a reservation for our wedding night at the Plaza Hotel on Central Park South. When we arrived at the bridal suite, there on the door was a brass plate and engraved on it was: Dr. and Mrs. Shearwood McClelland. We were thrilled. After a late dinner in the Oak Room downstairs, we returned to the elegant bridal suite and collapsed into bed. Other people say of their wedding night, "Oh, it was so wonderful." All Shearwood and I can say is, "Oh, we were so exhausted." In the morning our exchange went like this:

"Did you do anything?"

"No. Did you?"

"No."

"Well..."

Shearwood swung his legs over the side of the bed. "We've got the rest of our lives for that, Yvonne. Right now we've got to catch a plane to Hawaii."

The honeymoon was Shearwood's responsibility. I'd told him, "I'll take care of the wedding. You take care of Hawaii," and I'd proceeded to spend every penny of my thirteen-thousand-dollar savings, even in the end having to borrow from Daddy to pay for the flowers. "We shouldn't take a honeymoon," Shearwood had said. "We should spend the money on furniture." But then he saw my face and hastily added, "Okay, I've told you the practical thing to do. Now what do you want to do?"

"Furniture we can always buy, but a honeymoon is a one-time affair."

"Hawaii it is."

It is easy to sum up what we did on our honeymoon; we ate. We didn't go near the beach because neither of us knew how to swim and I wouldn't be caught dead in a bathing suit. In two and a half weeks we gained twenty pounds—each of us. To gain that much weight in that short a time takes really dedicated eating, and we were up to it. We quickly knew where every restaurant, coffee shop, service bar, and snack place was in the hotel and for blocks around. I no longer had to worry about fitting into my wedding dress, we both love to eat, and I suppose we were nervous. After all, neither of us had been married before and it does take a bit of getting used to. So we ate. And went back home convinced that after the most perfect wedding in the world, we'd had the most perfect honeymoon.

We were flat broke, of course, but it didn't matter because Shearwood was starting the first of his two years of residency at St. Luke's Hospital and I my second year of a four-year residency at Roosevelt, and we had a tiny apartment supplied by Roosevelt. And the band was still going on, so there was a little bit from that. Linda needed tuition money for her last year of dental school, and Rita for the University of Pennsylvania, where she had transferred. She had grown restless and discontent at NYU and thought she might like life better in Philadelphia, which was close enough for her to remain with the band. As musicians, we were so attuned to each other and by now so experienced that, even though we had no time to practice and had to accept fewer and fewer engagements because of our schedules, we still sounded great. There was no falling off in the beat and drive of the music, but the taste of college kids was changing. Drugs were becoming ever more prevalent, and what suited the drug scene were not bands and dancing but psychedelic music and strobe lights. By the end of the year, Daddy was saying, "What do you think, Cookie?"

"I'll be chief resident soon, Daddy, and time is really going to be a problem for me, plus Mommy isn't looking too well."

"And things are winding down at the colleges. I guess we should think about packin' it in."

"We've had a good run for our money."

"Yeah, and as fickle as people are, I never thought it would last this long."

"Look what the band's done for us: Linda's a dentist, Rita's in dental school, Jeanette has a doctorate in counseling psychology, Donna's studying to be a court stenographer, Betty's a nurse...."

"But I only got one doctor," he grumbled. "I set out to make five."

"They say the best way to reach a goal is to be aiming at something far beyond it. You wanted us all to be somebody, to be able to take care of ourselves, so you aimed at our being doctors.

We're not all doctors, but you ended up with six educated, independent women, so you really did reach your goal."

He thought this over for a few moments, then shot me one of his quick smiles. "Not bad, eh, Cookie? Not bad for an uneducated ditchdigger."

Linda graduated from New York University School of Dentistry in 1975. Because it takes money to set up a dental practice and because, being black and a woman, the chances of her being taken on as a junior partner in an existing practice were remote, she decided to join the army.

"The army!" I exploded. "Linda, their uniforms are ugly."

"I'm not joining for the uniform," she countered haughtily. "All the army dependents, their mouths are terrible, so I'll get lots of good experience. And the Armed Forces Dental Pathology Lab is better even than Harvard's."

I suspect Daddy had planted the idea of the army because Linda was unsuited to the hurly-burly of the world. She could bang the drums but she couldn't bang on doors; she could crash the cymbals but she couldn't crash gates. The army would give her security and a fine chance to grow in her profession. It was the right move for her to make, she and Daddy agreed, and one day in the summer he took her to Fort Monmouth to sign up.

"Sorry," the recruiter said. "We can't take you."

Linda, expecting a glad hand, was rocked by the cold shoulder. "But I was at the top of my class at NYU and the army needs dentists, they told me that in New York."

"It's not your qualifications," the recruiter explained. "It's your weight. We don't have a uniform that would fit you."

Linda was devastated. Mommy and Daddy had always said it was our brains that mattered, not our bodies, and nobody had ever made anything before out of our being overweight. Linda plummeted head first into a black depression, then surfaced grim with determination: if she was going to be denied what she wanted because she weighed 298 pounds, she would cease weighing 298 pounds by the simple but excruciating expedient of ceasing to eat. She did not intend to spend two years of her life getting the weight off at the approved rate of two pounds a week; she took the fast track and she had the willpower to stick to it, even when she was hospitalized with gastritis.

"What have you been eating?" the doctor said.

"Nothing."

"Nothing?"

"I've been fasting for two months."

"Good heavens! You've got to start eating."

But she did not. "I didn't care what that doctor said. I had a little diluted orange juice and went right back to not eating."

She began fasting in August and I didn't see her until November when we had a family gathering at our apartment in New York for Thanksgiving. When I opened the door, I saw this woman wearing a bright scarf around her neck. Her eyes looked familiar but I didn't recognize anything else about her. "Yvonne, it's me. It's Linda!" She had lost 120 pounds.

When she ended her fast, despite having exercised hard on a rowing machine, she had to have a tummy tuck and reduction mammoplasty to make her skin fit her new shape. With these procedures out of the way, she took two large steps: she married the man she'd been dating at NYU, Roger Braithwaite, a law school graduate, and she applied again to the army. This time the recruiter welcomed her. As for her wedding, she said, "Your wedding was gorgeous, Yvonne, but I'm not going through all that." Always a quiet person, she and Roger were quietly married by a justice of the peace.

That year of 1976–77, I was chief resident on the OB/GYN service at Roosevelt Hospital, loving it the way you love work that uses you fully and is triumphantly worth doing. Shearwood and I had been married for two years and had eased into the deepest kind of enriching contentment. Our time together was limited because he was as immersed in work at St. Luke's as I was at Roosevelt, absorbed in the curiously contradictory calling of orthopedic surgery, which can require both a delicate touch and brute strength as you wrest bones back into place or yank out a diseased hip socket that is to be replaced. But what time we did have together was filled with a kind of delighted tenderness. Sometimes I thought: *Now. Now I'm beginning to understand what Mommy and Daddy meant by love. It isn't a pounding heart and sighs and fervent embraces. It is this good, deep sense of being here together, come what may.*

On a winter's day in December, I was in the operating room at Roosevelt doing a vaginal hysterectomy when a message came that the medical center needed to get in touch with me and asked that I call as soon as I could. With the years of my residency at Roosevelt ending the following June, the chairman of the department had suggested that I consider continuing my studies to become a perinatologist, a specialist in maternal-fetal medicine and the problems surrounding complicated births.

"Because it's a new specialty, there are only a hundred or so perinatalogists in the country," he said, "and I think you'd be gifted at it."

I had asked Mommy what she thought, and she said, "I don't have the slightest idea what it is, Cookie, but if it means more education, do it." So I had applied to Columbia for a two-year postdoctoral fellowship in maternal-fetal medicine, and I presumed it was the medical center calling me now about some problem with the papers I had filled out. When I left the operating room, I asked the department secretary to get P & S on the line for me.

"No, it's Monmouth Medical Center in New Jersey that wants you. A Dr. Demaree."

Dr. Demaree was Mommy's doctor from the time of the kidney operation. When he came on the wire, he said, "Yvonne, your mother's in the hospital. Can you come?"

I paused just long enough to tell the department chairman where I was going, then raced to Long Branch. Daddy and Betty, who was an LPN at the hospital, were with Mommy, and Daddy told me what had happened. In the middle of the night, Mommy pounded Daddy awake. "Donald, take me to the hospital," she said frantically.

"She didn't say she was sick or anything?" I questioned Daddy.

"Just 'take me to the hospital.' Out of the blue. The middle of the night." His hands were shaking and he looked ill himself. "So I brought her here to the emergency room."

Betty had gotten a look at Mommy's chart. "Her pulse rate was up in the 120–130 range, her blood pressure was 240 over 120, her heart was wildly irregular. They've diagnosed it as a thyroid storm."

I was startled. "Mommy's never had any problem with her thyroid. She doesn't have a goiter."

"No, but that's what they're saying—Graves' disease of unknown origin."

Dr. Demaree confirmed this diagnosis when I saw him, adding that the storm had been quieted and Mommy's pulse rate brought down with medication, but the cardiac arrhythmia was continuing. "If her heart is still fibrillating by tomorrow, we'll have to cardiovert her."

I explained to Daddy that this meant they would administer a brief electric shock to the heart to restore a normal beat. "The body needs a strong heart," I told him, "and right now Mommy's heart is like a bowl of jelly."

Dr. Demaree had to obtain Mommy's consent to the procedure, and he warned her that, although complications were very, very rare, fibrillation could lead to blood clots, which, if jolted loose by the electric shock, could then travel to the lungs or brain. "But it's uncommon for anything to go wrong," he repeated.

I talked to Mommy and she was cheerful and feeling better. Linda was there, and Donna and Rita; Jeanette was on her way. Daddy seemed reassured, and after we persuaded him to join us for a quick sandwich in the coffee shop, the trembling in his hands disappeared and he told me to get on back to New York.

"Daddy, I gave Dr. Demaree my number and he'll beep me if you need me," I said as I kissed him goodbye.

The next day the call came. They had cardioverted Mommy. There was a clot, an embolism. It had gone to her brain. She had had a stroke.

I rushed back to the hospital. Mommy was paralyzed on her

right side. She could not talk. She drooled out of the side of her mouth. The rare complication had struck, with devastating consequences. I was too much of a doctor now to rail against fate, not to know that the unexpected can happen and it is no one's fault, but the human being inside me silently screamed. When the parents who have always been strong for you are suddenly incapacitated, one helpless with illness and the other helpless with worry and fright, it is as though someone has played cat's cradle with the world, turning it inside out, taking it from their hands and putting it into yours.

After several days Mommy began coming back. She could speak, although not clearly and only out of one side of her mouth. Physical therapy was started, and she could drag along for a yard or two with the support of a walker. All of us were at the hospital as often as we could be.

There was no one else there one afternoon when I arrived for a visit. "How're you doin', Mommy?"

"Oh, some better," she said, and gave me her hand to hold while we talked quietly. Her mind ranged back and she spoke of the Savoy Ballroom and this young boy asking her to dance and saying goodbye to Daddy on the subway steps when he went off to war and his mother ripping up her marriage certificate. I reminded her how she had been Daddy's hod carrier building the house and about our winning six times at the Apollo and the nights she'd be sewing our band dresses with the sewing machine needles breaking and popping sequins in her face and the times we had driven all night to make a date in Georgia or Kentucky and the cocoa she made when she woke me at three in the morning to study.

"You kids have been wonderful," she whispered.

All I could think of was a line from a movie. "Your children may be the miracle," I said, changing it to fit the truth of our family. "But you and Daddy are the miracle workers." She was lying with her head turned to one side and a tear came out from the corner of her eye and started down her cheek. I blotted it away. "I have to go back now, Mommy," I said gently. "I'm on call tonight. But I can phone and get someone to take my place if you want me to, if you need me here."

She said no, that I should go ahead. But then, as I started for the door, she suddenly said, "Honey, don't leave me."

"Sure, Mom. I'll call and change my schedule."

"No. No, I'm just being silly. You go on, honey. I'll be okay. I'll be fine."

In the night, another embolism lodged in her brain.

I talked on the telephone to the medical staff of the Intensive Care Unit, to the neurologist who was called in, and to Dr. Demaree, who warned me that the situation did not look good. With this new embolism, Mommy was totally incapacitated and they would have to put her on life support. "All right," I said. "Go ahead. Let's hope for the best."

I went down each day for the next three days. Mommy was on a respirator and she began to improve. She was clearly fighting and I was optimistic. But on the fourth day, a call came from Dr. Demaree. "Yvonne, I don't think your mother is going to make it."

"What do you mean, she's not going to make it? What does that mean?" I, as a physician saying that to a family member knew perfectly well what it meant. It meant "your mother is dying." But when it was my mother, I couldn't hear, I couldn't accept, I couldn't take in the meaning.

Understanding, Dr. Demaree said quietly, "She's not doing well. I want you to come as soon as you can." The same message went out to my sisters, and since they all lived in New Jersey, they were at the hospital before I got there. Linda met me coming down the corridor. "Mommy's not good, Yvonne. What do you think, should she be taken off life support?"

"I don't know. I have to talk to the doctor."

"He's already been here. He talked to Jeanette."

"Jeanette? What's he going to talk to Jeanette about?"

She shook her head. "He came out and said, 'I need to talk to you about your mother's condition. Which one of you is Dr. Thornton?' and Jeanette said that she was Dr. Thornton, so he started telling her about this count and that rate and this reflex and that sign. When he noticed a funny look on Jeanette's face, he stopped and said, 'What kind of a doctor are you?' She told him she had a doctorate in clinical psychology. 'Oh,' he said, 'then I need to speak with your other sister—the *real* doctor.'"

Rita had gone in search of Daddy, who was off finishing up a masonry job, Linda stayed with Donna, who was looking rocky, and Jeanette and I went into the Intensive Care Unit. We threaded our way past the IV poles and tubes and wires running to monitors, past the beeping machines and the busy screens, until we came to the foot of Mommy's bed. We hesitated there to see if she would open her eyes. In that moment we heard a high-pitched "Hmmmmm," and then "Code." Mommy's heart had stopped.

From her body came...it wasn't a mist; it was like looking through the trembling air that rises above a hot stove; a shimmer floated up and disappeared. I whispered, "Did you see what I just saw?" I knew from the whiteness of Jeanette's knuckles gripping the bed railing that she had indeed.

A split second later, doctors and nurses racing with the "crash cart" and shock paddles in hand converged on the bed. "No," we said, "it's too late. Leave her alone. It's over."

We went out to Donna and Linda. "Mommy's gone." It was all there was to say. It was Saturday, January 8, 1977. Our lives would never be the same.

The doctor asked for permission for an autopsy. "Not my Tass," Daddy cried over and over. "You're not going to cut my wife!"

The doctor appealed to me. "An autopsy would help us to know what happened, what caused your mother's death."

It had all happened so unexpectedly, the onset of the Graves' disease had been so sudden, that I understood his wish to discover if there had been other, unidentified factors involved. I put my arm around Daddy's shoulder and kneaded a knotted mass of muscle in his back. "Don't think of it as cutting Mommy," I said. "Think of it as the doctors trying to understand what happened."

"I don't want them to cut her. I can't see her being cut."

"All right, Daddy, I'll tell them no." I squeezed his arm and began to turn away.

"Do you think it's best, Cookie?"

"Not if you don't want it."

He thought a minute. "If it was something female, maybe they'd find something that could help you girls. All right, tell them it's okay."

The autopsy turned up nothing mysterious; the only finding was an enlarged thyroid.

I couldn't be angry. I couldn't blame God. I couldn't curse fate. I couldn't answer Daddy's anguished, "Why? Why? Why did it have to happen to my Tass?" All I could say was, "It was Mommy's time to go."

But that didn't lessen the loss, not for Daddy, not for me, not for Donna and Jeanette and Linda and Rita. It was not just that Mommy was our mother. She had played in the band with us. She was one of the Thornton Sisters. She was one of us, and we had taken her for granted. Because Daddy was the talker and she was the quiet one, had we given her enough credit? Had we given her enough love? I still wonder.

◆ 13 ◆

A Labor of Love

ON MOTHER'S DAY, the year before Mommy died, I telephoned a florist in Long Branch to have roses delivered to Mrs. Itasker Thornton. Mommy and Daddy were a devoted couple but not a demonstrative one; they never kissed or hugged in public, nor exchanged gifts, nor did Daddy ever bring home flowers, so I took it upon myself, after I grew up, to see that Mommy received a bouquet on her birthday and holidays. That last year I was on call at the hospital in New York and didn't get free until late in the day to telephone home.

"Hi, Mommy. Happy Mother's Day. How'd you like the flowers?"

She thought I was joking. "Those beautiful invisible ones?"

"You didn't get the roses I ordered?" She could hear the upset in my voice and tried to reassure me.

"Honey, I don't need roses. All I need is you to call once in a while to let me know how you're doing."

The florist apologized at length, saying they'd had so many orders that day that mine had somehow fallen through the cracks. Still, I felt that I had let Mommy down, like the time she waited in the attic at school for the promised check that never came.

I thought of this when we went to choose the flowers for Mommy's funeral. I asked the florist if he remembered me, that I was the person who had ordered flowers last Mother's Day that had never arrived. "Oh, I remember, Dr. Thornton. We felt so bad."

"Now the flowers are for her grave," I said harshly. I suppose I should not have made a point of it, but I couldn't get past the feeling that Mommy had somehow missed out all through her life

202

on the rewards she had earned with her patience, her fairness, her sweetness.

When it came time to make the funeral arrangements, we wondered if Daddy was going to be able to get through the ordeal. "I'll make it," he mumbled. "I got to do it for Tass. But you girls had better come with me 'cause I don't know about dresses and stuff."

The funeral parlor in Asbury Park was run by blacks for blacks, and the director kept assuring us we had come to the right place, telling us that, "A black person in a white funeral parlor, they don't know the makeup, they don't know what to do with the hair." He led us all downstairs to choose a casket.

"No pine box." Daddy was adamant about that. "My wife's got to have a lead casket so nothin' can get in at her."

"A pillow for her head?"

"A satin pillow."

"A coverlet, of course."

"Make that satin, too."

Back in his office, the funeral director suggested that we be seated while he figured the charges, but Daddy continued to stand, as though braced to bolt if it all became more than he could bear. There was an ancient adding machine on the funeral director's rolltop desk, and each time the director punched in a charge, he yanked the rasping handle of the machine down. "For the casket..." *Scrunch.* "For the pillow..." *Scrunch.* "For the coverlet..." *Scrunch.* "For the renting of the hall..." *Scrunch.*

With each *scrunch*, he ground down our hearts. The ugly sound was so disrespectful, so emphatically mercenary, so final, as though he were driving nails into the lid of Mommy's coffin.

"Being as how you've only got daughters," the director said over his shoulder to Daddy, "you'll need six pallbearers. Pallbearers..."

"Hold it!" The noise of the adding machine had sanded Daddy's nerves raw and he began to scream. "Nobody's touchin' my wife! Nobody's touchin' my wife! Nobody's touchin' my wife!"

"Daddy...Daddy, it's okay...."

"Nobody's touchin' Tass!"

"Uncle Reggie, Uncle Milford..."

"They never paid her no mind!"

"Daddy, somebody's got to carry the coffin."

"You'll do it! You girls!" The thought calmed him. "You'll carry your mother." We exchanged glances. A lead casket? The five of us plus Betty—the six of us carry a lead casket? Riding over our hesitation, Daddy insisted heedlessly, "Women can do anything."

"If that's what you want, Daddy..."

"That's what I want."

"Then we'll do it."

The funeral director raised his eyebrows but went on to his next item. "Who will lead the service? What's your minister's name?"

"No minister," ordered Daddy, and again he looked to us. "My girls'll take care of the service."

We wrote the eulogy that evening, all of us sitting at the round table, reliving the story of Mommy coming from West Virginia to New York, meeting Daddy at the Savoy Ballroom, having a baby alone when Daddy went off to the navy, raising us, helping Daddy build the house, overseeing our music lessons, making our clothes, playing in the band, and always, always insisting we study, and not only study but get A's. We titled her story, "A Suitcase Full of Dreams" because that is what Mommy came north with, and like so many other impoverished immigrants in a new world, she had made her dreams come true—but not for herself, for her children.

At the service, Jeanette read the eulogy, and after the eulogy I sang "Ave Maria," fighting off tears because there before me, in the open casket, lay Mommy, so lifelike but never to be alive again.

The date on which she was born was the date on which we buried her—January 12. She hadn't liked her birthday because she claimed that it always snowed on that date, and, true to form, at the cemetery a blanket of new sleet was on the ground and the wind swirled icy sharp crystals in our faces as we gathered at the back of the hearse to take our places, three on each side of the casket. The grave site was under a tree at the top of a hill. Could we carry the casket uphill through the snow without losing our footing and having it crash to the ground?

"Women can do anything," we whispered to reassure ourselves as we formed a circle to carry out our old ritual. We stacked our hands without touching, concentrated, broke away, and grasped the rails of the casket. The box was as heavy as our worst imaginings, but years of lifting amplifiers in and out of the car had so strengthened our arms, shoulders, and backs that, with Donna, Jeanette, and Betty on one side and Linda, Rita, and me on the other, we were able to go with measured steps up the hill to deliver Mommy to her final resting place. Only once did someone lose her footing. The rest of us braced ourselves; the slipping one steadied, and we went on. After we set the casket down at the graveside, we ranged ourselves around Daddy at the head of the grave and sang "The Lord's Prayer." And then it was over.

On the way home we drove in silence, mourning Mommy. We were almost back at the house before anyone spoke, and then it was to remark solemnly, "Gee, Daddy, you've got to go on a diet if you expect us to carry your butt up that hill."

It took us so by surprise that we started to laugh. And we laughed and laughed, Daddy more than anyone. It was the release we needed.

But the laughter was short-lived for Daddy. After we had all scattered again, he was miserably lonely, able to say little else when we called on the telephone but, "Oh, your mother's gone, oh, oh." Rita, in dental school in Philadelphia, became virtually a surrogate wife to him, traveling back and forth to cook his dinner, massage his feet, which were bothering him because of poor circulation due to his recently discovered diabetes, and just generally to be there to assuage his loneliness. It was a hard time for her as well as for Daddy, and none of the rest of us, except for Betty, was able to be of much help. The army transferred Linda to Germany, and after that to Korea. Donna had her husband and small child to look after. As chief resident, my time was not my own. And Jeanette was not only in practice as a counseling psychologist but, bored with administering IQ tests and stung by having been put down as "not a *real* doctor" at the time of Mommy's illness, she had decided to go to medical school and was making up the courses she needed to meet the entrance requirements. Jeanette was thirty-two years old by the time she started medical school at Boston University, which made Daddy snort that if she had listened to him in the first place she wouldn't have wasted ten years.

"All those detours. Running on empty. Wasting time you can't never get back."

"I know, Daddy," Jeanette agreed. "But I couldn't let you tell me what to do. I had to find myself."

"You could've found yourself a whole lot quicker goin' in a straight line."

He was easier on Rita than he was on Jeanette because he had counted so confidently on "Doc" to make it, to prove his point that his daughters could become doctors, that he was more cynical than pleased by this late decision of Jeanette's. As much as the decision vindicated him, it did not go far to repair the devastation he had experienced when she let him down originally. On the other hand, when Rita now decided to drop out of the University of Pennsylvania as she had dropped out of New York University, this elicited only an ordinary amount of disapproval and displeasure from Daddy. He ranted against her for not getting the job done but was inclined to excuse her because she was the youngest and had not had as long and as intensive an exposure to his teachings as we older ones. Having gone through Monmouth College in three years, it was patent that Rita was at least as bright, if not more so, as any of us, but she too was having trouble finding herself, and after two tries at dental school and one at medical school at the University of Medicine and Dentistry of New Jersey, she opted for a job teaching science at a private school. Of the five of us, Jeanette and Rita were the most independent and individual, while Linda and I were plodders and followers, but, as so famously happened in the story of the tortoise and the hare, we tortoises had plugged away and crossed the finish line first.

I was twenty-nine years old when Mommy died, and Shearwood and I had been married for three years. Concerning children, Mommy had said, not once but many times, "Your life as you know it is ended when you have kids, so do everything you want to do before you let yourself become pregnant. When it gets to the point where you can say, If God took me away right now, I've done most of everything I want to do, that's when it's okay to have kids." At twenty-nine, I was an M.D., the obstetrician I had wanted to be since I was eight years old, and I would be completing my residency in a few months. I decided it was okay now to have a child. Shearwood agreed.

But I couldn't seem to get pregnant. Shearwood's younger brother, Ricky, married a month before we were in 1974, had a daughter born in 1976. Elaine, Ricky's wife, taunted me on the telephone from Gary, Indiana. "Oh, you intelligent women, you study all your eggs away." That was silly, but when she sneered, "Well, you wanted to be a doctor," implying that if I wasn't willing to stay home and be a traditional wife to my husband, not being able to get pregnant was the consequence, I began to wonder if she was right. It got so I cried every month and every time I delivered a baby.

Shearwood, always the quiet voice of reason, scouted my fears. "You're a resident. I'm a resident. You're on call every other night. I'm on call every other night. When do we have time? Don't worry about it." I finished my residency and left the hectic world of the hospital to return to Columbia and enter the calmer world of research as a Fellow in maternal/fetal medicine. The very next month I became pregnant. Shearwood said, "See, I told you that as soon as you relaxed, it would happen."

For more than four years I had watched over, cared for, studied, and delivered pregnant women. But studying pregnancy and being pregnant are two entirely different matters, I discovered. I had genuinely sympathized with my patients' morning sickness and their aches and pains, but now I shared them. I realized that how you view yourself and how others view you drastically changes when you're pregnant. All your hopes, fears, and emotions seem to be distilled down to a single thought: *I hope my baby is all right.* Your concerns are about someone you've never even met. The bonding process has begun.

One day when I was about five months pregnant, I thought I felt the baby move. This was what I'd been waiting for, the moment all my patients spoke about reverently. Slowly, I lay down on the couch in our apartment, barely breathing so as not to confuse any other natural occurrence with the baby's movement. Sure enough, I felt it! It wasn't a kick as I had expected and as my patients and the textbooks described it. It was more like holding a fluttering butterfly in my cupped hands. It was an ecstatic experience. I felt life. I felt *my* baby. I couldn't wait to share it with Shearwood.

"Guess what!" I said as he came through the door that evening. "I think I felt the baby move!"

He looked down at me, pondered for a moment, and in a measured clinical tone asked, "Are you sure it's not gas?"

I was crushed. How could he be so unemotional about the most exciting happening in my life? I realized then what a chasm there can be between men and women. Men are at a distance from an experience central to a woman's existence.

As a medical student, resident, and now a Fellow, I had witnessed time and again what we referred to as the hospital jinx: a doctor, doctor's wife, or a nurse—someone closely connected with the hospital—came in for a simple procedure and ended up with a totally unexpected, life-threatening complication. Determined that this was not going to happen to me, I opted to go for Lamaze training so that I'd be able to get through labor without drugs or anesthesia. Shearwood balked at accompanying me, fearing he'd feel awkward and out of place, but I insisted and he quickly became a convert to the method. After six weeks of training, in the breathing exercises for me and as coach for him, we were as fine-tuned as soldiers ready for battle.

Time went by. And went by. I was one week, two weeks, three weeks overdue. The stretch marks on my tummy proliferated like cracks on a desert floor. Daddy called and joked, "Listen, turn the Pampers over to me. I can use them to polish my car." I stopped answering the phone because I didn't want to hear one more person sound incredulous over the fact that I hadn't delivered yet.

One Tuesday evening I was watching television and had just polished off a giant Blimpie submarine—over Shearwood's objections—when the pain struck. At first, I thought it was indigestion in just retribution for the sandwich, but the pain kept coming on and coming on, as unrelenting as a runaway locomotive. Soon it felt like a stun gun of fifty thousand volts being applied to my body every ten minutes, then eight minutes, then five minutes.

By six o'clock the next morning I was exhausted, having sat up through the night, all the while puffing in 4/4 time to the tune of "Yankee Doodle" in proper Lamaze style. I threw a shoe at Shearwood to wake him because the pains were so bad I couldn't get up from the chair. I asked him to call Dr. Bowe, my obstetrician. He said, "Why don't we wait, honey, until I can time the contractions so I can tell Dr. Bowe the precise intervals between them." I hurled the other shoe and threatened him with decapitation if he didn't call instantly.

It was my professional opinion that dilation must have progressed to at least six or seven centimeters out of a possible ten because of the amount of pain I had endured over the last twelve hours. Alas, upon arrival at the hospital, I proved to be at three centimeters. I couldn't believe it. Only *three*. I felt like the victim of a cruel joke.

Throughout the day, although it scarcely seemed possible, the contractions became even more intense. At one point, I decided I was having an out-of-body experience as I retreated to a corner of the room and watched this woman lying in bed being tortured every two or three minutes. Dr. Bowe held my hand and kept saying, "Roll with it, Yvonne." Shearwood did everything he could to support and encourage me. I was in agony, and still, not wanting anything to go wrong, I held out against epidural anesthesia, although I finally asked for and was given a small amount of Demerol.

At six o'clock that night, Dr. Bowe pronounced me fully dilated and gave me permission to push. From that point on, it usually takes another hour for delivery of a first baby, but I told Dr. Bowe not to go away, that I intended to get this over with. At 6:22 P.M. the baby was born. Without complications.

A boy, weighing in at 8 pounds, 15 ounces, and except for his little cone-shaped head because of all that labor, the most precious small creature I had ever seen. We named him Shearwood McClelland III, after his father and grandfather, and promptly called him Woody.

With the ordeal over, I luxuriated in the care and attention I received because I was a Fellow at the hospital. I had a large room with a spectacular view of the Hudson all to myself in the Harkness Pavilion, the wing for private patients in the same Presbyterian Hospital where I had been born. I was not unaware of the irony that thirty years earlier Mommy had been in a multibed ward while here was I in royal accommodations. But Mommy would have been the first to revel in the contrast, taking it as proof of how far and fast it is possible to rise in the world if you have the wit to value education. My only regret was that she wasn't there to look down at her first grandson as he lay in my arms, to take hold of his tiny fists and kiss him gently to welcome him into the world.

I took it for granted that Daddy would show up at the hospital as soon as he heard the news, pleased, proud, and excited that at last there was a boy in the family. He didn't come the next day or any other day. He merely said over the phone, "Are you okay? Is the baby okay? Fine." And on the rare occasions after that when he came to the apartment to visit, he treated Woody in the same casually affectionate fashion he responded to neighborhood kids in Long Branch. He would pick him up and bounce him on his knee, but that was just because he loved kids, not because of any special grandfatherly interest or attachment. He never brought

Woody a toy or a gift, never in the years after that sent him a birthday card.

I think, when Daddy gave me away that day in Riverside Church, he experienced it as quite literally giving me away to another man. No matter that he liked Shearwood, that he knew Shearwood would be a good husband for me and a good provider; on some unconscious level where ego and testosterone and territorialism mingle, he felt I had chosen Shearwood over him and in doing so had defected like a spy going over to the enemy. He had had his daughters so long in his life—we had been little pieces of clay that were his to mold—that he could not willingly release us, and when we left him to be with another man, it did not seem to him like a natural part of growing up but like a treasonable act. With his sons-in-law—Donna's Willis, Betty's Hubert, Linda's Roger, and my Shearwood, he was correct and polite but not warm, not friendly with them for their own sakes; not one of them ever called him anything but Mr. Thornton.

When I spoke of his lack of interest in Woody, Daddy shrugged. "He's yours and Shearwood's."

"But, Daddy he's also your grandson."

"Yeah, but that's not important. You're the ones who'll raise him up. I didn't want my parents interferin' in the raisin' of my kids and I ain't gonna interfere in the raisin' of yours."

Some men build businesses from the ground up. Some fashion paintings where before there was blank canvas, write books where before there was blank paper, make movies where before there was blank film, erect buildings where before there were empty lots. Daddy raised children. They were his blank paper, canvas, film, landscape, and like any creative person, the material had to be his own, to be shaped single-mindedly to his vision.

It was about this time that Daddy suffered a second blow, one that did not compare with losing Mommy but, like that incalculable loss, left him floundering and aimless. For thirty years he had worked at Fort Monmouth in menial capacities: as a laborer, as a janitor, in the motor pool. When offered promotions to more skilled work, he had refused the offers because the greater effort and energy involved might interfere with his holding down a second eight-hour job, while the increase in hourly pay would in no way match the money he could make on a second job.

One day he was called in and told that his current janitorial job was being abolished and that he would be transferred to be a laborer in the supply depot. He had once, briefly, put in some time in the depot and he knew the low-life civilians who staffed it to be bigots. He told the personnel officer, "Where you're sending me ain't gonna do nothin' but get me upset. If I was a young guy, I would try to put up with it. But I'm not young and I've put up with enough." He requested janitorial work elsewhere on the base or transfer to another kind of work, like running a copier or cataloging, saying he didn't care if it meant a downgrade and less money. "If you send me to the warehouse, I'm the one they'll have picking up the boxes, opening them, putting the stuff on the shelves, walking miles every day, and before I let myself get pushed around like that, I'll retire. I don't want to retire, but if I've got to go down there, I can't accept it, I can't put up with it, I'll bow out."

Bow out he did and was now doubly miserable: no Tass, no job to go to. When people tried to console him by saying he was in the enviable position of being able to do anything he wanted to, he answered flatly: "I've already done what I wanted to do. I looked after my kids and my wife. They depended on me and it was a challenge. I love a challenge, and now I ain't got a challenge no more."

To a suggestion that he might want to travel, he replied, "I took a vacation once for five days, and the thing that really hurt me and ruined the vacation was that I couldn't get it out of my mind that here I was, doin' nothin' when I could have accomplished so much in those five days, I could have got a step ahead."

Rita urged him to visit Linda in Europe. He vetoed that idea. "You go to Europe," he said. "You sit in a French house, you listen to French music, you eat some French pastry, you go back home. Once you realize that no matter where you go, you got to come back home, you know what you should do—stay home and eat French pastry."

What he did instead of vacationing or lazing around was to look for other work. He linked up with a man who had bought some dilapidated houses in Asbury Park that he wanted made over into apartments, and Daddy contracted to do the job single-handedly. He went to work gutting one house at a time, taking up floors and knocking out walls. He installed all new windows, walls, and floors; made kitchens, bathrooms, and closets; and grew happier.

"It's a funny thing," he commented, "but after working so hard for so many years, I can't stop. If I wake up in the morning and don't know where I'm going, I feel like I'm going crazy. And I do believe I would go crazy if I didn't have something to do."

For a feature story for Father's Day, a newspaper reporter interviewed Daddy about his dream of raising his five daughters to be doctors. Daddy spoke about working two and three jobs for twenty-five years and driving, sometimes hundreds of miles, on the weekends to make a band date, but then he reflected: "I think the biggest of all my hardships, of all the things I been through, is having my children not need me anymore. Some people can say about their kids, 'Oh, the hell with them,' but my kids, they're my children as long as I live. My life has been my children. They're still babies to me."

"But, Mr. Thornton..." the interviewer said.

"Yeah, I know," Daddy interrupted. "Kids grow up. I accept that but I don't have to like it. How can children that parents love so much drift away from them?"

"It's the way of the world."

He shook his head sadly. "The worst thing about marrying young is that you have a longer time to be lonely when your children are gone."

This was a very small part of the interview. Mostly Daddy talked about the music lessons and traveling to New York to make records so we could hear ourselves getting better, playing at the Apollo and the Brooklyn Fox, and then at colleges and debutante balls, and our studying in the car while he drove. Only at the end, when the interviewer was expressing admiration for what Daddy and his daughters had been able to accomplish, did he speak of his yearning to have it all to do over again. Another man might have hidden his loneliness but Daddy had the courage to be himself and transparent.

While he was working in Asbury the next summer, a young boy began hanging around, offering to fetch a tool Daddy needed or help hold Sheetrock in place until Daddy could anchor it with nails. Daddy began to look forward to seeing him each morning. He would be waiting for Daddy in front of one of the houses to help him carry his tools in, and when Daddy had to go to the lumberyard or hardware store for supplies, the boy went along and offered his advice, saying, "Mr. Thornton, let's get this. I think we're going to need it." While they worked, Daddy talked to him about life and the world like he'd talked to us, telling him stories about people and incidents and drawing morals from them.

Daddy regretted that he didn't have the lad with him all the time because, he said, "He's all right with me, but as soon as he goes home, his mind is twisted into a different kind of atmosphere, and when I see him again the next morning, he's lost some of the things he grasped the day before." And when the boy went back to school in the fall, Daddy lost him altogether, which set him to thinking. "Maybe I'll adopt another three kids," he ruminated, sounding out the idea with one or another of us when we called. "Maybe three brothers."

But when he did start over, it was with just one boy and the story did not have a happy ending.

◆ 14 ◆

Navy Blue and Black

BY 1979, SHEARWOOD HAD FINISHED HIS INTERNSHIP and residency in orthopedic surgery and I had completed my fellowship in maternal/fetal medicine. I had an offer to become an assistant professor and join the staff at a teaching hospital on Long Island, and I asked Shearwood what he had in mind to do.

"I want to get more experience working with trauma," he said. "I want to see more bones."

"Shearwood, you've been looking at bones for years. We have a new baby. You should be thinking about starting a private practice or getting on staff at a hospital."

He gave me a sidelong look, not sure how I would take what he was about to say. "I'll tell you what I think we both should do, Yvonne. What I think we should do is go into the military."

"What!"

"They're looking for black people. Besides which, the country has given us an opportunity to succeed and we should pay back what we've been given."

I wasn't sure that what we had been given was anything more than the same opportunities anybody who works hard is entitled to. But that was beside the point. "First of all," I said, "the military is with guns and killing people. I'm an obstetrician. I deliver babies. What am I going to do in the military?"

"You can come in as my dependent."

"I'm not going anywhere as anybody's dependent!"

"Don't get excited, Yvonne. Why don't we just look into it?"

I didn't like the idea. I didn't like it at all. Linda was in the military and they had shipped her to Europe and Korea. What if they separated Shearwood and me? I told him, "Shearwood, okay,

215

we'll look into it, but if it doesn't sound good, I'm taking the position on Long Island. Agreed?"

He agreed, and we went to a navy recruiting office—navy because, Shearwood reasoned, the army was like the dregs, the marines were heavy into killing people, and air force bases were on vast wastelands, while naval bases were on the water at attractive places like Newport and San Diego. We presented ourselves to the recruiter: two Ivy League–trained physicians volunteering to enter the service. The recruiter could not have been more surprised—or pleased, because all the physicians who opted out of the Vietnam war in order to complete their residency training under the Berry plan were now finishing up the years of service they owed the government and were returning to civilian life, leaving the military with a shortage of physicians. Also, he said, we had specialties that were in demand.

"Obstetrics?" I said, not sure I'd heard right.

"There are sixty thousand babies born in the military each year. Men come home from a six-month tour of duty abroad and..."

"Nine months later..."

"Boom."

"A baby boom."

"Right."

I could tell he wanted me to join up even more than Shearwood, so I figured we were in the driver's seat. "We'll think about it," I offered, "if we can go somewhere nice and posh, like Bethesda, somewhere affiliated with a medical school or a large teaching hospital."

"We can't give you any guarantees."

"In that case, we're not coming in," I announced.

It turned out that we could get a guarantee after all. Word came that we would be stationed at Bethesda. But we still didn't sign any papers because we decided to drive down and take a look at the place first. Bethesda is in Maryland, just outside of Washington, D.C., and it is the location of the National Institutes of Health and the National Library of Medicine, as well as the

National Naval Medical Center. It looked wonderful to us. And Shearwood looked wonderful to the chairman of the orthopedic department, who pumped his hand and enthused when he heard Shearwood might sign up: "Oh, my goodness, this is great. Let me take you around, son."

I laughed when I heard about his reception. "Boy, they must really be hard up if they're hugging you, Shearwood," I said, and indeed it proved to be that the navy had only forty orthopedic surgeons for the entire fleet, and what with broken legs and slipped disks, that wasn't very many.

So, Shearwood was all set, but I reminded him that we had made a bargain: if the chief of obstetrics didn't want me, then we weren't going in. "Right," he agreed, "but they'll be as anxious to have you as they are me."

I was interviewed by a Dr. Knab, chairman of the OB/GYN department and captain in the Naval Medical Corps. I sensed immediately that the man did not like me. He looked through my curriculum vitae and commented that it was most impressive. Then he settled back in his armchair, tented his fingers, and said, "But, unfortunately, Dr. Thornton, we don't need you."

"That's strange," I said. "I've just finished my fellowship in maternal/fetal medicine and there are fewer than one hundred such specialists in the whole country. There can't be too many here."

"Be that as it may, I can only thank you for coming to see me and repeat that the navy has no need of you."

Thank you, Knab, old boy, I said to myself as I left his office. *I didn't want to be in the military anyway. Just let me get out of here*.

"Pack up the car, Shearwood," I said when I got back to the hotel. "You're going to have to find a job in New York."

"Why? Dr. Slemmons loved me."

"Yeah, but Dr. Knab didn't love me. He says there's no room for me here."

Shearwood was disappointed, but he dutifully called Dr. Slemmons. "There's a Dr. Knab in the OB/GYN department who says there's no room for my wife, and my wife and I agreed that if we couldn't come in together, we wouldn't come at all."

"Hold on," Dr. Slemmons told him. "Let me look into it."

In almost no time at all, Dr. Knab was on the phone, saying smoothly that he had discovered one of the maternal/fetal specialists was about to be transferred to Portsmouth and so there was an opening for me after all.

"Oh, really? Are you sure?"

"Certainly. Any time you'd like to come, the position is here for you."

Someone else might have hesitated to go to work for a man who didn't like her and hadn't wanted her there, but I knew how eager Shearwood was to be at Bethesda and, besides, having to prove myself to men like Dr. Knab was nothing new to me. Like the others, he would be waiting for me to fail, which meant that I had to make very sure not to. I could never do less than my best. I had to have my wits about me always and take infinite pains with every procedure and every operation. Rather than making me tense, though, the pressure led me to be very good at what I did and, like Daddy, I enjoyed the challenge.

Dr. Knab, despite my credentials, obviously didn't believe that I was good. I had read in his eyes what he was thinking: "Oh, I had one like you taking care of me when I was a baby." Such men hate it because they can't treat you like a servant; they have to treat you as an equal on the surface but underneath they are seething. As a black woman all you can do is never give them any cause to say you're belligerent or that you're not professional; you just basically do your work and accept the fact that you are not welcome, merely tolerated.

It was July 1979 when we went into the military, and in September I discovered I was pregnant again. I informed Dr. Knab, who did not trouble to hide his annoyance. I was the only female on the attending staff in the department, and my pregnancy simply served to affirm his opinion that women in medicine were a nuisance because they had babies and disrupted the status quo. I assured Dr. Knab that being pregnant wouldn't interfere with my carrying out my duties, that the baby was due June 7 when I would be taking my month's vacation in any event.

Also at the end of that month, on June 30, I would be taking my specialty board examination in maternal/fetal medicine. In all, there were four examinations: written and oral exams in my basic specialty, obstetrics and gynecology, and written and oral exams in my subspecialty of maternal/fetal medicine; plus a postdoctoral thesis to be written, published, and defended as part of the oral examination.

By the time we went into the service in July, I had already passed my written exam in OB/GYN and my thesis was in its final stages of preparation. The oral exam was being given in November, which meant that all that fall, while getting accustomed to being in the service, I was studying furiously and at the same time suffering from such morning sickness that my dearest wish was that someone would take me out in the backyard and shoot me. The morning sickness hadn't in the least abated by November when I flew to Chicago for the exam, and a more wretched—and retching—person had never stood before the board of examiners, all of whom were male and were rumored never to pass female candidates if they could possibly find an excuse not to. I took as many antinausea pills as I dared, but even so...

When they said, "Dr. Thornton, give us a differential diagnosis on the basis of these slides," I had to say, "Excuse me, I have a touch of flu," and scurry to the bathroom.

I staggered back. "Are you all right?" the chief examiner asked, staring at the large drops of perspiration I had to keep wiping away. "Do you want to make this an incomplete and come back next year?"

"No, sir, I can do it. Just give me some time. I have this flu...." I excused myself again, staggered back again, glad of my black skin so they couldn't see how green I was. After that I was able to stay in the room, albeit feeling like a cat who has swallowed a poisoned mouse. I didn't care if I passed or failed; I just prayed for the ordeal to be over.

Days later, back in Bethesda, Dr. Knab nodded at me in the

hall. "You passed," he said, in a peevish tone that implied he wished I hadn't so he would have that failure to hold over my head. The occasion called for fireworks shooting off, or at least for a cheer or two, because even though you have completed all your training, if you're not board-certified, you haven't managed to catch the brass ring. But it was just, "You passed," from Dr. Knab, "Thanks," from me, and we continued on our ways. I wrote a little note in red ink to Shearwood, who was in the midst of a surgical procedure, and sent it into the operating theater: "Don't forget the milk and eggs on your way home, and by the way I PASSED MY BOARDS!" To this day, Shearwood carries the note in his wallet.

The morning sickness subsided and I set to work studying for the written board examination in June. As many as forty-five percent of candidates fail the boards each year, and I didn't intend to be among their number. Every night I set the alarm for 2:00 A.M., studied until 6:00 A.M., then went off to the hospital to see patients and operate. In the evening I came home and made dinner, studied some more, and fell into bed. If we hadn't had an angel named Bev Thomas to look after Woody, I don't know what I would have done.

One evening Shearwood arrived home with the news that, as of January 1, he was being sent to Okinawa for three months. "Okinawa!" I screamed. "I'm four months pregnant, we've got a small child, and you're going to leave me? Tell them you're not going!"

"Yvonne, we're in the military. I can't tell them I'm not going. They'd send me to Leavenworth."

"You got me into this and you're leaving in January for the South Pacific—twelve thousand miles away!"

"I'll be back in three months."

"Don't bother coming back!" I stormed, which was how upset I was.

But, of course, when December 31 came and I drove him to the airport, we were both tearful. It would be the first time we'd ever really been apart since medical school. As I held Woody in my arms and watched Shearwood go through the gate, I thought: *This is how Mommy must have felt when Daddy disappeared down the subway steps on his way to the war.* Woody picked up on my desolate feeling and began to cry. "Here, honey, have a biscuit," I said, which cheered him up but my cheeks were wet all the way home.

When we got back to the house, the telephone was ringing. It was Shearwood. A flap had fallen off the plane and the passengers had been returned to the terminal to wait until it was fixed. I was sorry for Shearwood's sake that he had hours of idleness ahead, but, oh, it was as reassuring as warm milk just to hear his voice one more time.

After he finally arrived in Okinawa, we talked every night, at first using the military's system of hopping from station to station for free, but that could take as much as three hours to get a call through, so we gave up on that and called person-to-person and ran up bills of two thousand dollars a month. I didn't care. I had to hear his voice. I had to say, "Shearwood, it's really bad," and hear him say back, "You can make it, Yvonne."

I wasn't at all sure I could. That February, Maryland had the worst snowstorm on record. While the snow was still falling, the hospital called; a patient had been transferred to Bethesda with preeclampsia and needed to be delivered. It was nine o'clock at night. I had to get there. Five months pregnant, I shoveled and shoveled so I could get the car out of the driveway. The baby in my belly was kicking and kicking. "Oh, Lord," I moaned, "I'm going into preterm labor."

Bev, struggling through snow and black ice, arrived to look after Woody. I climbed into the car. It wouldn't start. I roused a neighbor and asked him to drive me to the hospital. At the hospital there was an air of crisis: "It's twins and her blood pressure is 210/120."

"Stabilize her. We'll do an immediate cesarean section under general anesthesia," I ordered. "Let's go."

The anesthesiologist said, "I'm not going to give her a general. I want to use an epidural."

"Do you know how long it takes to get going with an epidural? I'm the responsible physician here. She needs to have a general. Put her out now so we can deliver these babies."

"I'm going to put in an epidural."

I stared at him, then ordered, "Get your superior in here."

His superior arrived, and when he saw me, he got that look on his face. "I don't know whether or not you're even *qualified* to do a cesarean section," he said. "I have to assume you are or your boss wouldn't have sent you down here. Nevertheless, we're going to do this the way *we* want to do it."

Thirty minutes went by as they tried to get the epidural into the woman's spine. Forty-five minutes. By now it was obvious even to them that time had run out. They gave up and administered a general anesthetic, and I delivered the twins at one o'clock in the morning.

I arrived back home crying and raging. *I assume you know what you're doing.* If I'd been a man, he wouldn't have talked to me like that. If I'd been white, he wouldn't have questioned my ability to do what was right for my patient. I tossed and turned, unable to sleep. I got out of bed and drafted letters to the Bureau of Medicine and Surgery, the Surgeon General of the Navy, and to the commanding officer of the National Naval Medical Center, letters that outlined what had happened. Each letter ended with: "Now you know why not many black people come into the navy, especially black officers, because we are treated with such disdain." In the morning I put the letters in the interoffice mail.

Almost immediately I received a call from Admiral Horgan, the commanding officer of the base. "Dr. Thornton, can you come to my office?"

"Yes, sir. Will ten o'clock be all right, after morning rounds?"

"That'll be fine."

At nine o'clock, Dr. Knab came in search of me. "What happened last night?" he demanded. I outlined the facts. "The next time something like this goes on, you are to call me."

"At one o'clock in the morning?"

"Well, then, next time write this kind of letter to me. This is a real fan-hitter."

"Sir, I was the attending physician of record, and it was the chairman of the anesthesia department who was talking to me. My understanding is that the only person who can reprimand the man is the base commander, that you can't do anything because he's not in your department."

"That's right. But, nevertheless, next time come to me first."

"Yes, sir."

Nothing was more predictable than that if I'd gone to Knab, he would have said, "Okay, I'll take it from here," and that would have been the end of it; my hands would have been tied because I then wouldn't dare go over his head, and the arrogant actions that jeopardized the health of my patient would have gone unaddressed. Instead, I had acted on advice my mother had long ago given me: "Things trickle down but they never trickle up, Cookie, so start at the top when you've got a complaint."

The admiral was a different story from Dr. Knab. "I will not put up with this sort of thing at the medical center," he said unequivocally, then added a personal note of understanding. "I know the aggravation my mother went through in trying to establish the right of women to practice medicine and be treated professionally." He got up to escort me to the door of his office and patted me on the shoulder. "Not to worry, Dr. Thornton," he said. "What you did was right and proper. If you have any other problems, come and see me."

Both the Bureau of Medicine and Surgery and the Surgeon General of the Navy wrote me letters of apology after an investigation of the incident, and the chairman of the anesthesiology department, who had been slated for promotion to admiral, was denied his promotion and was asked to leave the National Naval Medical Center. After that, after I had gone to the top as Mommy had taught me "because the top person can win your battles for you," I had no further problems at Bethesda.

My problems were with studying for the boards and being

pregnant and snow and ice and praying to God that I wouldn't fall and kill myself and the baby and being on call and Bev having to go home in the evenings to look after her own child and having a husband who was just a voice over the phone saying, "It's really warm here in the Pacific."

"I don't want to hear how it is over there!"

"I'll bring you back something."

"Don't bring me anything!"

In April Shearwood arrived home, walking off the plane with the uncertain diffidence of a puppy who is anticipating a major scolding. But I was too glad to see him to lash him with too many words—until, that is, we heard about another officer who had just come into the navy and who had refused to go overseas because his wife was pregnant and he wanted to be with her. Then I was furious all over again.

June came and I started on my month's vacation. The baby, due on the seventh of the month, did not put in an appearance. Woody had been eighteen days late so I wasn't too surprised that I was running over, but the board exam was on the thirtieth and I was consumed with anxiety to have the baby born and be back to normal well in advance of that date. The fifteenth of June came and went. I couldn't study for my boards at home because even with Bev there to look after two-year-old Woody, he'd search the house crying, "Mommy!" if he suspected I was around. Instead, I went to the hospital and studied in the library. But the decibel level began to rise there and Shearwood suggested, "There's a little conference room in the back of the orthopedic department. Nobody will bother you there and I can pick you up each day and drive you home."

The baby still hadn't arrived by the twenty-sixth of June. I was to take the exam on Monday, the thirtieth. By Friday, the twenty-seventh, I was in despair. If I went into labor on Monday, all the studying would have been for nothing; I'd have it all to do over again the next year. If I went into labor on Sunday, maybe I could drag myself to the exam, which was being given at the medical school on the campus of the naval hospital at Bethesda. But even if I managed to get there, in all probability I would flunk the exam. As I sat there alone in that little conference room on Friday, I began to cry, and with no one there to hear me, I let out a long wail of anguish.

A strange yet soothing voice came from behind me. *Why are you crying? Have I ever forsaken you?*

I wheeled around to see who had come into the room. There was no one there.

Oh, my God, am I going crazy? My mind leaped back to the moment when Mommy died and the vapor rose from her body. I hadn't known how to explain that. I didn't know how to explain this.

But my despair had vanished. A feeling of calm crept over me. A little bit of hope seeped into my soul. "Let me just get back to studying," I said to myself, "and perhaps things will work out."

The next morning, Saturday morning, I awakened with a burning sensation in the pit of my stomach and said to Shearwood that I seemed to have some indigestion. "I don't think so," he said. "I think you may be in labor."

"It's indigestion! What do *you* know? I'm the obstetrician," I told him. "I'll take some Mylanta." I got up, dressed, and fed Woody his breakfast. Every time I grimaced, Shearwood looked at his watch.

"Let me just call Dr. Knab," he said. "Just to be on the safe side."

"It's not even painful yet. It's not contractions. You'll make me look like a fool."

"You can come home again if it's nothing."

We argued back and forth, and Shearwood won. Thank heavens, because by the time he hung up the phone the contractions were hitting me left and right. Bev arrived to look after Woody, and as Shearwood and I hurried to the car for the drive to the hospital, the contractions suddenly went from every fifteen minutes to every three minutes.

"Go around back of the hospital," I gasped. "I don't think I'll make it if we go in the front." I was remembering when I was eight and the baby was born in the elevator.

We arrived in the labor and delivery suite at 12:00 noon. At 12:22 Kimberly Itaska McClelland was born, weighing eight pounds, eight ounces. If I'd hesitated any longer at home, she would have been born in the car or on the stairs, which would have been pretty embarrassing for a specialist in maternal/fetal medicine. With Woody I had been in labor for twenty-three hours. Textbooks decree that the second baby arrives in half the time of the first, which meant that I should have had twelve hours to get to the hospital. In fact, I had about twelve minutes, proving, as I had long suspected, that the only thing certain about obstetrics is that you cannot be certain about anything.

After my episiotomy incision had been stitched up and I was settled in bed in a private room, I said, "Shearwood, if you'll fetch my books for me, dear, I'll just get on with my studying."

The nurse asked, "Do you want rooming in? Are you breastfeeding?"

The answer was no to both. "Please take my baby to the nursery. As much as I'd love to hold her, I've got to study."

The board exam started at 12:00 noon on Monday. Shearwood arrived to escort me across the campus. Said the navy nurse on the floor, "You're not going anywhere. You could have a postpartum hemorrhage. I cannot allow this."

"I'm going to take my boards. It's just across the way at the medical school. I'll be back in four hours. I'll take full responsibility."

"I'll have to call Dr. Knab."

If Dr. Knab had refused permission for me to leave, I think I would have knocked the woman down and stepped over her fallen body to get to that exam. My walk to the medical school on Shearwood's arm was an exceedingly gingerly excursion on account of the episiotomy stitches, and I still had the hospital bracelet on my arm when he left me at the door of the examination room. "Are you sure you're all right?" he asked worriedly.

"I have to be all right. It's only four hours and then it will all be over."

But what a four hours, sitting on a wooden seat with those stitches in my bottom. I summoned up Daddy's phrase, as I had done for final exams at Monmouth College: "You do what you got to do," and at the end of the four hours I was satisfied that I had made a good job of it, that I would not be among the contingent who failed. Sure enough, when the letter came saying I had passed, it contained the additional note that I had scored among the top 1 percent of all those taking the test.

I didn't forget, ever, that my parents had had a lot more struggles than I had, but that first year in the navy was tough for me, juggling one baby, pregnant with another, working with people who despised the color of my skin, studying for my boards, Shearwood in Okinawa, shoveling snow to make it to the hospital to deliver babies, giving birth to my own baby. When it was over, I exulted: "I am woman! Hear me roar!"

I decided that Daddy was right: there is nothing women can't do, up to and including whatever it takes to get the job done.

◆ 15 ◆

Civilians and Civility

"I SHOULD GET ANOTHER BATCH OF KIDS," Daddy kept saying. "I need another batch of kids."

"So, what are you waiting for?" we encouraged him. "Get some kids from the state. Be a foster parent. Get yourself three or four more girls and bring them up like you did us."

"No, no girls. This time I'm gonna get me a boy." Daddy's voice softened when he said this and his eyes grew dreamy, as though girls were okay, but a son...that was different. The first time around he had played the hand he was dealt, but this time he was doing the dealing and he intended to deal himself a boy.

I said to him, "Daddy, don't you think that when you talk like that you're kind of saying that Mommy wasn't good enough to give you a son and we were a disappointment to you because we were girls?"

I was trying to be reasonably tactful, but I did want him to sense our resentment that he was, in effect, downgrading his daughters, making us feel second-class and inadequate. Each of us had experienced over and over the world's dismissive view of women, and now our own father, who had taught us to be so good at what we did that we could not be shoved aside, was doing the same thing, indicating that a male has value simply by virtue of his maleness while women have to earn and re-earn every scrap of respect they get.

He brushed aside our resentment. "I don't want to hear it, Cookie. I ain't sayin' nothin' about what's been. I'm sayin' what's gonna be, and it's gonna be a boy."

The boy was Alfred, a fourteen-year-old who had already been in several foster homes and had been moved out and on

228

because he was wild. Wildness was all right with Daddy; he wanted a tough case because he figured that was a child he could make a real difference with. He started right in disciplining Alfred. Soon after Alfred arrived, he and Daddy were shopping in the grocery store together and Daddy, selecting potatoes from a bin, turned and saw Alfred eating a grape. Alfred described what happened.

"Your father whacked me across the face so hard that the grape was, like, hanging out of my mouth. He said, 'You haven't paid for it, have you?' I told him I pick up stuff all the time, and he tells me, 'If you haven't paid for it, it's stealin'. Don't ever do that again.'" Alfred laughed. "And I don't guess I'm about to, at least not when he's around, that's for sure."

Daddy said, "I'm teachin' Alfred manners and proper countenance, which nobody bothered him about before." At the same time, he was teaching him masonry and Alfred worked side by side with him on some of his jobs. "Finally," Daddy bragged, "finally I've got me a son." So bewitched was Daddy by the satisfactions of this that before very long Alfred discovered he could get around Daddy quite easily. With a bit of care and subtlety and a show of loving attention, he chivied Daddy into buying him silk underwear, handsomely tailored suits, and the most expensive shoes from the best stores. The trap Daddy had excoriated women for falling into of buying men clothes because they wanted the guy to look nice when they went out together, he now succumbed to himself. Even more to the point, however, was the fact that, for fear of alienating Alfred, he eased off giving him unwelcome news about the necessity of getting an education, about dignity and responsibility, about sizing people up and keeping your word. His handling of Alfred and the way he had raised his daughters began to be as different as day and night.

He said, in effect, at every turn, "Oh, Alfred knows this. Alfred knows that. Alfred's smart. Alfred, he's my main man." After a while, anything Alfred wanted, Alfred got. No lectures. No cautions. No goals set. No pressure to get good grades. The ending was predictable. Alfred dropped out of school, began doing drugs, and stole money from Daddy whenever he needed five or ten dollars.

When Daddy caught on to Alfred's stealing, his indulgence ended abruptly and he confronted the boy with: "Okay, you think you're a man. Come on. We're going to fight it out." Alfred swaggered along behind as Daddy marched to a nearby empty lot. He was seventeen, Daddy in his fifties. Alfred assumed all the advantage was on his side. They squared off. Alfred swung. Daddy ducked and countered. His blow landed, splitting Alfred's lip and dislocating his jaw.

"You ready to get up?" Daddy demanded, looming over Alfred as he writhed on the ground. "No? Then I got only one thing to say to you: don't you ever steal from me again. And just to make sure you don't, I'm throwin' you and your things outa my house."

It was the first and only time Daddy used his fists rather than his mind to best someone else.

Daddy hated to talk about Alfred after the boy was gone, but once when we were sitting at the roundtable having a cup of coffee together, he admitted: "Maybe God was trying to tell me something when he sent me all girls because if Tass and I had had a son, he would probably have ended up just like Alfred. That would have been my own son I hit out there because I wouldn't have been strict with him like I was with you girls and he would've gone bad." Daddy took a long reflective sip of his coffee and sighed. "I blew it. I wanted a son so bad, I really blew it."

It was a lesson in how to raise children that I took very seriously. If I'd been inclined to spoil Woody and Kimmie—and I was tempted to because I loved them so dearly—I had only to compare how we girls had turned out with the mess Alfred was making of his life to realize that the way to express love is not by giving children whatever they want but by giving them values and structure and lively explanations of the difference between needs and wants. When one of our children really needs something, Shearwood and I do everything we can to provide it. But when the material thing is merely wanted, then we consider it is time for a clear talk about purposes and meaning.

But all that was still in the future because Kimmie had just been born. I had told Dr. Knab that, with the baby due June 7, I would be back to work when my vacation was up at the end of June. However, with Kimmie having waited so long in the wings, I decided to take the full six weeks' maternity leave the military allows and use the extra time to study for my last hurdle: the oral examination and defense of my thesis that was to take place in Chicago in December. After I reported back to duty in August, Dr. Knab put me on call immediately, but whenever I had an evening off, Shearwood baby-sat so I could study.

Because the military paid the board-certification fees, I traveled to Chicago in uniform, which fortunately fit nicely again because I'd eaten carefully while pregnant, not wanting to gain sixty pounds as I had with Woody. Actually, on a Weight Watchers diet, I had gained exactly three-quarters of a pound, and that plus another twenty dropped off soon after Kimmie was born. Flying to Chicago, I felt trim and confident; I wasn't pregnant, I didn't have the flu. The only worry I had concerned which examiners I would get because the grapevine had it that there was one examiner who was exceedingly tough, another who never passed anybody, and a third who was only interested in esoterica.

When I was introduced to the panel, I recognized the name of one examiner to be that of the tough fellow, but I had escaped the other two, which I was glad of. The tough one proved to be fair as the panel posed such problems as: "Give the mechanism of calcium metabolism in a hyperparathyroid mother. Tell how you would treat her." The trick, I knew, was to discuss the case dynamically, talking to the examiners as I would to an attending physician when I was called in as a consultant on a case.

When I had done that, the tough examiner went on to question me about my thesis: "This part here, what methods did you employ for your statistical analysis? How did you analyze these data? How did you arrive at that?" When he was satisfied that I really had done the work and written the thesis, not had someone else do it for me, he returned to case problems.

"Your next patient comes in with a family history of Tay-Sachs disease. Her cousin has Tay-Sachs disease and her husband is a carrier. How do you counsel her about her risk of having a child with the disease?" I constructed a family pedigree, went through all the calculations, and he nodded, satisfied.

The next question concerned the mechanism of drugs that cause birth defects in humans, with specific reference to thalidomide. After discussing at which point during a pregnancy the drug has to be ingested for it to cause birth defects—specifically, twenty-one to forty days after conception—I referred to the fact that testing of the drug on laboratory rats had shown no adverse effects because thalidomide itself is not toxic; rather, the drug is converted in the liver to a chemical derivative called an arene oxide metabolite, and that is what causes the damage. This conversion, I said, takes place only in the livers of humans, rabbits, and monkeys, not in rats, which is why the problems with thalidomide had not been detected sooner.

"Is that right?" the tough examiner said with some surprise.

"Yes, it is, sir."

"Well, then, I've learned something." He was extremely polite and thanked me as I left the examination room.

Weeks later a guest lecturer speaking at the National Naval Medical Center remarked to Dr. Knab in front of all the attendings, "Hey, Doug, they tell me that one of your staff was terrific on the orals. The examiners couldn't remember when they'd seen such a knowledgeable candidate."

"Oh, that must have been Bill O'Brien." O'Brien was Dr. Knab's fair-haired boy.

"No, it was a woman, a Dr. Thornton."

Dr. Knab glared at him, ready to spit tacks because the visitor had mentioned this in front of the assembled staff. He had probably done it thinking that my performance was a credit to Dr. Knab, but Knab wanted no reflected glory from me, any more than he wished praise to come to me.

I was double board-certified now, a specialist in obstetrics and gynecology with a subspecialty in maternal/fetal medicine, the first person of my race to pass the boards in maternal/fetal medicine. I felt that I had paid my dues, and I had complete confidence in my skills and knowledge. People might not like me as a black woman but they had to respect my expertise. They had to listen when they came up against a problem and I, asked my advice, said, "This is what must be done."

All my life people have prejudged me. Before I open my mouth, they tell themselves that I should be in somebody's kitchen doing the cooking and the cleaning. Since I know that I am very different from the person people assume I am based on my looks, I always wonder if that person I'm meeting might also look one way but be quite another, so I try not to make up my mind about a new acquaintance too quickly. I follow Daddy's technique, which he said was to "throw out something and see how they respond." If, for instance, someone says to me, "What do you think of women in medicine?" I answer noncommittally, "You know, they're working hard," and wait for the other person to reveal himself by the opinion he may then go on to express. Or, to take a specific example, when I was in medical school, I asked one fellow what he thought about a woman's keeping her own name after she married. "Oh, no," he said. "Any woman who marries me is going to have to take my name." Shearwood's answer to the same question was, "I think she should. Her parents have put a lot of time in on her." The contrasting answers told me almost everything I needed to know about the two men.

This way of being noncommittal until the other person reveals himself has stood me in good stead in the male-dominated medical profession. A woman physician needs to protect herself because many men deliberately try to make her look bad. I honestly believe that I have had more problems because I'm a woman than because I'm black. Male doctors would rather deal with a black male than with a woman of any color. If they have an antipathy toward blacks, they tend to keep their feelings well concealed because they know blacks have been oppressed and they are sympathetic, but it is somehow socially acceptable to be scornful of women.

Male or female, an obstetrician, particularly one in private practice, needs stamina, the ability to just plain keep going through the long hours until the baby is delivered. It can be trial by fire, and you have to dig down deep into your reserves of strength and endurance. Oddly enough, the time when I had to dig deepest came not in civilian life but in the military where, theoretically, there should be quite enough staff on hand to help out. But one time there wasn't, and I went fifty-two hours without sleep.

A call came in from the naval base at Beaufort, South Carolina, that one of the two obstetricians on the base was out with appendicitis and they needed the loan of an obstetrician to cover for him. The base was next to the marine training center at Parris Island, which was under the umbrella of the navy, and I quickly gained the impression that Parris Island was a rabbit hutch, so numerous were the pregnant wives. It was February 1981, Kimmie was seven months old, when I was ordered down there to help out. When people heard where I was going, they told me to take my tennis racket along because the beautiful resort of Hilton Head was nearby.

"Sounds great," said I, and threw my suitcase and racket in the trunk of the car and started out. A day later, when I pulled into the hospital parking lot in South Carolina, a nurse came running to the car. "We thought you'd never get here! Are you Dr. Thornton? Oh, please, God, you've got to be Dr. Thornton!"

"I am indeed," I said as she pulled at me to drag me from the car. "What's going on here?"

"We've got a patient ready to deliver and there's no obstetrician!"

"How come? I was told there was a Dr. Peterson here."

"He fell out of a tree and broke his arm."

"What!"

"The cat went up a tree. His daughter went up after the cat. He went up after his daughter. His daughter and the cat got down all right, but he fell out of the tree and broke his arm. Oh, please hurry!"

I didn't stop to take my suitcase from the car, just raced into the hospital after the nurse and delivered the baby. And another baby. And another. I did a forceps delivery. I did C-sections. I manned the clinic, the emergency room, and the operating room. Day became night. Night became day. I can't remember eating or going to the bathroom. After forty-eight hours I was moving in a surrealistic world, putting one foot in front of the other as though I were walking underwater. "I can't function," I finally said. "This is no good for the patients. Get me a telephone." I called Dr. Knab.

"Where's Dr. Peterson?" he demanded.

"He fell out of a tree. I'm here alone and these marine wives are having babies like you wouldn't believe."

"Why didn't you call me sooner?"

"Sooner? I couldn't even get to the bathroom, let alone to a phone."

"Oh, Yvonne..." For the first time, I detected a human warmth in his voice, as though he might just have been concerned about me. "I'll call Charleston," he said. "They'll have to send somebody there immediately."

At the fiftieth hour a nurse hauled me into the delivery room. "The mother's fully dilated but the baby's head won't come down." The patient's feet were in the stirrups, her knees up. As I moved toward her, the baby's head popped out. It was enormous. I started to say, "If this is the head, imagine what the shoulders are like," when I saw the baby's head begin to turn blue. His head was wedged; the circulation to it was being cut off. Even though I'd witnessed the situation only once before, I recognized the problem immediately—shoulder dystocia. I had observed it as a resident when I was assisting an attending physician who went crazy trying to get the baby out before it strangled to death. That's what happens: the head is out but the shoulder is wedged, and before you can free it, the baby dies.

"Get me a pair of scissors!" I yelled at the nurse. I did an instant large episiotomy, cutting all the way down into the rectum and opening it up so I could try to maneuver the baby's shoulders. The mother's knees were flexed near her shoulders. I was attempting to corkscrew the baby's head with my hand. The nurses were on the mother's lower abdomen pushing, pushing, *pushing*, trying to press the baby's shoulders out from under the pubic bone where they were hooked. The mother was fully conscious and I was shouting at her, "Push! Push!"

Suddenly the baby came free. It was out. It started to cry. It was alive! I looked to the heavens and breathed, "Thank you, Jesus." A living baby. A ten-pound, twelve-ounce baby. Now I had to make repairs to the poor mother. Just as I finished stitching her up, the obstetrician sent from Charleston arrived and someone led me to a bed. I collapsed and slept for twenty-four hours. The new doctor began calling after fifteen hours because by then he felt he had to have help, but I didn't even hear the phone ring. Eventually, he became so worried that he sent a nurse down to see if I could be roused.

He and I were the only obstetricians on duty for the next two weeks, and I never set foot outside the hospital. Someone fetched my suitcase from the car, but the tennis racket stayed in the trunk and to this day I have never laid eyes on Hilton Head.

This episode and another made me argue with Shearwood against reenlisting when our three-year tour of duty was drawing to a close. The tune in the department had changed considerably by then. Now it was: "Dr. Thornton, everybody loves you. You're such a marvelous obstetrician, such a caring doctor. You can't leave us now." Oh, yes, I can, if the navy is threatening to send me to the Persian Gulf.

The hostage crisis was on in Iran, and I received word that I had been assigned to the Surgery II team. "But I'm an obstetrician," I protested.

"Doesn't matter. You're a surgeon, and we can teach you gut surgery in twenty-four hours."

"I don't want to do gut surgery, and I've got two little children."

"Sorry. Surgery I team is over there now on a hospital ship, and Surgery II is the backup."

That night I fumed at Shearwood, "Why don't they take you?"

"I suppose because I went to Okinawa."

"You weren't being shot at in Okinawa! You weren't on a ship that could get bombed!"

Luckily the hostages were released, things quieted down in the Middle East, and I didn't have to learn gut surgery. But I no longer wanted to be in a position where a snap of the fingers could send me thousands of miles across the world from my children. "Okay," Shearwood agreed, "we're outa here," and we wrote letters resigning our commissions, giving as the explanation that "the vicissitudes of military life do not permit us to provide a stable environment for our children."

Our resignations were accepted, but everyone predicted, "You'll be back because it's tough out there in civilian life." I was well aware that it is difficult to establish a private practice, particularly if you're black and not part of an old-boy network that will refer patients to you. You're beating the bushes, you're taking Medicaid patients, you're doing anything to get a patient in your office who will pay even a few dollars. And if you're an obstetrician, you're working all hours. You tell your child, "Of course, I'll come to see you in the school play, dear," only to have to say later, "Gee, honey, I'm sorry but I had a delivery." That was one reason I had taken so much advanced training: so that my expertise would qualify me to serve as a consultant in an academic setting where I would have a base salary and relatively regular hours and wouldn't have to neglect my children.

One of the places I applied when I knew we would be leaving the military was The New York Hospital/Cornell Medical Center in New York City. I sent them my curriculum vitae, which was an absolutely neutral document as far as my race was concerned—I didn't attend Howard or Meharry; I wasn't a member of the National Medical Association—and when the people at Cornell called my former professors and mentors at Columbia and Roosevelt for references, no one apparently thought to mention that I was black, only that I was a hard worker and a good one. Dr. Roy Petrie at Columbia teased me by telling me: "I had this guy from Cornell really drilling me about you so I told him you were a terrible person and hated your patients."

Whatever he told the people at Cornell, it was enough to persuade them to hire me sight unseen, and when I showed up, they were dumbfounded. As a member of a minority, you become adept at reading nonverbal communication: the slackness around the mouth that indicates the jaw is on the verge of dropping, the furrow between the brows, the tilt of the body as though the person is instinctively about to back away. Then comes the hesitant question: "Are you . . . Dr. Thornton?"

"Yes," I said to the department head at Cornell, "I'm Dr. Thornton. Is there a problem?"

"Oh, no. No, there's no problem. Well, there is the problem that we've run out of space on the B level where the faculty offices are, so we'll have to put you on the subbasement level, which will be convenient to the clinic."

"The clinic?"

"The clinic director has left, so you'll be taking her place."

"But I am a maternal/fetal medicine specialist."

"Well, yes, but that's the only opening we have for you right now."

How would Daddy handle this? He'd say, "Kill 'em with a smile, Cookie."

"Clinic director?" I said. "Fine. Subbasement? Fine."

A few more surprises were delivered by the other maternal/fetal medicine specialists on staff. He said, "You're going to have to conduct a private practice, you know."

"No, I didn't know. I was under the impression that maternal/fetal medicine specialists were consultants to other obstetricians and that's how we acquire patients and generate revenue for the department."

"Oh, no, you need to have a private practice. You have to see patients and deliver babies."

"I don't mind delivering babies, but I don't want to have a one-on-one practice as though I were an obstetrician when what I am is a perinatalogist."

"That's the way it is here at Cornell. You get paid a third of your salary and the rest of it you have to generate yourself from your practice, with all income over that going to the OB/GYN department."

"And how will I get patients?"

"Don't worry about that. The rest of us will send you our overflow."

I am still waiting for their overflow—their overflow of paying patients, that is. They sent me their patients on Medicaid, they sent me addicts and indigents, but not one patient who could pay. Realizing that this was a way of forcing me to leave because they would have the excuse that I was not generating revenue for the hospital, I took stock and hied myself off to a two-day seminar in how to succeed in a medical practice.

"You can have an office full of patients," the seminar director lectured us. "You can put in fifteen hours a day and you can end up making five dollars for the day because the patients are not paying you. That is not the way to succeed."

"But you're helping people," someone objected.

"Wake up and smell the coffee. You're in a business. What you really need is a bank president to look after the money end, but you're not going to be that lucky so you'll have to do it yourself."

I didn't get a bank president; I got Mrs. Kiman. At sixty-two, she'd been laid off from her job in a bank. "You know how to deliver babies," she said. "I know about accounts receivable. Give me a chance. Let me show you what I can do."

I hired her as my office manager, and fifteen minutes after she went to work, she had the Blue Cross participating number that I had been trying to get for four weeks. A month later she announced, "We're here all day and we're making thirty dollars. From now on when a patient calls for an appointment, I'm going to say the fee is fifty dollars, cash or check, no insurance. If they want reimbursement, they'll have to see to it themselves. If they say they can't afford fifty dollars, I'll tell them to come to the clinic, that you're the director of the clinic and they can see you there."

In the next couple of months, only one patient came. But that one person said, "You're so nice; you really take time with your patients" (not knowing that all I had was time), and she told her friends and they told their friends, until by the end of the second year my practice was generating half a million dollars a year. At the same time I was running the clinic, delivering babies, consulting on problematic cases, and squeezing in some research time at The Rockefeller University.

Experiences like this have convinced me that being black is like being the frog in a muscle-wasting experiment. A researcher interested in determining how rapidly immobilized muscles atrophy tied down one of the frog's back legs and left the other free. The frog pushed so hard and struggled so long against the fetters that the tied-down leg got stronger and stronger and soon was far more muscular than the free leg. Just so, the more you struggle against the fetters of being black, the stronger you become.

But before I even got to New York Hospital and Shearwood to Harlem Hospital where he had signed on as Acting Chief of Orthopedic Surgery, we had to find a place to live in the metropolitan area. We were leaving the navy on July 8 and were taking our vacations the month of June to give us time to get settled in our new home, which we planned to find by driving to New Jersey every weekend in May to go house-hunting.

The first real estate agent we contacted arranged to show us a house in Franklin Lakes that was within our price range. The owners looked at us rather oddly as we were being introduced, but I was paying attention to the house, not the owners, and deciding that it wasn't really to our taste. At the next house we went to, the owner asked the agent to step into the kitchen while we stayed in the living room. Her voice was clearly audible. "Get the niggers out of my house," we heard her say.

Shearwood looked at me. I looked at Shearwood. This was New Jersey in 1982?

Outside the agent apologized, saying how sorry she was. "It's their house," I said, but I was hurt and I was angry because we had the children with us and this was something we did not want them to hear, not when they were still so young. Now I knew how Daddy felt when he said, "It don't mater what you do to me, but don't hurt my kids."

The real estate agent didn't seem to have any more houses to show us after that, so I called an old classmate from medical school. "Oh, forget it," she said. "Franklin Lakes is too far from the city anyway. I have a good real estate agent. Her name is Mary LaBelle, and she'll take care of you."

Mary LaBelle proved to be a lovely lady with an Irish accent. I explained that I was an obstetrician and had to have a house close to a major highway so I could get to New York Hospital quickly. "No problem," she said. "We'll find just the right place for you."

Just the right place proved to be a handsome house in Paramus, New Jersey, but by the time we found it, we had used up so many weekends in looking that there wasn't enough time left before we had to move to arrange for a mortgage and all the other necessities like a title search and survey. Mary LaBelle suggested that we rent with an option to buy, which seemed an excellent solution. The owners, whom we hadn't met, agreed to this plan in a long-distance phone call. We put down a deposit with Mary, returned to Maryland, and I ordered a refrigerator and washer and dryer from Sears to be delivered to the house.

Shearwood had decided that he needed more training in hip-replacement surgery since, for the most part, naval personnel were not of an age to need such surgery and he had little experience in it. Consequently, he had applied for a fellowship to Ohio State and was leaving in July to be away until January. With the house question settled, I felt I could mange without him for that length of time.

On June 3, Mary LaBelle telephoned. "Dr. Thornton, I'm afraid you can't have the house because the people don't want you in there. The wife said to tell you that she's decided to give the house to her son, but I don't want to lie to you. What she really said was that they would burn the house down before they'd let niggers move into it."

I cried and cried and cried. Shearwood, trying to soothe me, said, "We'll find another house."

"When? Where? You're going to Ohio! The kids and I have to have some place to live!"

"Yvonne, don't get so upset."

"This is blatant racial discrimination! It's not right! It's not fair!"

"Yvonne, calm down."

I couldn't calm down. I grabbed the phone. I called Senator Bill Bradley of New Jersey. I called the *Bergen Record*, the county newspaper. I called CBS News. I said, "Here we are, doctors, naval officers. We've been putting our lives on the line for these people—my husband went to Okinawa; I was about to be sent to the Persian Gulf—and they are denying us a place to live!" Everyone I talked to was outraged on our behalf but could think of no action to take. I called the NAACP, both the New York City and Bergen County chapters, and was told they could do nothing unless twenty or thirty black persons were involved, in which event they would bring a class action suit. I told myself so often that I wanted *justice* that I finally looked in the Washington, D.C., Yellow Pages under *Justice* and came upon a listing for the Department of Justice. I called there and repeated my story.

"Let me give you Mr. Hadley," the person listening to me said. "He deals with the New Jersey area."

I repeated my story to Mr. Hadley, who said, "Dr. Thornton, this is really bad. I've never heard of this happening before."

"You've never heard of this happening?" I was stunned. "I'm not lying to you. We have two children. We have to move out of our Maryland house in a couple of weeks. We have to tell the military where to send our furniture, and it's not right. It's not right!"

"I agree with you," he said. "I suggest that the person you need to talk to is Lee Porter. She's the director of the Fair Housing Council in Bergen County."

I called Ms. Porter and told my story again—and finally I was being listened to by someone who had an answer. "We'll get on this immediately, Dr. Thornton. We'll have our lawyer get an injunction against these people which will prevent them from selling or renting to anyone else." I could hear the red tape being cut over the phone.

"Good," said Shearwood when I told him. "That means we can go ahead and move."

"Shearwood, I can't move into that house. I'd be terrified— you off in Ohio and me alone with the kids at night and them alone with a sitter during the day. I'd be frightened to death that someone might harm them."

Mary LaBelle understood and found us a three-bedroom apartment in a highrise in Hackensack, New Jersey. I hated being on the tenth floor and felt we might just as well be living in the city, but at least we had a place to put our furniture and a roof over our heads. And I discovered that a dear friend from Roosevelt Hospital, a nurse named Ruth Horton, lived on the next block. She was company for me when Shearwood went to Ohio and an emergency baby-sitter when I was summoned to the hospital in the middle of the night.

Kimmie was two; Woody was four and went to nursery school during the day. Both children went to bed at six o'clock in the evening, and during the day they weren't running around because I didn't want them on the terrace for fear of their somehow falling off. One day I came home to find a note slipped under the door: "If you don't keep your kids quiet, I will." From that moment on, I didn't feel safe in the apartment. Each time I went down to the laundry room in the basement, each time I took Woody and Kimmie to the park, I searched the faces of the people in the elevator. *Did you write that note? Do you intend harm to my children?* Now I could imagine what it was like to live in the South, never knowing when the Ku Klux Klan was going to strike because of some offense, real or imagined.

I called Shearwood in Ohio to tell him, "I'm going to find a house. I'm not waiting until January when you get back." I asked Mary LaBelle to start looking for me. "We're not in a rush this time," I said, "so let me tell you what I want. I want a house with a circular driveway. . . ."

"Why?"

I couldn't say why. For years I had fantasized about a house just as I had once fantasized about my senior prom and my wedding, and in my mind's eye the house had a circular drive, was built of brick because Daddy claimed brick was as lasting as rocks in the earth, was set back far enough so the children wouldn't run into the street and be killed, and had a big backyard for them to play in. And practically speaking, the house had to have four bedrooms and a room on the first floor that could be made into a library.

Within a week Mary LaBelle called. "Dr. Thornton, I have your house. It's big but it's not too big. It's on a busy street but the street is not too busy. It's next to a major highway but the house is very quiet."

"What kind of a house is this?"

"You have to see it because I can't describe it. It was going for $279,000 but it's been on the market for four years and you can get it for $145,000."

Mary was busy on Sunday so we agreed that she would take me on Monday to see the house. I went to bed Saturday night thinking about the house and woke up Sunday morning thinking about it, thinking about it with such a sense of excitement that I called the office and asked if there wasn't somebody else who could show it to me right away. A gentleman obliged, and as we approached the house, he pointed to it. The house had a circular drive! It was built of brick! It was my house; I was sure of that before I even got out of the car.

Well landscaped, it looked from the front like a one-story, handsome but unpretentious, rather snug house, but inside, across the wide living room was a wall of windows, and beyond them the skyline of New York City. The land sloped down, so that under the first story was a second story, and the whole opened up into a four-thousand-square-foot mother-daughter house, with a huge backyard yard and a swimming pool and off to the right a patch of woods shielding the house from Route 80, the superhighway that would get me to the George Washington Bridge in under ten minutes. The bedrooms were on the opposite side of the house and the house was 1960s vintage and solidly built, so the hum from the highway was not a problem. The house had been rented to a U.N. delegation from a third-world island nation. The chandeliers had been ripped out and the swimming pool was cracked and peeling, which was why the house had been on the market for such a long time and the price had been almost halved.

I rummaged in my purse for my checkbook. "I want the house," I told the real estate agent. "I'll give you a binder."

"Are you sure you don't want to wait until your husband sees it? I've had this with other wives. They give me a binder and then the husband finds something wrong with the house and I have to return the binder."

"I like the house. My husband will like the house," I said firmly. But then I thought maybe he was right and I'd better check with Shearwood. I reached him in Ohio. "Shearwood, I've found our house and I want to put a binder on it. What do you think?"

"Honey, houses and homes are for women. I could live in a tent. Whatever house you want, that's fine with me."

Our bonuses for joining the military made up the $10,000 down payment, and we obtained a VA mortgage for $135,000. The house needed patching and painting, which meant taking out a bank loan. We needed more furniture. Another bank loan. The utility bill for the first month was $1,200 because the heating system was electric. Obviously we couldn't afford a bill like that every month, so we paid $8,000 to have the house converted to gas. Another bank loan. But none of that mattered. We had a lovely house, and by luck rather than good management, we had fetched up in a town, Teaneck, which welcomes ethnic diversity and has a school system second to none.

Daddy came to see the house and pronounced his verdict. "You done good, Cookie."

The path to getting settled in civilian life had been a rocky one, but then nothing in my life had come easy. "Hey," as Daddy said, "it builds character."

Incidentally, we won the racial discrimination suit against the Paramus people and the settlement paid for wall-to-wall carpeting throughout my dream house.

♦ 16 ♦

The Gospel According
to Donald

THE WEATHER PREDICTION for Friday, February 11, 1983, was for snow; a storm was coming up from the South. But the day was still clear when I left home for the twenty-five-minute drive into the city and to the hospital. Friday was one of the assigned days in the faculty practice group for seeing private patients, and I was counting on getting through my schedule in time to be safe at home for the weekend before the storm hit.

One of the last patients in my office that morning was a woman with a history of having missed two periods who was experiencing crampy lower abdominal pain and some vaginal spotting. Her urine pregnancy test in the office was negative. I did a pelvic exam and discovered an area of extreme tenderness and fullness on the right side. Since the patient had no fever, which would have suggested an infection, my presumptive diagnosis was a possible ectopic pregnancy, that is, a fertilized egg lodged in a fallopian tube rather than in the uterus where it would normally begin to develop. The next step was to determine whether the fallopian tube had ruptured and the patient was bleeding internally. I warned the patient that what I was about to do was going to hurt but that I didn't feel comfortable sending her home on a Friday into a possible snowstorm without having established exactly what was going on.

I inserted a needle into the area of fullness and the syringe promptly filled with dark red blood. The patient was indeed bleeding internally. An immediate operation was imperative. I had the patient admitted to the hospital, and met her in the operating room a brief time later. Her fallopian tube proved to be too damaged to be saved and I had to remove it. When the patient had regained consciousness, I checked on her again and listened to her whispered apology for keeping me at the hospital for so long. We both could see the snow coming down outside the windows, but I told her not to worry, that it was worth having to drive home in the snow to know that she was out of danger. I was not looking forward to the drive, however. I was tired after a full complement of office patients and then the emergency surgery. The distance between hospital and home was only eleven miles, but I would be glad when I had negotiated it.

I called Shearwood, who was at home with the day off from Harlem Hospital in observance of Lincoln's Birthday, and he offered to come get me, but I said no, that there was no sense in two of us being out in the storm. He suggested that perhaps I should stay put at the hospital, and again I said no, that I didn't want to get stuck for the weekend away from him and the kids.

When I pulled out of the underground garage at the hospital, it was two o'clock in the afternoon and I had three-quarters of a tank of gas. I turned up First Avenue, heading for the East River Drive. After thirty minutes I had gone half a block, so snarled was the traffic by stalled cars. It took me two more hours to negotiate the six blocks to the entrance to the Drive. The wind was blowing at what seemed like hurricane force, piling the swirling snow into entrapping drifts and plastering huge flakes against the windshield. The wipers were laboring to clear the icy slush, the heater was going full blast becasue it was deadly cold, and I had the headlights on, trying to gain some slight visibility, which had closed to a few feet in front of the creeping car. Everywhere, there were abandoned cars, but I in my large Chevrolet and a few other determined souls in heavy cars kept pressing on.

I did not have a car phone at the time so Shearwood had no way of reaching me, but every once in a while he beeped me to reinforce my courage. He had no way of knowing whether I was buried in a drift, immoblized in a tangle mass of cars like a bumper car in an amusement park, or was still inching along. All he could do was beep to convey his concern.

By eight o'clock that evening I had less than half a tank of gas left and I had struggled only as far as the foot of the ramp leading to the George Washington Bridge, where I was blocked behind several other cars and had several cars stopped behind me. Every time a driver pulled out to try to make it up the ramp, his car slipped and slid and fishtailed and spun its wheels, only to end up back where it had started. One driver after another made a run at the ramp. No car made it.

In the blinding storm, a man climbed from his car and made his way from car to car, saying, "If we don't help each other, none of us will get up the ramp." It was clear that he was right. One by one we ventured from the shelter of our cars and gathered behind the first car in line. With the driver steering, we pushed the car up the ramp. Then the next car was pushed. And the next. And the next, until we were all at the top of the ramp. It felt like wartime, with people making common cause to survive.

Slowly, slowly, slowly, I slewed over the bridge and onto Route 80. This superhighway is a major route to Pennsylvania, Ohio, and the West and is ordinarily solid with fast-moving cars and trucks. Now, nothing was moving. All was silent and still. I had entered a ghost world. Abandoned cars and trucks were strewn like dead carcasses in every lane. It was a constant fight to maneuver around them in the storm and, with all markers obliterated, to keep from driving off the highway altogether. Inch by inch, I fought my way along, crying now as I faced the prospect that, alone in the night, marooned in the drifts, I might very well freeze to death so close to home.

The Teaneck exit is the first exit off Route 80. It was ten o'clock when I made it there, and I was down to less than a quarter tank of gas. Now it was an uphill climb to the intersection of my street, but if I could get that far, if I could make a left-hand turn there, I would be just a few blocks from home. I started up the hill. It was a graveyard of abandoned cars blocked from going farther by a jackknifed tractor-trailer at the intersection. The car groaned and spun and slipped as I wormed and squirmed my way through this obstacle course—back, forward; back, forward—struggling for every bit of traction I could get. Hours later I made it to the intersection and somehow crept around the tractor-trailer, whether on the road or sidewalk or someone's front lawn, I had no idea.

Now the gas tank was on empty and I still had half a mile to go. I spun sideways. I slipped backward. The rear of the car sashayed like a fan dancer. My eyes blurred from the intensity of my stare through the iced windshield at the featureless wastes of snow; my hands were numb from the intensity of my grip on the steering wheel.

At last I saw the house, ablaze with light as though Shearwood was trying to provide a beacon for me in the storm. I crawled on, the wheels spinning uselessly around and around but now and again gaining a little bit, a littel bit, a little bit. I was almost there when the car coughed, spluttered, died—out of gas. It was two o'clock in the morning—twelve hours after I had started out to drive the elven miles home.

I struggled to push the car door open against the weight of snow. I pushed, pushed harder, battered the door against the snowbank. I squeezed my arm out, my shoulder, my head, and twisted and shimmied and struggled until I was out of the car and clawing my way up the bank. I stumbled, fell, got up, fell, crawled, fell against the front door of the house. It opened and Shearwood snatched me up into his arms, hugging and cradling and crooning to me as though I had returned from the dead. And I clung to him and sobbed as though I had.

My exhausted sleep ended the next day only when Shearwood stood by the bed with a breakfast tray. The eggs were underdone, the toast was overdone—Shearwood is no cook—but what he was communicating was clear: *I love you with all of my heart and I was dreadfully afraid I had lost you.* He sat by the bed while I ate, never taking his eyes off me and now and again reaching out to pat the blanket over my legs as though to make certain I was solidly there.

I was giving some thought to suggesting another way of proving I was really there when the telephone rang. It was Uncle Milford calling from Long Branch.

"Yvonne, your father's in the hospital."

"What! Why?"

"I'm afraid he's had a stroke."

"Oh, God, oh, God, oh, God. Is he conscious?"

"No."

"What was he doing—shoveling snow?"

"He came over to our house this morning to see how we were doing after the storm, and he was walking down the driveway when he said he had a headache and slumped to the ground. He's been unconscious ever since."

The day was brilliantly sunny. The storm had passed and crews were working to plow and sand the highways, which were still buried under snow and down to two lanes, but passable. Shearwood shoveled the driveway to get his car out while I dressed. Our housekeeper had been wiser than I and had not tried to get home in the storm, so she was there to look after the children. It was a long, slow, cautious drive to Long Branch, but this time Shearwood was at the wheel.

At the hospital the neurologist who had been called in said that Daddy's vital signs were stable, he did not require life support measures, but that he was unresponsive. We went in to see him and I was struck by how peaceful he looked. And, even lying in bed, how sturdy and strong. A nurse who came in the room to turn him said it was as though he were made of concrete, so deceptively heavy he was.

He continued in a coma though the day and night. By the following day it was clear he was going downhill. We watched and waited in a fog of unreality. Surely he would open his eyes. Surely his laugh would ring out and that rough, affectionate, matter-of-fact voice would come again. It could not be the end, not for this vital, undefeated man. His daughters waited and prayed as his strong heart beat on—the daughters he'd loved so much, the daughters he had given life to and who had been his life.

But the next day was the end. With a little smile on his face as though he were going to meet his dear, dear Tass, Daddy died on February 15, 1983, a month short of his fifty-eighth birthday.

All of us—Donna, Linda, Rita, Betty and I—were at his bedside, all of us except Jeanette.

Jeanette was in Nigeria. She had gotten her M.D., and during her first year of internship, she had met Emil Powe, a Fellow taking postgraduate training in gastroenterology. She brought him home to meet Daddy, and Daddy said, as he had about Shearwood, "That's a good man," and Jeanette had married him.

By coincidence, I had known Em long before Jeanette met him when I was a resident at Roosevelt and moonlighting one day a week at an adolescent clinic in the Chelsea section of New York. He was a lot like Shearwood: quiet, steady, thoughtful—qualities that Daddy picked up on and approved of, particularly since it was obvious that Em adored Jeanette and thus fulfilled the requirement of loving his woman so much that he would stick by her through thick and thin.

He and Jeanette were in Africa because, by the terms of a grant Em had received, he was obliged to put in a year in public health service and had elected to serve in Nigeria. They were on the verge of starting for home when cabled word of Daddy's death reached them. Jeanette cabled back that she would come as quickly as possible, but since we did not know when that would be, we went ahead with plans for the funeral.

While daddy had ultimately given his consent to Mommy's autopsy, we knew how abhorrent the idea was to him. Thus, there was no autopsy, and, also on the basis of his strong wishes expressed at the time of Mommy's death, the casket was closed because, "If they didn't come around to see me when I was alive, I don't want 'em gawking at me when I'm dead. Let 'em wonder: Is he really dead or is he still hangin' 'round some place?"

This time the undertaker did not suggest that we hire pallbearers but simply assumed that Donald's six daughters would carry him to his grave as we had carried our mother. Could we manage it? We were older. The snow on the ground was deeper. Daddy was heavier. The climb to the grave site was still as steep, and we had not been wrestling amplifiers in and out of college buildings in recent years. We resolved our doubts the same way we had before, by telling each other, "Women can do anything they put their minds to."

Gathered in the living room of the house that Daddy built and we grew up in, we talked about what we wanted to say at his service. I commented that, even though the last line was not appropriate, the poem, "If—" by Kipling had always reminded me of Daddy. I was thinking of lines like these: "If you can trust your-self when all men doubt you . . ." and "If you can force your heart and nerve and sinew/ To serve your turn long after they are gone,/ And to hold on when there is nothing in you/ Except the Will which says to them: 'Hold on!' " and "If you can fill the un-forgiving minute/ With sixty seconds' worth of distance run . . ."

"It sounds as though it was written about Daddy," Linda said when I quoted the poem.

"Except that it ends: 'Yours is the Earth and everything that's in it/ And—which is more—you'll be a Man, my son.' "

"That's okay," Rita said. "He *was* a man, and we can start the eulogy by saying, 'But our father never had a son; he had all daughters, and he said to himself, *Well, daughters is what I've been given, so let me just see what I can do with them.' "

That struck us as a good idea, and starting from there, using phrases contributed by all of us, we fashioned a tribute to Daddy. Never was one more deeply felt. We described how he was born into poverty, one of twelve children, and grew up poor, unedu-cated, and black; how he met and married our mother and to-gether they formulated a dream that their children would be educated; how he started as a ditchdigger at Fort Monmouth and worked two and three jobs simultaneously to keep us fed and buy us music lessons; how he had served as road manager of the band and driven us thousands of miles. We recounted how many a person remarked to him, "Donald, you work so hard, you'll kill yourself," and his reply that he would rather kill himself trying than have his children experience the hunger, poverty, and prej-udice he had known. We described how he had given all he had of his time, his energy, and his heart so that we, his children, could rise to stand on equal terms with anyone, man or woman, rich or poor, white or black.

We spoke most of all of his single-minded devotion to his family. "If loving my family is wrong," he often said, "then I don't want to be right." He *was* right. And good and honorable and strong and clearheaded, with a wisdom all his own and a great store of common sense that he used in the service of, first, set-ting a seemingly impossible goal for his daughters and then coaxing, coaching, and guiding us in the struggle to achieve it, relentless in his quest to have us go beyond the limits set by others for his daughters. We ended our tribute by saying that with deep love for him and profound gratitude for his being the person he was, we now laid him to rest beside our mother, a rest he had truly earned and richly deserved.

Jeanette walked in the door just as we were putting our coats on to leave for the funeral service. Startled, she said, "You were going ahead without me?" She was not remembering, as we were, that there had been many a time that we'd had to go ahead without her. She went alone to the funeral parlor to say goodbye to Daddy; she, the daughter most like him, who had been both his pride and his grief. Like Daddy, she done it "My Way," the song he had told us he wanted sung at his service.

The rest of us joined her and the service began. I read the poem, Donna shared the reading of the eulogy with Jeanette, then Linda, her voice as big and true as ever, started "My Way," and one by one we each came in, the Thornton Sisters singing together again, for the last time.

At the cemetery we gathered at the rear of the hearse, stacked our hands without touching, silently concentrated, broke away, and lifted the flag-draped coffin.

As determined in death as in life not to let our father down, the ditchdigger's daughters delivered him without a stumble to his grave beside his beloved wife.

Curiously, despite the absolute centrality of Daddy to our lives, we did not experience the grief we had felt at Mommy's death, perhaps because we had such a strong sense of completion. Daddy had done what he set out to do in his life, and after we were grown and did not need him anymore, he had lost his reason for living. He had not been able to find another challenge to absorb his energies, and he sorely missed Mommy. Now he had joined her, and we could not help but feel that he was happier.

Back at the house, we made coffee and gathered around the table where Mommy and Daddy had sat every morning of our young lives, the command post, in effect, from which they had directed our lives while teaching us about the world and prodding us to excel in it. I looked around the table. We were six women. Six black women. No more or less intelligent, no more or less gifted, than any other black women. As little girls, there had been nothing special about us, nothing to set us apart from the other black children in Long Branch, New Jersey. By any ordinary expectation, we should have grown up to graduate from high school and get factory or clerking jobs, that is, if we had been lucky enough to avoid getting pregnant and becoming high school dropouts, perhaps single mothers living on welfare and having an illegitimate child every other year or so.

Instead, here we were: Betty, a nurse, and Donna, a court stenographer, each in a stable marriage to a man with a civil service job, each with one child and no intention of having more; Linda, a dentist, an army major married to a lawyer; Rita, the head of the science department in a private school; Jeanette and I, both doctors and married to doctors, me with two children, Jeanette childless by choice. Women of accomplishment, independent women, women capable of taking care of themselves.

"How did he do it?" I mused aloud. "How did Daddy turn out six women like us? He had no education to speak of, nobody to learn from. He never read a book or a newspaper. Where did he learn to be such an extraordinary father to us?"

"I've often wondered about that," Betty said. She knew the family he came from, his mother and father, his sisters and brothers, knew them better than any of us because she had been a foster child in that family from the time she was a baby until Nanna died and she had come to live with us. "Donald was different from the rest of his family. He wasn't like any of them."

"But why?" I persisted. "Where did he get his ideas?"

"Roger asked Daddy that once," Linda said, referring to her husband.

"What did Daddy say?"

"All he said was, 'I just did what I thought was right to do. I never thought I was worth a dime unless I could be some help to my kids.' "

"Unless," Jeanette amended, with a trace of the old bitterness, "he could run his kids' lives."

I bit my tongue not to remind Jeanette that she would have been a doctor years sooner and with a lot less anguish for all of us if she had listened to Daddy; it was not a time to open old wounds. "He wanted to run our lives," I agreed. "It was the best thing about him, but finally it was his Achilles' heel."

I was remembering what he had said when he was interviewed for a story about the family for *Ebony* magazine: "I didn't want to let them go. I didn't want them to grow up. When they were all babies, they depended on me. I loved that. I used to love to see them smile when I gave them something."

"It's understandable when you think about it," Donna said. "Where else but in his own family can a man who is a ditchdigger feel important, feel like a big man?"

Rita, who had seen the most of Daddy after Mommy died, said, "He told me he wished that when any of you came to see him, you'd come by yourselves."

"Without our husbands?"

"So it would just be family again, so he'd have his girls back."

"Without any men around. He never did want other men coming around."

"In a way he was right. If he hadn't been so strict, we'd be living in the projects over at Garfield Court with a raft of kids."

"Instead, we're out in the world living the gospel according to Donald."

The gospel according to Donald. It was true. I sometimes said to Shearwood that I doubted whether I had ever had an original thought in my life. I might phrase something differently, use longer words, but I could trace my beliefs, the words I lived by, the guideposts I steered by, to ideas I had heard Daddy express.

We began to reminisce about the gospel according to Daddy, starting with: "You're black and you're ugly and you're girls, and the world's already written you off. You can grow up and be a bag lady. You can be on the streets and the world won't give a damn whether you live or die. But if you listen to me, we can get out of this."

And after that: "If you're a musician, they can break your fingers. If you're an athlete, they can break your kneecaps. But . . ."

Here he always paused dramatically. "*But* if you are educated, the only way they can get to you is to kill you. There is no way they can take anything out of your brain. Once you've got something in your head, it's yours as long as you live."

What we should have in our heads, in the gospel according to Donald, was something the world needed because then it would not be important that we were black. "A man can be a Ku Klux Klan member who hates blacks, hates niggers, won't shake hands with 'em, but if he's layin' in the road hurt and bleedin' and you tell him you're a doctor, he's gonna beg you to help him. It don't make any difference to him then what color you are because he needs you."

Jeanette said thoughtfully, "Sometimes I wonder if we weren't real lucky to be born black. If we'd been high yella, if we'd had skin the color of Lena Horne's . . ."

"Forget it!" we chorused, and Donna quoted more of the gospel according to Donald: "If you're high yella, you can get over on your looks. Or if you're rich. Or if you're male. But if you're a dark-skinned woman . . ."

"Forget it!" we chorused again. I picked up the refrain. "You can have babies and be written off. If you think you can get any place above that by being cutesy, just forget it." We could all quote Daddy word for word, and the older we got and the more we observed how the world works, the more right we knew him to be, not only about the prejudice among whites against dark-skinned people but among our own race. With equal degrees of talent, as a dancer, say, it would be the lighter-skinned person who'd be chosen to perform, even when the person doing the hiring was a black. Daddy had worked to make sure we did not have to live our lives subject to that kind of judgment.

But neither did he consider being black, being *black* black, an excuse for nonachievement, only a reason to work harder, so that people who might pass you over for the way you look *have* to turn to you for what you know. "Work hard and you'll make it," he said. "It's a natural law, like gravity. This country gives blacks a lot of grief. But it gives them a lot of opportunities too. Work hard and people will help you, doors will open."

"If the door doesn't open," he always added, "go around and climb through a window. If the window is closed, try to get in through the cellar. If that's locked, go up on the roof and see if you can get in through the chimney. There is always a way to get in if you keep trying."

"Look for your opportunities in the cast-off areas of life," he had told us, and it had worked for me recently in my work. Believing a new esoteric procedure in diagnostic fetal testing was almost certain to prove worthless, the department chairman had tossed the opportunity of learning it to me. Not only had the technique turned out to be valuable, but now I was in demand to teach it to doctors in other hospitals. As Daddy said: "Take what they give you and make something of it so they'll say, 'Wow, that's pretty good,' where before there wasn't nothin' there."

One by one the others came in with their remembrances of how Daddy had phrased similar ideas:

"How you get ahead in the world is by being the best at what you do."

"Do it with enthusiasm instead of whining, 'Oh, God, I got another thing to do.' Nothin's gonna come from whinin'."

"Never dread anything. Just go ahead and do it."

"He and Mommy both used to say, 'You waste more time dreading. Whatever happens, happens. Just go ahead and do it.'"

Linda said, "I remembered that every time I had an exam."

"Me too."

"Me, too."

"Get the job done," I quoted.

"Get the job done," Rita said, and Linda said it too. We were remembering the days when the three of us had carried on with the band.

"Everybody says it can't be done until somebody goes ahead and does it."

We smiled at the echoes of Mommy and Daddy bouncing around the room. We smiled because people had said the Thornton sisters could not do it and we had done it.

"Daddy was the bow, we were the arrows," someone said, "and he aimed high. He didn't say midwives, he said doctors. He didn't say dental assistants, he said dentists."

A bit ruefully, a bit defiantly, Donna said, "It didn't work with me."

"Ah, but if you and Jeanette hadn't rebelled," I told her, "we probably would have. It was you two bucking him and our seeing the trouble and unhappiness it caused that made the rest of us shut up and get on with it."

Rita asked something I had sometimes thought about. "Do you think he sat down and said to himself that the way out for blacks is athletics or music and girls are not going to do much with athletics so it had better be music?"

"I doubt it," Jeanette said. "I think he was like a guy in a traffic jam who takes any opening he sees, just trying to get a little bit ahead."

"Right. He always said if it hadn't been music and the band, he'd have found another way."

"He was a determined man."

"If he hadn't been determined, we wouldn't have been the Thornton Sisters."

"If he hadn't gone right on being determined, we'd still be the Thornton Sisters and blowing our brains out in some honky-tonk bar."

"Instead we're professional women, respected, strong. . . ."

"You'd better believe we're strong! We carried Daddy's butt up that hill. . . ."

"In the snow . . ."

"Without dropping him . . ."

We started to laugh then and kid around. And soon we were gathering our things together and getting ready to go our separate ways. We had each taken the mementos we wanted. Betty and her husband would move into the house. Whatever money there was had been spent on the funeral. Mommy was gone. Daddy was gone. It was over.

Except that it will never be over. This past spring, ten years after Daddy's death, sixteen after Mommy's, I was asked to be one of the speakers at the annual meeting of the American College of Obstetricians and Gynecologists in Orlando, Florida. As the speakers filed onto the dais, I looked around. Here I was, a black woman—the only woman, the only black—surrounded by distinguished, white-haired men.

I had been asked to speak on "The Whole Patient." When it came my turn, I began by saying that, as specialists, we had been trained to evaluate, examine, and treat parts and that we were sometimes in danger of forgetting that what we were dealing with was not just a uterus but someone's mother, sister, wife, or daughter. I reminded my colleagues that all of us had taken a sacred oath upon becoming physicians—the Hippocratic oath—that we had vowed to practice medicine in the best interests of our patients, not in the best interests of attorney, HMOs, or hospital administrators.

I argued, with all the persuasive powers I could muster, that we as physicians had to be stewards of the high standards of our profession. "We are at a crossroads," I said, "where our patients are being reduced to codes, invoices, and hospital utilization units, and it is up to us to keep the humanity in medicine. We must insist on quality health care for our patients, because if we don't fight for our patients' health, who will? If we don't fight for our patients' dignity and right to be treated as a whole person, who will?"

When I had finished speaking, the audience applauded. I began to turn away from the podium but the applause swelled and went on. I smiled and nodded to acknowledge my thanks. Again, I began to turn away, but one person stood up, then another, and another. Suddenly the whole audience of doctors was on its feet and I was being given a standing ovation—me a black, me a woman. I raised my eyes heavenward and silently said, as I have said over and over and over in my life, *Thank you, Mommy. Thank you, Daddy.*

I say it once more as I come to the end of their story. *Thank you, Mommy and Daddy. We would have been nothing and done nothing without you. And it will not stop with us. Our children's lives, too, and the lives of all the people we touch will be immeasurably different because we were the ditchdigger's daughters.*

◆ Afterword ◆

It has been twenty-five years since my father's death and more than a decade since the first printing of *The Ditchdigger's Daughters*. Many readers have asked: "What happened to the daughters?" "What are they doing?" "Where are they now?" This new edition of *The Ditchdigger's Daughters* has given me an opportunity to answer those questions.

My parents' dream was to have all of their daughters become physicians. Victor Hugo once said: "There is nothing like a dream to create the future." Little did my parents know that their dream would blossom into a future for their daughters that continues to bear fruit. Over the past decade, the book has garnered many accolades, including a nomination for the Pulitzer Prize and recognition by former President Bill Clinton. It also has become a national bestseller and an award-winning film.

Now for the update: My oldest sister, Donna (tenor sax), never celebrated her fiftieth birthday. She lost her battle with lupus in 1993 and died at age forty-eight. Although Donna chose not to graduate from college, she still recognized the value of education. Her daughter, Heather, is an alumna of the University of Virginia and the University of Pennsylvania. She is a social worker now living in San Francisco with her husband and young son.

Betty and her husband still reside in "The House That Donald Built" in Long Branch, New Jersey. Betty will soon be retiring after almost forty years of being a geriatric nurse.

Jeanette (electric guitar) continues to practice psychiatry in Albany, New York, in her subspecialty of Addiction Psychiatry. She has been married for over twenty-five years to her husband, a gastroenterologist. Although they have no children, Jeanette remains involved in many civic activities.

Over the past twenty-five years, Linda (drums and percussion) has since retired from the United States Army as a Lieutenant Colonel. She is now one of the very few female board-certified prosthodontic oral surgeons in the country and holds a master's degree in Healthcare Administration. Currently, Linda is an associate professor on the faculty of Temple University School of Dentistry in Philadelphia, Pennsylvania, where she serves as the course director for removal prosthodontics.

Rita, my kid sister (piano and keyboards), has had a more circuitous route to her present career. After leaving her position as a science teacher, she enrolled in Seton Hall University School of Law and received her law degree at the age of forty. Not being satisfied in the legal profession, Rita changed her path, entered the New Jersey Institute of Technology and, in 2006, at fifty-four years of age, became the first black woman at NJIT to receive a Ph.D. in Environmental Science.

As for me, since 1983 (when the book ends), my life has been occupied with trying to balance my roles as a mother, wife, professor, obstetrician/gynecologist, and author. I am still married to my medical school sweetheart, Shearwood. It will soon be thirty-four years. Where does the time go?

I have been affiliated with several teaching hospitals and universities since the book was published in 1995. The academic achievement of which I am most proud is my climb to the faculty position of Professor of Obstetrics and Gynecology at Cornell University Weill Medical College in New York, and my delivery of 5,542 babies. I am presently a consultant in High-Risk Obstetrics (Perinatology).

My mother always told us: "No amount of success in your profession can ever make up for being a failure at home." With that said, my greatest life accomplishment has been (with my husband) rearing two exceptional children. Our daughter, Kimberly, is a graduate of Stanford University and is now completing her graduate studies in socio-medical sciences in the Master of Public Health program at Columbia University.

During her years at Stanford, Kimberly, distinguished herself by being asked to sing for then-President Clinton and Mrs. Clinton.

Our son, Woody (Shearwood, III), is a Life Chess Master and has had a stellar career in the world of chess. He was the 1997 United States Junior Open Chess champion, became a member of the All-American Chess Team and won the United States Chess Federation Scholar–Chessplayer Award before entering Harvard University. Woody graduated *cum laude* from Harvard and began his medical studies at Columbia University College of Physicians and Surgeons (our alma mater). When he graduated from P & S, my husband and I ascended to the stage and presented him with the diploma of Doctor of Medicine. He is currently in his residency, training to be a neurosurgeon.

I again want to thank Dafina Books and Kensington Publishing for continuing my parents' legacy. By keeping their story alive, others may be inspired and motivated by their vision, their struggle, and their triumph. My parents are no longer with us physically, but their indomitable spirit will live on in the next generation and in generations thereafter.

Although we may not have all become physicians, the four remaining daughters of Donald and Itasker are all doctors. We were born daughters of a ditchdigger, continued together in the music arena as "The Thornton Sisters," but we are now living our parents' dream as the Doctors Thornton.